THE CLASSICS ON REVIVAL

The Classics on Revival

Edited by Robert Backhouse

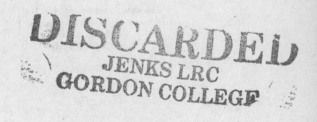

Edition and selection copyright © Robert Backhouse, 1996

First published in Great Britain 1996

The right of Robert Backhouse to be identified as the editor of
the Work has been asserted by him in accordance with the
Copyright, Designs and Patents Act 1988.

1 3 5 7 9 10 8 6 4 2

British Library Cataloguing in Publication Data
A record for this book is available from the British Library

ISBN 0 340 66910 1

Typeset by Watermark, Cromer, NR27 9HL
Printed and bound in Great Britain by

Hodder and Stoughton Ltd
A Division of Hodder Headline PLC
338 Euston Road
London NW1 3BH

Contents

My heart is broken within me;
   all my bones tremble.
I am like a drunken man,
   like a man overcome with wine,
because of the Lord
   and his holy words.

Jeremiah 23:9

Lord, I have heard of your fame;
   I stand in awe of your deeds, O Lord.
Renew them in our day,
   in our time make them known;
   in wrath remember mercy.

Habakkuk 3:2

Will you not revive us again,
   that your people may rejoice in you?
Psalm 85:6

Do not get drunk on wine, which leads to debauchery. Instead, be filled with the Spirit.

Ephesians 5:18

A man who does not know what has been thought by those who have gone before him is sure to set an undue value upon his own ideas.

Mark Pattison

INTRODUCTION

This is an overview of revivals and teaching about revival from the days of our Lord's apostles to the beginning of the twentieth century. It is not easy to find a single definition of revival to explain the subject matter of this book satisfactorily, but the following quotations do give a good idea of the flavour of the book.

'I would define a revival,' writes Martyn Lloyd-Jones, 'as a large number being baptised by the Holy Spirit at the same time; or the Holy Spirit falling upon, coming upon a number of people assembled together. It can happen in a chapel, in a church, it can happen in a district, it can happen in a country.'[1] Lloyd-Jones also writes, in his book *Revival*, what he believes is the essence of revival: 'Suddenly they are aware of God's presence, they are aware of the majesty of the awe of God. The Holy Spirit literally seems to be presiding over the meeting and taking charge of it, and manifesting his power and guiding them, and leading them, and directing them. That is the essence of revival.'[2] Elsewhere Lloyd-Jones writes, 'Does our doctrine of the Holy Spirit, and his work, leave any room for revival either in the individual or in the church? . . . Does our doctrine allow for an outpouring of the Spirit – the 'gale' of the Spirit coming upon us individually and collectively?'[3]

Dr Packer suggests this as his definition of revival: 'Revival I define as a work of God by his Spirit through his word bringing the spiritually dead to living faith in Christ and renewing the inner life of Christians who have grown slack and sleepy. In revival God makes old things new, giving new power to law and gospel and new spiritual awareness to those whose hearts and consciences had been blind, hard and cold. Revival thus animates or reanimates churches and Christians groups to make a spiritual and moral impact on communities.'[4]

This book amply illustrates Guy Chevreau's assertion that 'God has not *just* made himself known in biblical times and then disappeared; there is continuous and documented evidence of his disclosure throughout the history of the Church.'[5]

Dunn expresses a similar conviction in this way: 'The earliest Christian community was essentially charistmatic and enthusiatic in nature, in every aspect of its common life and worship . . . The fact is that ecstatic and physical phenomena have been a regular concomitant of religious awakening and revival movements within the history of Christianity.'[6]

Rob Warner points out the distinction between revival and evangelism: 'Revival is not simply organised evangelism; it is a mighty visitation of the Spirit of God. And where God comes powerfully among his people there are always physical signs of his presence . . . Where there is revival, and the Spirit is outpoured in power, strange and strong manifestations can be expected.'[7] Perhaps the simple phrase 'days of heaven on earth' goes some way to encapsulate what revival is all about.

This potted history of revivals, with quotations from over one hundred people, is presented in chronological order, starting with the leading theologians of the second century, such as Clement of Rome, Ignatius, Hermas, the Didache, Celsus, Justin Martyr, Irenaeus, Tertullian, the much maligned Montanists, the Phrygian prophets, Hippolytus, Athenagoras, Bishop Melito, and Origen. The thoughts about revival of many of the most famous Christians teachers over the successive centuries are gathered together here, as well as those of many less well-known individuals, such as Macrina the Younger, Isaac the Syrian, Joseph Hazzaya, Rupert of Deutz, Agnes Blannbekin of Vienna, Augustine Baker, August Hermann Francke, Thomas Walsh and Stephen Bradley.

This anthology has been compiled by using different types of quotations. First, there are numerous 'soundbites' about revival from well-known Christian theologians. Secondly, there are descriptions of revivals. These are often gleaned from the journals of people involved in revivals, such as Fox, Whitefield and Wesley

– Wesley's *Journal* runs to twenty-six volumes, so we are not short of details about the revivals he engaged in. A third type of quotation could be termed personal experiences of the Holy Spirit. Rob Warner writes that 'the leaders of revivals are characterised by intense personal encounters with God, both in their conversions and in moments of powerful anointing for public ministry.'[8]

A number of such experiences are set out in this book. They have been labelled in various ways – conversion experiences, anointing by the Holy Spirit, baptism in the Spirit, a second blessing, etc. – and it is often not easy or wise to try to pigeon-hole such spiritual experiences with one particular theological name. Some of the visions and revelations that have been received over the centuries by a wide variety of people, from Contantine to Teresa of Avila, from Madame Guyon to Mrs Jonathan Edwards, and from Pascal to mystics, in the Eastern Orthodox tradition, are included in this book. Often, these intensely personal encounters were pivotal experiences in the lives of the individual Christians. It was so with the present Archbishop of Canterbury, George Carey.

Dr Carey says that he was converted when he was seventeen. Twenty years later he was lecturing in an evangelial Anglican theological college and was by that time particularly upset about his lack of spirituality. He goes so far as to say that he experienced a 'spiritual void or ennui'. This came into sharp focus when he was lecturing on St Paul's doctrine of the Spirit. He became acutely aware of the great gulf between Paul's triumphant assurance and his own 'spiritual poverty'.

Things changed for George Carey in Canada. He read a book called *Aglow with the Spirit* by Robert Frost just before he was due to preach in Little Trinity Church, Toronto. He recalls that he unexpectedly found himself on his knees. He told his Lord that he had been so busy in serving him that he had somehow lost him. He asked to be filled again with God's Spirit. He knew that without this he could not go on.

George Carey recalls that nothing special happened immediately after this except that he kept on hearing the word 'Shamayim, Shamayim, Shamayim' repeated. It is the Hebrew

word for 'heaven'. Later he understood that what he had experienced that evening was a foretaste of heaven as the Holy Spirit
had become so real to him.

He felt that this experience was a turning point in his Christian life. Dying embers had been fanned by God's Spirit into a
fire. He could now move on again.[9]

A fourth type of quotation used in this book is from the com-
mentataries of such classic writers as J. C. Ryle, John Calvin,
Charles Hodge, C. H. Spurgeon and J. B. Lightfoot, where they
write on parts of the Bible that are on the subject of revival.

'Vineyard' churches, among many other groups, are studying
the writings of one man on revival more than any other – Jonathan
Edwards. J. I. Packer writes of Edwards, 'Jonathan Edwards, saint,
scholar, preacher, pastor, metaphysician, theologian, Calvinist,
revival leader, lived from 1703 to 1758. In 1734–5 and 1740–2 he
saw remarkable movements of the Spirit of God in his congregation and, in the latter case, throughout all New England.'[10]

Richard Lovelace explains why Edwards' writings are so pertinent to the subject of revival today:

Jonathan Edwards, the Puritan theologian who has been called
the greatest mind produced by America, was also the greatest
theologian of revival. When we talk about renewal in the con-
temporary church church, Edwards' writings provide us with
the best standards available to help us judge what is genuine,
what is spurious, and what is a mixture waiting to be purified.[11]

Many of Edwards' views about revival cut right across some of
the cherished, traditional beliefs about revival. Professor Lovelace
points out:

Edwards' model of revival and decline, based on the ebb and
flow of spiritual warfare, implied that an awakening might be
more like a street fight than a spring morning. A revival movement might be diluted, disfigured, or even invaded by the resist-
ing forces of sin and Satan.[12]

Edwards writes:

In the apostolic age, there was the greatest outpouring of the Spirit of God that ever was, both as to his extraordinary influences and gifts, and his ordinary operations, in convincing, converting, enlightening, and sanctifying the souls of men. But as the influences of the true Spirit abounded, so counterfeits did also abound: the devil was abundant in mimicking both the ordinary and extraordinary influences of the Spirit of God, as is manifest by innumerable passages of the apostles' writings. This made it very necessary that the church of Christ should be furnished with some certain rules, distinguishing and clear marks, by which she might proceed safely in judging of the true from the false without danger of being imposed upon. The giving of such rules is the plain design of this chapter [1 John:4], where we have this matter more expressly and fully treated of than anywhere else in the Bible. The apostle, of set purpose, undertakes to supply the church of God with such marks of the true Spirit as may be plain and safe, and well accommodated to use and practice; and that the subject might be clearly and sufficiently handled, he insists upon it throughout the chapter, which makes it wonderful that what is said here is no more taken notice of in this extraordinary day, when there is such an uncommon and extensive operation on the minds of people, such a variety of opinions concerning it, and so much talk about the work of the Spirit.[13]

Parts 1, 2 and 3 of Edwards' *Distinguishing Marks of a Work of the Spirit of God* are included in this book, almost in their entirety, as they are of quite exceptional help in discerning the characteristics of genuine revival. Referring to this book, Lovelace writes:

Edwards begins by stating that there are many elements in the revival that are neither sure signs of the Spirit nor marks of the flesh or the Devil, but that are simply indifferent – a kind of accidental package surrounding the real core of spiritual awakening. It proves nothing that revivals emerge from protracted meetings or that they seem to cause strange bodily effects. Strong preoccupation with religion or imaginative visions prove nothing either way. If revival phenomena seem to spread by contagion or imitation, this is again inconclusive. Imprudence and irregularity, satanic delusions, and even the subsequent apostasy of some converts do not disprove the real activity of the Spirit in a revival. More positively, Edwards finds five biblical marks of a genuine revival: it exalts Jesus Christ; it attacks the powers of darkness; it exalts the Holy Scriptures; it lifts up sound doctrine; and it promotes love to God and man.[14]

Selections from Edwards' *Religious Affections* are also included, as Edwards firmly believed that 'true religion, in great part, consists in the affections [emotions]'. Had these two works of Edwards' been widely read by Christians living today, many of the false suspicions about revival and much of the undiscerning acceptance of spurious, non-spiritual outward signs would have been recognised for what they were, and so a great deal of the heat from the controversies about revival, speaking in tongues, miracles, Pentecostals and charismatics and so on might have been avoided.

In addition to articulating some of the most inspiring and profound thoughts about revival, Edwards was among the sternest critics of hollow revivals. In this connection Professor Lovelace writes:

A revival movement that finds itself replicating compulsive laughter, spiritual drunkenness, pecking like chickens or roaring like lions as expected aspects of spiritual awakening may be playing into the Enemy's hands. It is in the Devil's interest to make Christians weird. He does not need possession to do this; he can manage by suggestion. The goal of his strategy is to create a church that is so institutionally strange that unbelievers will detour around it. The goal of revival is conformity to the image of Christ, not imitation of animals. . . . Edwards' own final approach to the Great Awakening was to subject it to the most rigorous critique, on the one hand, and to solicit extraordinary prayer for its advancement, on the other. These are strategies we need to follow today.[15]

The great majority of quotations in the book present the speakers and writers in a favourable and positive light: most of them support revival. However, it would be possible to select certain quotations so that their author's views are misrepresented. It is often said that a Bible text out of context can easily become a pretext, and this is equally true of any other writing or speaking. Often the quotations in this anthology need to be set in their context if their authors are not to be seriously misunderstood. For example, R. A. Torrey said that Pentecostals were 'founded by a sodomite'; and the Puritan John Owen wrote about the class of 'gifts which in their own nature exceed the whole power of all our faculties' [such as tongues, prophetic disclosures and the power to heal] that 'dispensation of the Spirit is long since ceased, and where it is now pretended unto by any, it may justly be suspected as an enthusiatical delusion.' If those quotations were all we knew about Torrey and Owen, we might conclude that they were set against revivals. But a different picture emerges when we know a little about the background to these quotations. J. I. Packer introduces Owen's quotation as follows: 'It was partly, no doubt, Owen's experience of such people [claimants to prophetic and healing powers, particularly in the wild days of the forties and fifties, when the signs of 'enthusiasm' (fanatical delusion) and mental unbalance were all too evident] which prompted him to write.'[16] The other selections from Owen in this book also reveal how much he favoured the work of the Holy Spirit. As far as Torrey is concerned, John White comments on the quotations as follows: 'Torrey . . . never lived to see the subsequent development of the pentecostal movement, or [his] words might have been more charitable.'[17]

One striking fact that becomes apparent from looking at the history of revivals in the Christian church is that few revivals existed without great opposition. Some of the thoughts of opponents of revival are included in this book. It is clear that revivals are often written off because people involved in them were too enthusiastic, too ardent, were 'drunk' (as the first were accused of being: 'they are filled with new wine' (Acts 2:13)), or were extremists. One none too friendly critic viewed Fox's bizarre behaviour as that of a psychopath:

No one can pretend for a moment that in point of spiritual sagacity and capacity, Fox's mind was unsound. Everyone who confronted him personally, from Oliver Cromwell down to country magistrates and jailers, seems to have acknowledged his superior power. Yet from the point of view of his nervous constitution, Fox was a psychopath or *détraqué* of the deepest dye.[18]

James then proceeds to quote from one of the strangest entries in Fox's Journal:

As I was walking with several friends, I lifted up my head, and saw three steeple-house spires, and they struck at my life. I asked them what place that was? They said, Lichfield. Immediately the word of the Lord came to me, that I must go there. Being come to the house we were going to, I wished the friends to walk into the house, saying nothing to them of whither I was to go. As soon as they were gone I stept away, and went by my eye over hedge and ditch till I came within a mile of Lichfield; where, in a great field, shepherds were keeping their sheep.

Then was I commanded by the Lord to pull off my shoes. I stood still, for it was winter: but the word of the Lord was like a fire in me. So I put off my shoes and left them with the shepherds; and the poor shepherds trembled, and were astonished. Then I walked on about a mile, and as soon as I was got within the city, the word of the Lord came to me again, saying: Cry, 'Wo, to the bloody city of Lichfield!' So I went up and down the streets, crying with a loud voice, Wo to the bloody city of Lichfield! It being market day, I went into the market-place, and to and fro in the several parts of it, and made stands, crying as before, Wo to the bloody city of Lichfield!

And no one laid hands on me. As I went thus crying through the streets, there seemed to me to be a channel of blood running down the streets, and the market-place appeared like a pool of blood. When I had declared what was upon me, and felt myself clear, I went out of the town in peace; and returning to the shepherds gave them some money, and took my shoes of them again. But the first of the Lord was so on my feet, and all over

me, that I did not matter to put on my shoes again, and was at a
stand whether I should or no, till I felt freedom from the Lord
so to do: then, after I had washed my feet, I put on my shoes
again.

After this a deep consideration came upon me, for what
reason I should be sent to cry against that city, and call it The
bloody city! For though the parliament had the minister one
while, and the king another, and much blood had been shed in
the town during the wars between them, yet there was not more
than had befallen many other places. But afterwards I came to
understand, that in the Emperor Diocletian's time a thousand
Christians were martyred in Lichfield. So I was to go, without
my shoes, through the channel of their blood, and into the pool
of their blood in the marketplace, that I might raise up the
memorial of the blood of those martyrs, which had been shed
above a thousand years before, and lay cold in their streets. So
the sense of this blood was upon me, and I obeyed the word of
the Lord.[19]

Some books on revival are thinly disguised attacks on somebody
else's theological viewpoint, or on some group of Christians who
think and behave differently from them. As John White has
pointed out, 'A manifestation of power is not a sign of God's special approval of one's person or of one's theology, nor does it vali-
date one's assessment of a national situation. God is grieved by our
party spiritedness and does not bestow power to prove one group
right and other wrong.'[20]

Perhaps the advice of Cyril, the fourth-century patriarch of
Jerusalem, needs to be heard again by some rather bombastic
Christians who sometimes set themselves up as gurus on the sub-
ject of revival:

Truly, I need spiritual grace if I am to speak about the Holy
Spirit. I do not mean, to enable me to speak as the subject
deserves, for that is not possible, but simply to run through what
is said in holy Scripture without imperilling my soul. For what is
written in the gospels, of Christ saying unequivocally, 'anyone
who speaks against the Holy Spirit will not be forgiven, either in

this age or in the age to come' (Matthew 12:32), truly makes one very much afraid. Frequently, there is good reason to fear that a person may incur this condemnation for saying what he should not say about the Holy Spirit, either through ignorance or through mistaken piety.

Let us say about the Holy Spirit exactly what Scripture says and nothing else, and do not let us pry where Scripture does not answer. The Scriptures were spoken by the Holy Spirit himself, and what he said about himself is exactly what he pleased, or we could comprehend. So, let what he spoke be said, which is to say, let us not dare to utter anything that he did not.[21]

Footnotes

1. D. Martyn Lloyd-Jones, *Joy Unspeakable: Power and Renewal in the Holy Spirit* (Eastbourne: Kingsway Publications, 1985), p. 51.

2. D. Martyn Lloyd-Jones, *Revival: Can We Make it Happen?* (London: Marshall Pickering), p. 100.

3. D. Lloyd-Jones, *The Puritans: Their Origins and Successors* (Edinburgh: Banner of Truth, 1987), p. 302.

4. J. I. Packer, *Among God's Giants: Aspects of Puritan Christianity*, (Eastbourne: Kingsway, 1991), p. 42.

5. Guy Chevreau, *Catch the Fire: Toronto Blesing – An Experience of Renewal and Revival* (London: Marshall Pickering, 1994), p. 41.

6. James D. G. Dunn, *Jesus and the Spirit: A Study of the Religious and Charismatic Experience of Jesus and the First Christians as Reflected in the New Testament* (London: SCM Press, 1978), pp. 189, 194.

7. Rob Warner, *Prepare for Revival* (London: Hodder and Stoughton, 1995), p. 44.

8. *ibid.*, p. 38.

9. Robert Backhouse, *Invaded by Love: A Collection of Christian Conversions*, (London: Marshall Pickering, 1993), pp. 58–9.

10. J. I. Packer, *Among God's Giants*, p. 408.

11. Richard Lovelace in *Christianity Today*, 11.9.95, p. 28.

12. *ibid.*, p. 30.

13. Jonathan Edwards, *The Distinguishing Marks of a Work of the Spirit*

of God: Part 1, introduction.

14. Richard Lovelace in *Christianity Today*, 11.9.95, pp. 30–1.

15. *ibid.*, p. 32.

16. J. I. Packer, *Among God's Giants*, p. 290.

17. John White, *When the Spirit Comes with Power, Signs and Wonders Among God's People* (London: Hodder and Stoughton, 1992), p. 148.

18. William James, *The Varieties of Religious Experience* (London: Collins, 1960), p. 30.

19. George Fox, *Journal*, vol. I, pp. 100–1.

20. John White, *When the Spirit Comes with Power: Signs and Wonders Among God's People* (London: Hodder and Stoughton, 1992), p. 48.

21. Cyril of Jerusalem, *Catechetical Lecture* 16,1.

2ND CENTURY

Clement of Rome
(150–215)

Clement of Rome was one of the first of the early group of Christian teachers known as the Apostolic Fathers.

But what must we say of David that obtained a good report? Of whom God said, 'I have found a man after my heart, David the son of Jesse.' Yet he too saith unto God, 'Make a clean heart within me, O God, and renew a right spirit in mine inmost parts. Cast me not away from thy presence, and take not thy Holy Spirit from me. Restore unto me the joy of thy salvation, and strengthen me with a princely spirit.'

Letter to the Corinthians.

Spiritual gifts

Let our whole body be preserved in Christ Jesus, and let each man be subject to his neighbour, since he has had his place given by his spiritual gift. Let the strong not neglect the weak, and let the weak respect the strong.

   Let the pure in flesh [i.e., the ascetic] not boast, as he knows that Another supplies his self-discipline.

Letter to the Corinthians.

19

Ignatius
(35–115)

Bishop of Antioch, martyred in c. 115

Ignatius in prophetic mode

When I was among you I cried out (I spoke with a loud voice, with God's voice): 'Give heed to the bishop and the presbytery and the deacons.'

There were some who believed I said this because of the previous division among you. But he in whom I am bound is witness that I was not informed by human agency. It was the Spirit that preached, saying: 'Never act without the bishop. Keep your body as the temple of God. Love union; shun divisions. Be imitators of Jesus Christ, as he was of his Father.'

To the Philadelphians, 7.

Saying from the apostolic era
(up to AD 100)

'If you see a brother who is sick and do not heal him, his blood will be on your hands.'

Hermas

Hermas refuted the teaching that Christians who sin cannot repent again.

The prophetic gift assessed

Try the man who has the Spirit of God by his life. First, he who has the Spirit of God which proceeds from above is meek, and peaceable, and humble and refrains from all iniquity and the vain desire of this world, and contents himself with fewer wants than those of other men; he does not speak privately [i.e., a true prophet speak from the Lord during a church meeting, as Hermas later explains] and the Holy Spirit does not speak at the whim of man, but only when God wishes.

Hear about the spirit which is earthly, empty, powerless and foolish. First, the man who seems to have the Spirit exalts himself, and wishes to have the first seat, and is bold and impudent and talkative and lives surrounded by many luxuries and many other delusions, and takes rewards for his prophecy.

Try by his deeds and his life the man who says he is inspired.

Shepherd, Mandate 11.

The angel of the prophetic spirit

When the man who has the divine Spirit comes into a synagogue of righteous men, who have faith in the divine Spirit, and intercession is made to God by the synagogue of those men, then the angel of the prophetic Spirit, who is in contact with him, fills the man, and the man, filled with the Holy Spirit, speaks to the congregation as the Lord pleases.

Shepherd, Mandate 11.

The Holy Spirit is choked by the evil spirit

Be, said he, long-suffering and prudent and you shall have power over all evil deeds and shall do all righteousness. For if you are courageous the Holy Spirit who dwells in you will be pure, not obscured by another evil spirit, but will dwell at large and rejoice and be glad in great cheerfulness, having well-being in himself. But if any ill-temper enter, at once the Holy Spirit, who is delicate, is oppressed, finding the place impure, and seeks to depart out of the place, for he is choked by the evil spirit, having no room to serve the Lord as he wishes, but is contaminated by the bitterness.

Shepherd, Mandate 5.

The Didache

The Didache is a church manual of primitive Christianity or of some section of it. It is called 'The Teaching of the Apostles' or 'The Teaching of the Twelve Apostles.' Its author is unknown.

Concerning the apostles and prophets

But concerning the apostles and prophets act according to the instruction of the Gospel. Let every apostle, when he comes to you, be received as the Lord; but he shall not abide more than a single day, or if there be need, a second day. But if he stays three days, he is a false prophet. And when he departs let the apostle receive nothing except bread, until he finds shelter. If he asks for money he is a false prophet. And any prophet speaking in the Spirit you shall not try neither discern; for every sin will be forgiven, but this sin will not be forgiven.

However, not everyone who speaks in the Spirit is a prophet, but only if he walks in the ways of the Lord. From his actions, therefore, a false prophet and a true prophet may be recognised. And no prophet when he orders a table in the Spirit will eat from it; otherwise he is a false prophet. And if any prophet who is approved and found true does something as an acted parable with a typical meaning for the church, but does not teach you to do what he does himself, he must not be judged by you; the Lord is his judge, for the prophets of old did the same. If any one says in the Spirit, 'Give me money' – or anything else – you are not to listen to him. But if he asks you to give it for others who are in need, let no one judge him.

The Didache, 11:3–12.

A prophet is worthy of his hire because of his prophetic ministry

Every true prophet who wishes to settle among you is worthy of his maintenance. So also a true teacher, like the labourer, deserves his maintenance. So you must take every firstfruit of the produce of your wine-vat and threshing-floor, of your oxen and sheep, and give it as a firstfruit to the prophets, for they are your chief priests. If you have no prophet, give it to the poor.

If you make bread, take the firstfruit and give it according to that commandment. In the same way when you open a jar of wine or oil, take the firstfruit and give it according to the prophets; and take the firstfruit of money and clothing and every possession, as seems good to you, and give it according to the commandment.

The Didache, 13: 1–5.

Instructions for meetings who have no resident prophets

Appoint for yourselves therefore bishops (superintendents) and deacons (ministers) worthy of the Lord, men of meekness, not lovers of money, true and approved; for these also perform for you the service of prophets and teachers. So you must not despise them [even if they are not prophets], for they are your honourable men along with the prophets and teachers.

The Didache, 15:1–2.

Celsus

Celsus, a pagan philosopher who criticised Christians bitterly, calling them 'worms' on one occasion, gives this description of Christian prophets he heard.

Celsus listens to a Christian prophesying

'I am God, or the Son of God, or the Holy Spirit. I am coming. The world is passing away, and you people are going to destruction because of your sins. I will save you. You will see me coming back with heavenly power. Blessed is he who now serves me; but on all the others I will make eternal fire to rain down on the cities and the countryside. It will be useless for mankind, unaware of its due punishments, to repent and groan; but those who believe in me I will preserve for ever.'

In Origen, 7, 9–11.

Justin Martyr
(100–65)

The first Christian writer to try to reconcile faith and reason.

Driving out demons

But 'Jesus', his name as man and Saviour, has also significance. For he was made man also, having been conceived according to the will of God the Father, for the sake of believing men, and for the destruction of the demons. And now you can learn from this what is under your own observation. For numberless demoniacs throughout the whole world, and in your city many of our Christian men exorcising them in the name of Jesus Christ, who was crucified under Pontius Pilate, have healed and do heal, rendering helpless and driving the possessing devils out of men, though they could not be cured by all the other exorcists, and those who used incantations and drugs.

The Second Apology of Justin, chapter 6.

The gifts of prophecy remain with us, even to the present time

The prophetical gifts of the Jews were transferred to the Christians. For the prophetical gifts remain with us, even to the present time. And hence you ought to understand that the gifts formerly among your nation [the Jews: Trypho, to whom Justin is writing was a Jew], have been transferred to us [Christians].

Dialogue with Trypho.

Among us women and men possess gifts of the Spirit of God

The Scripture says that the powers of the Spirit have come on Christ, not because he stood in need of them, but because they would rest in him, that is, would find their accomplishment in him, so that there would be no more prophets in your nation after the ancient custom: and this fact you plainly perceive. For after Christ prophet has arisen among you. Now, your prophets each received one or two powers from God . . . Solomon possessed the spirit of wisdom, Daniel that of understanding and counsel, Moses that of might and piety, Elijah that of fear, and Isaiah that of knowledge . . . Accordingly the Spirit rested, that is ceased, when Christ came, after whom, in the times of this dispensation wrought out by him among men, it was requisite that such gifts should cease from you; and having received their rest in him, should again, as had been predicted, become gifts which, from the grace of his Spirit's power, he imparts to those who believe in him, according as he deems each man worthy. I have already said, and do say again, that it has been prophesied that this would be done by him after his ascension to heaven. It is accordingly said, 'He ascended on high, he led captivity captive, he gave gifts unto the sons of men.' And again, in another prophecy it is said: 'And it shall come to pass after this, I will pour out my Spirit on all flesh, and on my servants, and on my handmaids, and they shall prophesy.'

Now, it is possible to see among us women and men who possess gifts of the Spirit of God.

Dialogue with Trypho.

The prophetic Spirit we worship

But both him [i.e., the Father] and the Son who came from him and taught us these things, and the host of the other good angels who follow are made like him, and the prophetic Spirit we worship and adore.

Second Apology, chapter 1.

Irenaeus
(140–203)

Bishop of Lyon, biblical theologian.

It is not possible to number the gifts of the Spirit in the church

For which cause also his true disciples, having received grace from him, use it in his name for the benefit of the rest of mankind, even as each has received the gifts from him. For some do, really and truly drive out demons, so that those who have thus been cleansed from evil spirits frequently believe and join themselves to the church. Others have foreknowledge of things to come: they see visions, and utter prophetic expressions. Others still, heal the sick by laying their hands on them, and they are made whole. Yes, moreover, as I have said, the dead even have been raised up, and remained among us for many years. And what shall I more say? It is not possible to name the number of the gifts which the church, [scattered] throughout the world, has received from God, in the name of Jesus Christ.

Against Heresies.

Where the church is, there is the Spirit of God

If you do not join in what the church is doing, you have no share in this Spirit. For where the church is, there is the Spirit of God; and where the Spirit of God is, there is the church and every kind of grace.

Against Heresies, 3.24.1.

Tertullian and Montanism

Tertullian was a North African theologian who became so influential that he was called the 'Father of Latin theology'. He embraced Montanism towards the end of his life.

'*About the middle of the second century a new prophetic movement began in the heart of Asia Minor where Montanus began to "speak in tongues". Associated with him were two women, Maximilla and Prisca, who also had the gift of prophecy, or speaking with tongues – ecstatic speech that needed interpreting*' (Records of Christianity, *vol. 1, p. 91*).

'*The chief manifestation of prophetism in the post-apostolic age was the rise of the Montanist movement, which spread from its home in Phrygia to other parts of the Christian world*' (*F. F. Bruce,* The Spreading Flame *(Paternoster Press, 1958), p. 218*).

The false prophet speaks in a trance

The false prophet speaks in a trance, which induces irresponsibility and freedom from restraint; he begins by deliberate suppression of conscious thought, and ends in a delirium over which he has no control. A prophet must not be expected to speak in ecstasy.

De Praescriptione Haereticorum (A Demurrer to the Heretics' Plea), v.17.

Visions

The majority, almost, of men learn from visions.

New wine of Montanism too potent for old wineskins of a too rigid organisation

Briefly, its characteristics were these:

1. A strong faith in the Holy Spirit as the promised Paraclete, present as a heavenly power in the Church of the day.

2. Specially a belief that the Holy Spirit was manifesting himself supernaturally at that day through entranced prophets and prophetesses.

3. An inculcation of a specially stern and exacting standard of Christian morality and discipline on the strength of certain teachings of these prophets. And increase in the numbers and prosperity of the church having brought an increase of laxity, it was not unnatural that attempts should be made to stem it by a rigorous system of prohibitions.

4. A tendency to set up prophets against bishops, the new episcopal organisation being probably favourable to that large inclusiveness of Christian communion in which the Montanists saw only spiritual danger.

5. An eager anticipation of the Lord's Second Coming as near at hand, and a consequent indifference to ordinary human affairs.

F. J. A. Hort, *The Ante-Nicene Fathers* (1895), pp. 100–1.

'Not prophecy, as they call it, but Pseudo-prophecy'

Some short time ago I visited Ankara in Galatia and found the local church deafened with the noise of this new craze – not prophecy, as they call it, but pseudo-prophecy, as I will now demonstrate. As best as I could, with the Lord's help, I spoke out, day after day, in the church about these matters and answered all their arguments. The church was delighted and confirmed in the truth and the enemy was defeated for the moment.

In a village near Phrygia, in Mysia, they claim that Montanus first exposed himself to the attacks of the devil in his unbridled desire for leadership. A recent convert, he became possessed by a spirit, and suddenly began to rave in a kind of ecstatic trance, and to babble in unknown words, prophesying in a way the church was most unused to and not according to the traditions that had been handed down from the earliest of times.

Some people who heard his corrupt utterances rebuked him as if he was possessed by a devil, as they recalled how our Lord had warned his disciples to be on their guard against false prophets. Other people, however, were taken in, and believed that they were possessed by the Holy Spirit and had the gift of prophecy. Montanus also encouraged two women and filled them with this corrupt spirit, so that they became demented and full of disturbing sayings. Such people blasphemed the whole catholic church under heaven, under the influence of their presumptuous spirit, because the church did not recognise or honour this false spirit of prophecy. The faithful in Asia often met to debate this matter in many places throughout Asia. They rejected the heresy and the followers of the heresy were thrown out of the church and debarred them from communion.

An unknown author, who dedicated his writing to Abercius, bishop of Hieropolis in Phrygia; quoted by Eusebius, *Church History*, Book 5, 16.

A Montanist sister and the corporeal soul

We ascribe to the soul corporeal lineaments, not only from the confidence in its corporality supplied by rational thought, but also from the assurance given by grace through revelation. [This Montanist sister regularly received revelations during divine service which she then recounted to the esoterics at the end of the service.]

'Among other things there was shown me a soul in bodily shape, and the spirit remained in view. It was not insubstantial and void of qualities, but such as to suggest that it might be grasped; it was soft and shining and of the colour of mist, and its shape was in all respects human.'

Your own common sense will suggest that the soul cannot be thought of as having a human appearance, in fact the outward shape of the particular body which it informed. The corporeality of the soul was solidified by compression, and its appearance formed by a moulding process. This is the inner man, distinct from the outer, though identical with it as its replica.

It has its own eyes and ears; Paul had to have them to see the Lord and to hear the Lord (2 Corinthians 12:1–4). It has also the other members, with which it acts in thoughts and dreams. Thus in the underworld the rich man has a tongue, the poor man a finger, and Abraham a bosom (Luke 16:22ff).

Tertullian, *On the Soul*, 9.

The prophetess Prisca

That was an illuminating remark which the Paraclete made through the prophetess Prisca about those people who deny the bodily resurrection, 'They are things of flesh, and they hate the flesh.'

Tertullian, *On the Resurrection of the Body*, 11.

The New Prophets [i.e., Montanism]

Whereas you say that the church has power to remit sins, I have a greater reason for acknowledging and asserting this, in that I find the Paraclete saying, through the New Prophets, 'The church has power to remit a sin; but I will not do it, lest they commit other sins.'

Tertullian, *On Modesty*, 21.

The coming of the Paraclete identified with the appearance of Montanus

Hardness of heart reigned till Christ came, weakness of the flesh reigned till the Paraclete came.

Tertullian, *De monogamia*, 14.

Jerome on the Montanist doctrine

[According to Montanist teaching:] God, having failed to save the world by the two first degrees [of his revelation] came down through the Holy Spirit into Montanus, Priscilla and Maximilla.

Letter xxvii, to Marcella.

The church of the Spirit and Montanism

What about your church, worldly man? The power of binding and loosing will link to spiritual powers, to an apostle or prophet as far as they show same qualities as Peter's declaration of faith. For the church is correctly and primarily the Spirit, in whom is the trinity of the one divinity, the Father, Son, and Holy Spirit. The Spirit creates the assembly of the church, which the Lord established in three persons. And so all those who have grown together in this faith are given status in the church by the church's author and consecrator. There the church does indeed remit sins, bit it is the church of the Spirit, through the agency of a spiritual man, not the church as a number of bishops. For the right judgment belongs not to the servant, but to the Lord; not to the priest but to God himself.

Tertullian, *On Modesty*, 21.

Montanism and the Holy Spirit

The Paraclete has 'many things to teach' (John 16:13) which the Lord reserves for him, according to his prearranged plan. First, he will bear witness to Christ and our belief about him, together with the whole design of God the Creator; he will glorify him and remind us of him; and then when the Paraclete has thus been recognised in the matter of the primary rule of faith, he will reveal many things which relate to discipline. These revelations will be attested by the consistency of their proclamation. They are new in the sense that they have only been revealed now. They are burdensome, even though they are not at the moment being borne. However, they remain the demands of Christ who said that he had many more things which the Paraclete would teach us. These things would be just as burdensome to men today as they were to Christ's disciples, who were not yet bearing them.

Tertullian, *On Monogamy*, 2.

Losing consciousness

Peter, at the transfiguration, 'did not know what he was saying' (Luke 9:33). Why was that? Was it because of an aberration, or because of the rule that a state of ecstasy, of being out of one's mind, accompanies the work of grace? For a man who is 'in the spirit', especially when he beholds the glory of God and when God speaks through him, must inevitably lose consciousness, as he is overshadowed by the divine Power.

Tertullian, *Against Marcion*, iv,2.

The New Discipline of the Paraclete

The Paraclete is introducing nothing novel when he forbids marriage. He is making clear what he has already hinted at, and makes demands which up to now he has forborne. If you reflect on these things you will quickly conclude that since the Paraclete could have forbidden marriage completely, he had much more right to proclaim against remarriage, and that it is even more credible that he should have restrained what he might correctly have abolished. You will understand this if you have Christ's mind on this subject. In this matter you ought to recognise the Paraclete as your advocate and supporter, in that he excuses your weakness as you strive for complete continence. We have demonstrated this by showing that the discipline of the right to marry once only is nothing new nor something imported into Christianity. Rather, it is an ancient and characteristic discipline of Christians; so that you must think of the Paraclete as One who restores, rather than one who innovates.

Tertullian, *On Monogamy*, 3–4.

Let the weakness of the flesh end its reign now the Paraclete has come

Christ abolished the commandment of Moses. Why, then, should not the Paraclete have cancelled the indulgence granted by Paul ['each one has a special gift from God' and so is allowed to marry (1 Corinthians 7:9); 'if a husband dies, a married woman is free to marry' (1 Corinthians 7:39)]? 'Hardness of heart' (Matthew 19:8) held sway until Christ came. Let weakness of the flesh end its reign now the Paraclete has come. The New Law abolished divorce. The New Prophecy abolished second marriage.

Tertullian, *On Monogamy*, 14.

Guidance, reformation and interpretation through the Holy Spirit

The Lord has sent the Paraclete for this very purpose, that discipline might progressively be guided, ordered, and brought to perfection by his representative, the Holy Spirit. The province of the Holy Spirit is exactly this: the interpretation of Scripture, the guidance of discipline, the reformation of the intellect, and the advance towards better things. All things have their proper time and await their due season. So righteousness was rudimentary to start with, when nature feared God; then through the Law and the Prophets it progressed to infancy; then, through the Gospel, it reached adolescence, and now through the Paraclete it reaches maturity.

Tertullian, *On the Veiling of Virgins*, 1.

Expelling demons and healing

All this might be officially brought to your notice, and by the very advocates who are themselves also under obligations to us, although in court they give their voice as it suits them. The clerk of one of them who was liable to be thrown upon the ground by an evil spirit, was set free from his affliction; and was also the relative of another, and the little boy of a third. How many men of rank (to say nothing of common people) have been delivered from devils, and healed of diseases! Even Serverus himself, the father of Antonine, was graciously mindful of the Christians; for he sought out the Christian Proculus, surnamed Torpacion, the steward of Euhodias, and in gratitude for his having once cured him by anointing, he help him in his palace till the day of his death.

Tertullian, *To Scapula*.

To pagans who mocked at Christ

This is a test case. Bring someone before your judgment-seats who is obviously demon-possessed. Told to speak by any Christian, this spirit, so surely as he pretends to deity elsewhere, will truly own himself a demon. Mock as you will at our Christ and his 'fables' – his resurrection, his ascension, his coming again to judge the world; mock as you will, but get the demons to mock with you! Let them deny that Christ is coming to judge every human soul. All the power and authority we have over them stems from pronouncing the name of Christ and from reminding them that they are under God's judgment which is in Christ's hands. So as we breath one them [as a sign of giving the Holy Spirit, see John 20:22] the demons are expelled, unwillingly and distressed, from their bodies at our command.

Tertullian, *Apology* [Defence of Christianity], 23.

Montanism

Montanus' claim

[Montanus said:] 'Behold, man is like a lyre and I [i.e., the Spirit] strike that lyre as a plectrum would strike it. Man sleeps and I awake. Behold, the Lord is he who throws the heart of men into ecstasy, and gives to men a new heart.'

Epiphanius, *Heresies*, 48:4.I.

[Words attributed to Montanus:] 'Neither an angel, nor an ambassador, but I, the Lord, the Father, am come.'

Epiphanius, *Heresies*, 48:11.

Maximilla: the last prophet

[Maximilla said:] 'After me there will be no more prophets, but only the final End.'

Epiphanius, *Heresies*, 48:2.4.

Maximilla's claim

[Maximilla said:] 'The Lord has sent me as an adherent, preacher and interpreter of this affliction and this covenant and this promise; he has compelled me, willingly or unwillingly, to learn the knowledge of God.'

Epiphanius, *Heresies*, 48:13.I.

'I am chased like a wolf'

'I am chased like a wolf [this illustration is from Matthew 7 where Jesus talks about true and false prophets]; I am word, and spirit, and power.'

Eusebius, *Ecclesiastical History*, 5:16.

Montanus said: 'I am the Father, the Word, and the Holy Spirit.'

Didymus, *Of the Trinity*, III. xli.

Maximilla said: 'I am the word, and spirit, and power.'

Eusebius, *Ecclesiastical History*, 5.16.

The 'Phrygian' prophets

The 'Phrygian' prophets, like the Montanists, lived in expectation of the imminent end of the world. They believed that the holy city (see Revelation 21:1–10) would descend from heaven at Pepuza, a country town between Peltai and Dionysopolis.

Prisca's dream

[Christ] caused wisdom to sink into her heart and had revealed to her that this was a holy place, and here would Jerusalem descend out of heaven.

Epiphanius, *Heretics*, 49,1,3. 48,14,1.

Hippolytus
(170–236)

An important theologian of the Roman Church

The Apostolic Tradition

At the time set aside for baptism the bishop will give thanks over the oil and put it into a vessel. This oil is called the oil of thanksgiving. The bishop then takes other oil and exorcises over it. This oil is the oil of exorcism. Let the deacon carry the oil of exorcism and stand on the left of those to be baptised and another deacon oil of thanksgiving and stand on the right hand side. As the presbyter takes of each person who is to be baptised, let him say these words of renunciation:

'I renounce you, Satan, and all your service and all your works.'

After he has said this the presbyter anoints him with the oil of exorcism, saying, 'Let all evil spirits depart far from you.'

Then he takes him to the presbyter who is standing in the water. Let them stand in the water naked. And let a deacon also go down with him into the water.

The Apostolic Tradition, 18–20.

Priscilla and Maximilla are held to be prophetesses

They have been deceived by two women, Priscilla and Maximilla, whom they hold to be prophetesses, asserting that into them the Paraclete spirit entered. They magnify these women above the apostles and every gift of grace, so that some of them go so far as to say that there is in them something more than Christ. These people agree with the church in acknowledging the Father of the universe to be God and Creator of all things, and they also acknowledge all that the Gospel testifies about Christ. But they introduce novelties in the form of fasts and feasts, abstinences and dies of radishes, giving these women as their authority.

Refutation of All Heresies, 8, 19.

Athenagoras

Christian apologist and philosopher.

[The prophets], lifted in ecstasy above the natural operation of their minds by the impulses of the Divine Spirit, were inspired to utterance, the Spirit making use of them as a flute-player breathes into a flute.

Tillemont, *Persecution under Marcus Aurelius*, ix.

Melito
(died c.190)

Bishop of Sardis, and a prolific writer.

A second century example of prophecy

Who will contend against me? Let him stand before me.
It is I who delivered the condemned. It is I who gave life to the dead.
It is I who raised up the buried. Who will argue with me?
It is I, says Christ, who destroyed death. It is I who triumphed over
   the enemy,
And trod down Hades, and bound the Strong Man,
And snatched mankind up to the heights of heaven. It is I, says
   Christ.
So then, come here all you families of man, weighed down by your
   sins
And receive pardon for your misdeeds. For I am your pardon.
I am the Passover which brings salvation. I am your life, your
   resurrection.
I am your light, I am your salvation, I am your King.
It is I who bring you up to the heights of heaven.
It is I who will give you the resurrection there.
I will show you the Eternal Father. I will raise you up with my own
   right hand.

Prophecy, xxi.

Origen
(c.185–254)

Alexandrian biblical exegete, theologian and spiritual writer.

Exorcism, and ten thousand things beside

Some people show signs of having received some more incredible through this faith. I refer to the cures they perform. They call on God, who rules over everyone, and on the name of Jesus as they pray over all those in need of healing. We ourselves have seen many people set free from terrible illnesses and insanity, and ten thousand things beside, which neither men nor demons could cure.

Contra Celsum, III, 24.

The gift of wisdom through the power of the Spirit of God

The grace of the Holy Spirit is added so that those people who are not holy in themselves may be made holy by participating in the Spirit. So they derive existence from God the Father, rationality from the Word, and sanctity from the Holy Spirit. Again when they have once been sanctified through the Holy Spirit they are made capable of receiving Christ, as he is 'the righteousness of God' (1 Corinthians 1:30), and those who have deserved to advance to this stage through the sanctification of the Holy Spirit will go on to attain the gift of wisdom through the power of the Spirit of God and his work in them.

Thus the work of the Father who gives existence on all, proves more splendid and impressive when each person advances and reaches higher stages of progress through participation in Christ as wisdom, and as knowledge and sanctification; and as a man has become purer and cleaner by participation in the Holy Spirit he is made worthy to receive, and receives, the grace of wisdom and knowledge.

On First Principles, 1. iii. 8.

3RD CENTURY

Cyprian
(c.200–58)

Bishop of Carthage, who allowed repentant, lapsed Christians to rejoin Christian fellowships.

Under our hand they stand bound and tremble

If only you would see how [your gods] (who, in Cyprian's eyes are demons), under our command are . . . cast out from possessed bodies . . . As they experience the lashings and floggings they howl and groan, as they hear man's voice and feel God's power, and they confess that judgment will come. Observe that what they say is true. You believe them and even worship them, so take note of what they say! You will see that they plead with us, those whom you plead with; and you will see that we are feared by those whom you fear and worship. You will observe that under our hand they stand bound and tremble as captives, those people you worship and admire as lords.

To Demetrianus, 15.

Novatian
(210–80)

Rival bishop of Rome who was martyred. Wrote an important work on the Trinity.

Gifts of charismata

They were armed by the same Spirit, having themselves the gifts which this same Spirit distributes, and appropriates to the church. This is he [the Spirit] who places prophets in the church, instructs teachers, directs tongues, gives powers and healings, does wonderful works, offers discrimination of spirits, affords powers of government, suggests counsels, and orders and arranges whatever other gifts there are of *charismata*; and thus make the Lord's chuch everywhere, and in all, perfected and completed.

Treatise Concerning the Trinity, chapter 29.

Two eras contrasted: before and after Christ's resurrection

'In the last days, I will pour out my Spirit,' prophesied the prophet Joel. In the former times [before our Lord's resurrection], the Spirit was occasional, in the latter [times, after our Lord's resurrection] always – in the former times not always being in the prophets and apostles, but in the latter times as abiding always in them. In the former times the Spirit was distributed with reserve, but in the latter times he is liberally bestowed. The Spirit was not yet manifested before the Lord's resurrection, but conferred after the Lord's resurrection.

Treatise Concerning the Trinity, chapter 29.

Desert Fathers

In about 269 St Antony retired to the Egyptian desert, to seek after purity of heart and fight against demons. Soon, hundreds of people also went to various deserts in Egypt, Palestine and Sinai. Collections of sayings of these Desert Fathers (Apophthegmata Patrum) *circulated widely.*

Antony
(251–356)

Demons disappear at the name of Christ

Once, a very tall demon appeared with a procession of evil spirits and said boldly: 'I am the power of God, I am his providence. What do you wish that I grant you?' I then blew my breath at him, calling on the name of Christ, and I tried to strike him. I seemed to have succeeded, for, immediately, vast as he was, he and all his demons disappeared at the name of Christ.

Life, Athanasius' biography of Antony, chapter 40.

Demons and visions

A vision of the holy ones comes so quietly and gently that instantly joy a gladness and courage arise in the soul and the thoughts of the soul remain untroubled and unruffled, so that in its own bright transparency it is able to behold those who appear. On the other hand the attack and appearance of the evil ones at once begets terror in the soul, disturbance and confusion of thoughts.

Life, 35.

The state of his soul was pure. I feel confident that if the soul is pure through and through and is in its natural state, it becomes clear-sighted and sees no more and farther than the demons.

Life, 34.

Hilarion
(291–371)

Founder of the anchorite life in Palestine

Immediately cured

Facidia is a small suburb of Rhinocorura, a city of Egypt. From this village, a woman who had been blind for ten years was brought to be blessed by Hilarion. On being presented to him by the brothers (already there were many monks with him), she told him that she had bestowed all her substance on physicians. To her the saint replied: 'If what you lost on physicians you had given to the poor, Jesus the true Physician would have healed you.' Whereupon she cried aloud and implored him to have mercy on her. Then, following the example of the Saviour, he rubbed spittle on her eyes and she was immediately cured.

There would not be time if I wanted to tell you all the signs and wonders performed by Hilarion.

Jerome, *Life of Saint Hilarion*, 15:254–5, 262–3.

4TH – 5TH CENTURIES

Constantine
(c.276–337)

Roman Emperor who united the Christian church to the secular state by close ties.

Constantine's vision and dream

When Constantine overthrew his rival Maxentius at the Milvian Bridge in 312 and thus became master of the western empire, the change which this portended in the fortunes of the church was such that it came to be looked upon as practically a Christian victory. Constantine had hitherto been a worshipper of the 'Unconquered Sun,' whom he regarded as his patron deity. But he ascribed his victory at the Milvian Bridge to the direct intervention of the Christians' God. Before he marched into Italy against Maxentius, he had (according to Eusebius's account, based on Constantine's own later testimony) seen a vision of the cross in the sky ['What Constantine probably saw was a rare, but well-attested, form of the "halo-phenomenon," says A. H. M. Jones in *Constantine and the Conversion of Europe* (London: Hodder & Stoughton, 1948), p. 96], and in a dream the night before the battle at the Milvian Bridge he was commanded to mark his soldiers' shields with the monogram of Christ, a monogram formed of the two initial letters of the Greek name of Christ – X (ch) and P (r) – and to

use the same monogram combined with the cross as his standard
or labarum. The accounts of the vision and dream were naturally
embellished in later legend, but Constantine did from that time
forth consider himself to be in a special sense under the tutelage of
the God of Christianity.

F. F. Bruce, *The Spreading Flame* (Paternoster Press, 1958), p. 294.

Hilary of Poitiers
(310–67)

Hilary, known as 'the Athanasius of the West', wrote On the Trinity *and
a* Tract on the Psalms, *and his books influenced both Augustine and
Ambrose.*

Commenting on 'Streams of living water will flow from within him' (John 7:39)

The Holy Spirit is likened to a river. When we receive the Holy
Spirit we are made drunk.

We can prophecy and speak with wisdom . . . We receive gifts of
healing. Demons are subject to us.

These gifts come to us like gentle rain . . . At first they are small
streams, then they become raging rivers.

Tract on Psalm 64:6ff.

St Cyril of Jerusalem
(315–86)

*Patriarch of Jerusalem, later honoured as doctor of the church. He prob-
ably instituted the ceremonies of Holy Week.*

The gift of prophecy

If you have faith you will not only receive remission of your sins, you will also do things beyond the power of men, and, please God, you will receive the gift of prophecy.

Catechetical Lectures 17, 37.

A well bubbling out of his mouth (tongues?)

He heard Ephraim speaking as it were a well bubbling out of his mouth, all in good order, and knew that what came through the lips of Ephraim was from the Holy Spirit.

Apophthegmata Patrum, Ephraim 2.

Great are the Holy Spirit's gifts

Great indeed is the Holy Spirit, and in his gifts, omnipotent and wonderful. Think how, however many of you are sitting here now, there is present that number of souls. On each one, the Holy Spirit is at work for his good purpose. He is present with us and knows what we are thinking in our minds. He knows what we say, think and believe. Saying this might appear to be enough, but it is not. For, with your minds enlightened by the Holy Spirit, I urge you reflect on how many Christians there are in the diocese, and then in the whole province of Palestine, and in the whole Roman Empire, and beyond that, in the whole world: Persia, India, the nations of the Goths, Gauls, Spaniards, Moors, Libyans, Ethiopians, and countries which have no names. Then think about all the bishops, presbyters, deacons, celibates, virgins and all the other lay people in these countries of the world. Finally contemplate the great guardian and dispenser of their various graces, who, throughout the world, gives to this person chastity, to that person lifelong virginity, and to another to be a generous giver, and enabling another person to become detached from his worldly goods, while he bestows on another person the gift of driving out evil spirits. And just as daylight, by one act of the sun's radiation, enlightens the whole earth, so too the Holy Spirit gives light to everyone who has eyes to see. For if anyone is not granted such grace because of his blindness, let him not put

the blame on the Holy Spirit but his own faithlessness.
Catechetical lecture 16, 22.

Gregory of Nyssa
(330–95)

Bishop of Nyssa, the younger brother of Basil; he was deposed by Arians. His most famous writing was The Life of Moses. *He wrote the following account of the healing of his younger sister, Macrina.*

The hand of God restores sight to the blind Macrina the Younger (328–79)

There was with us our little girl who was suffering from an eye ailment resulting from an infectious sickness. It was a terrible and pitiful thing to see her as the membrane around the pupil was swollen and whitened by the disease.

I went to the men's quarters where your brother Peter was Superior, and my wife went to the women's quarters to be with St Macrina. After an interval of time we were getting ready to leave but the blessed one would not let my wife go, and said she would not give up my daughter, whom she was holding in her arms, until she had given them a meal and offered them 'the wealth of philosophy'. She kissed the child as one might expect and put her lips on her eyes and, when she noticed the diseased pupil she said, 'If you do me the favour of remaining for dinner I will give you a return in keeping with this honour.' When the child's mother asked what it was, the great lady replied, 'I have some medicine which is especially effective in curing eye disease.'

We gladly remained and later started the journey home, bright and happy. Each of us told his own story on the way. My wife was telling everything in order, as if going through a treatise, and when she came to the point at which the medicine was promised, interrupting the narrative, she said, 'What have we done? How did we forget the promise, the medicine for the eyes?'

I was annoyed at our thoughtlessness, and quickly sent one of my men back to ask for the medicine, when the child, who happened to be in her nurse's arms, looked at her mother, and the mothers, fixing her gaze on the child's eyes said, 'Stop being upset by our carelessness.' She said this in a loud voice, joyfully and fearfully. 'Nothing of what was promised to us has been omitted, but the true medicine that heals disease, the cure that comes from prayer, this she has given us, and has already worked; nothing at all is left of the disease of the eyes.'

As she said this, she took our child and put her in my arms, and I also then comprehended the miracles in the gospel which I had not believed before, and I said, 'What a great thing it is for sight to be restored to the blind by the hand of God, if now his handmaiden makes much cures and has done such a thing through faith in him, a fact no less impressive than these miracles.'

On the Lord's Prayer and the Beatitudes, xxiv.

Basil
(330–79)

Basil the Great, Archbishop of Caesarea, founder of the ideal of monastic community life.

From the Spirit comes understanding of mysteries

From the Spirit comes foreknowledge of the future, understanding of mysteries, apprehension of what is hidden, the distribution of wonderful charisms [gifts].

On the Holy Spirit.

Ambrose
(339–97)

Bishop of Milan. Helped Augustine to become a Christian. With Jerome,

Gregory the Great and Augustine, Ambrose is one of the four traditional doctors of the Latin church.

God still bestows tongues and healings

Behold, the Father established the teachers; Christ also established them in the churches; and just as the Father gives the grace of healings, so the Son also gives it; just as the Father gives the gift of tongues, so the Son also has bestowed it.

The Holy Spirit

Augustine
(354–430)

Bishop of Hippo in North Africa. Apart from biblical writers, Augustine is the most influential Christian theologian of all time.

Augustine's conversion experience

I threw myself down under a fig tree and collapsed in tears . . .

'How long, O Lord, how long will you be angry? For ever? Do not hold against us our former sins' [cf. Ps. 79:5–8 and Ps. 85:5] – for I felt I was bound by them . . . 'Tomorrow and tomorrow? Why not now? Why isn't there an end to my dirtiness here and now?'

I was talking like this and crying with most heartfelt bitterness when I heard a voice (perhaps a child's voice, I'm not sure) coming from a nearby house. I was chanting and repeating the words 'Pick it up and read it!' Immediately my face changed and I began seriously to wonder whether children used these words in any of their games, but I couldn't remember ever hearing anything like them. So, subduing my tears, I got up, thinking it must be nothing other than a command from God to open the book and read the first chapter I found. For I had heard that Antony, coming in during the reading of the Gospel, received what was being read as a warning to himself: 'Go, sell your possessions and give to the poor, and you will have treasure in heaven. Then come, follow me' (Matthew 19:21). And he was immediately converted to you by this message.

Then I ran back to where Alypius was sitting; for, when I left him, I had left the Apostle's book lying there. I picked it up, opened it, and silently read the passage (Romans 13:13–14). I first set eyes on: 'Let us behave decently, as in the daytime, not in orgies and drunkenness, not in sexual immorality and debauchery, not in dissension and jealousy. Rather, clothe yourselves with the Lord Jesus Christ, and do not think about how to gratify the desires of the sinful nature.' I didn't want to read any further, and it wasn't necessary. As I reached the end of the sentence, the light of peace seemed to shine on my heart, and every shadow of doubt disappeared.

Confessions, Book 8, Section 12.

Renewal does not happen in one moment of conversion

Renewal does not happen in one moment of conversion, as the baptismal renewal by the forgiveness of all sins happens in a moment, so that not even one small sin remains unforgiven. But it is one thing to throw off a fever, another to recover from the weakness which the fever leaves behind it; it is one thing to remove from the body a missile stuck in it, another to heal the wound it made with a complete cure. The first stage of the cure is to remove the cause of the debility, and this is done by pardoning all sins; the second stage is curing the debility itself, and this is done gradually by making steady progress in the renewal of this image. These two stages are seen in Psalm 103:3, where we read, 'who forgives all your sins,' which happens at baptism, 'and heals all your diseases,' which happens by daily advances while the image is being renewed. The apostle Paul speaks about this quite clearly in 2 Corinthians 4:16: 'Though outwardly we are wasting away, yet inwardly we are being renewed day by day.'

Sermons, on Psalm 103.

Miracles

Miracles, which were performed to make the world believe, have not stopped now that the world does believe.

It is sometimes objected that the miracles which Christians claimed to have occurred no longer happen. The truth is that even today miracles are being wrought in the name of Christ, sometimes through his sacraments and sometimes through the intercession of the relics of his saints.

It is a simple fact that there is no lack of miracles even in our day. And the God who works the miracles we read of in the Scriptures uses any means and manner he chooses.

The City of God, Book 22, chapter 28.

A miracle at Milan

A miracle took place while I was in Milan when a blind man had his sight restored. This became widely known in Milan, since Milan is an important city and because the emperor was visiting there at that time. A huge crowd had gathered to view the bodies of two martyrs, Protasius and Gervasius, and the miracle took place in front of all those witnesses. These bodies had been had been lost and nobody knew where they were, but the place where they were hidden was revealed to Ambrose, bishop of Milan, in a dream, and the bodies were found. It was there that the darkness, in which this blind man had lived so long, was banished, and he saw daylight.

The City of God, Book 22, chapter 28.

Miracles galore!

What am I do to now? I must keep my promise and complete writing this book. But this means that I will not be able to relate all the miracles I know about. Doubtless many of my Christian friends will be sad to see that I have left out so many of the miracles that are familiar both to them and to me.

The City of God, Book 22, chapter 28.

The gift of the Spirit is separate from water baptism

[Preaching on Paul's words, 'We being many are one bread, one body.']
Understand and rejoice: unity, truth, piety, charity. 'One bread': who is that one bread? 'Many are one body.' Remember that bread is not made from a single grain, but from many.

When you were exorcised, you were, so to speak, ground.

When you were baptised, you were, so to speak, watered.

When you received the fire of the Holy Spirit, you were, so to speak, baked.

Sermon 273.

The distinction between baptism and the Holy Spirit

And so this distinction between the reception of baptism and the reception of the Holy Spirit shows us clearly enough that we should not think that those whom we do not deny to have received baptism forthwith have the Holy Spirit.

Sermon 269.

6TH–7TH CENTURIES

Gregory of Tours
(540–94)

Bishop of Tours, theologian and historian of the Franks

Eleutherius, abbot of St Mark's monastery, lived with me for a long time in my monastery at Rome and died there. His disciples say that he raised a dead person to life by the power of prayer. He was well known for his simplicity and compunction of heart, and undoubtedly through his tears this humble, childlike soul obtained many favours from almighty God.

I will tell you about a miracle of his which I had him describe to me in his own simple words. Once while he was travelling, evening came on before he could find a lodging for the night, so he stopped at a convent. There was a little boy in this convent who was troubled every night by an evil spirit. So, after welcoming the man of God to their convent, the nuns asked him to keep the boy with him that night. He agreed, and allowed the boy to rest near him. In the morning the nuns asked him with deep concern whether he had done anything for the boy. Rather surprised that they should ask, he said, 'No'. Then they acquainted him with the boy's condition, informing him that not a night passed without the evil spirit troubling the boy. Would Eleutherius please take him along to the monastery because they could no longer bear to see him suffer. The man of God agreed to do so.

52

The boy remained a long time in the monastery without being troubled in the least. Highly pleased at this, the old abbot allowed his joy at the boy's healthy condition to exceed moderation. 'Brothers,' he said to the monks, 'the Devil had his joke with the sisters, but once he encountered real servants of God, he no longer dared to come near the boy.' That very instant, hardly waiting for Eleutherius to finish speaking, the Devil again took possession of the young boy, tormenting him in the presence of all. The sight of it filled the old man's heart with grief, and when his monks tried to console him he said, 'Upon my word! Not one of you shall taste bread today until this boy is snatched out of the Devil's power.'

He prostrated himself in prayer with all his monks and continued praying until the boy was freed from the power of the evil spirit. The cure was complete and the Devil did not dare molest him any further.

Dialogues.

Gregory I (the Great)
(540–604)

Pope from 590. One of the four traditional doctors of the Latin Church.

'The miracles of the Fathers which were done in Italy'

One day at Subiaco, the little monk Placidus, the future apostle of his [Gregory's] Order in Sicily, went to the lake to draw water, but overbalanced himself and fell in. Benedict, who was sitting in his cell, was supernaturally aware of the occurrence, and cried out hastily to his disciples Maurus: 'Run, Brother Maurus, for the child who went to fetch water has fallen into the lake, and the stream has carried him a great way.' Maurus ran down to the edge of the lake, and then, 'thinking still that he went on dry land, he ran on the water', caught the drifting boy by the hair and brought him safely back. It was only when he stood again on the firm ground that Maurus realised that a miracle had taken place, and 'much astonished, he wondered how he had done that which knowingly he would not have dared to venture.'

Dialogues, in F. Homes Dudden, *Gregory the Great* (1905), vol. I, p. 334.

Isaac the Syrian
(c.620–c.690)

Isaac of Nineveh, or 'the Syrian' is the best known Syriac mystical and spiritual writers. His main work was The First Part of the Teaching of Mr Isaac on the Monastic Life.

The world is ennobled and uplifted by the boundless love of Jesus which possesses his heart and pours itself over all creation

At times I felt a burning love for Jesus Christ and for all God's creation. At times sweet tears of thanks to the Lord streamed involuntarily from my eyes. At times a comforting warmth of the heart streamed through my whole frame and in rapture I felt all around me the presence of God.

Not only in my inmost soul did I feel this, but also all outward things appeared to me to love and give thanks to God; men, trees, plants, beasts – everything seemed so familiar, everywhere I found the imprint of the name of Jesus Christ.

Vide, pp. 39–40

Joseph Hazzaya
(Seventh century)

A seventh-century monk and Syrian theologian, known as 'The Seer'.

Four marks of the presence of the Spirit

The first sign of the effective working of the Spirit is God's love burning in the heart of a man, like a fire.

The second sign consists in true humility being born in your soul.

The third sign of the working of the Spirit in you consists in the compassion which represents within you the image of God, through which, when your thoughts extend to all men, tears flow form your eyes like fountains of water, and you affectionately embrace them and kiss them, while your pour your kindness on all.

The fourth sign of the working of the Spirit . . . is a spiritual speech and the knowledge of both worlds: of the one that has passed and the one that shall pass, and also a consciousness of the mysteries of future things, the fine sounds of the spiritual intelligences: joy, jubilation, exultation, glorification, songs, hymns, and odes of magnification.

Quoted in Alphonse Mirgana's *Early Christian Mystics* (Cambridge: Heffer, 1934), pp. 165–6.

8TH–10TH CENTURIES

St Symeon the New Theologian
(949–1022)

One of the greatest of the Byzantine mystics.

New eyes, a new power, and the new perception in the glorified man

He is made worthy to look upon the revelation of great mysteries. I speak of mysteries because, whereas all can see them clearly, they cannot understand. He who is glorified by the new-creating spirit receives new eyes and new hearing.

Quotation in Holl, *Enthusiasmus und Bussgewalt beim Griechischen Monchtum* (Leipzig: Hinrichs, 1898), p. 81; quoted by N. S. Arsenev in *Mysticism and the Eastern Church* (London: SCM Press, 1926), p. 71.

Filled with the Holy Spirit

Do not try to be a mediator on behalf of others until you have yourself been filled with the Holy Spirit, until you have come to know and to win the friendship of the King of all with conscious awareness in your soul.

Enthusiasmus und Bussgewalt beim Griechischen Monchtum: Eine Studie zu Symeon dem neuen Theologen (Leipzig: Hinrichs, 1898), Letter i, 10.

A vision of divine light

[Symeon, speaking in the third person, is referring to himself.] While he was standing one day and saying the prayer, 'God, have mercy on me, a sinner' (Luke 18:13), more with his mind than with his mouth, a great divine light suddenly appeared above him and filled the room. As this happened the young many lost all realisation of where he was, inside the house or outside it. All he could see was light, everywhere. He did not even know if his feet were still standing on the ground. He felt as if he was wholly united to non-material light and that he had himself turned into this light. He was oblivious of all the world, and became overwhelmed with inexpressible joy, tears and exultation.

Catechesis XXII, 88–100.

William of St Thierry
(1085–1148)

Abbot of the Benedictine monastery of St Thierry, near Rheims, and monk of the Cistercian house of Signy.

This embrace of the Holy Spirit

He who is the communion of the Father and of the Son, who is love, who is friendship, who is the embrace, he is everything in the love of the Bride and Groom. While he is majesty of a consubstantial nature there, he is the gift of grace here. While he is dignity there, he is condescension here; remaining the same Spirit, all the time. The embrace starts here and is completed there. 'Deep calls to deep' (Ps. 42:7). This ecstasy dreams about nothing than it sees, so the one secret sighs for another secret, one joy imagines another joy, and one sweetness looks forward to another sweetness.

Canticle 132.

Rupert of Deutz
(1075–1129)

Twelfth-century mystic and visionary abbot in the Cistercian tradition. He appealed to the visions he had as a source for his teaching.

I saw him not with corporeal vision: a consolation given by the Holy Spirit

My eyes were open and I saw the Son of God. I was awake and yet I saw the living Son of Man on the cross. I saw him not with corporeal vision, but my physical eyes suddenly disappeared so that I had much better vision – my interior eyes were opened. What did the Son of God look like? There are no human words to describe this. Suffice to say that I saw for a moment what he said so truly: 'Learn from me, for I am gentle and humble in heart' (Matthew 11:29).

The Glory and Honour of the Son of Man.

Hildegard of Bingen
(1098–1179)

A twelfth century German abbess, called the 'Sibyl of the Rhine', and, 'the first great woman theologian in Christian history'.

A beyond consciousness experience (known as 'excessus mentis' or, 'exstasis')

I saw a wonderfully mystical vision which made my whole womb convulse and cut dead all my other physical powers of sense. I received knowledge in some other way, as if I no longer knew myself. Like drops of gentle rain God's inspiration filled my mind, just as the Holy Spirit came into John the Evangelist when he suckled deep revelations from the breast of Jesus.

Life.

12TH–14TH CENTURIES

St Francis of Assisi
(1181–1226)

Italian founder of the Franciscan order of friars.

Drunk in spirit

Francis of Assisi, after the decisive break with his former life, can no longer contain his inward exaltation – it presses outwards, he is as though 'drunk in spirit'. He shouts and sings. And in the Italian text of the noble old *Legenda di tre compagni* we read about the 'unbounded joy and delight in the Holy Spirit' experienced by him and by his disciples.

Quoted by N. S. Arsenev, *Mysticism and the Eastern Church* (London: SCM Press, 1926), p. 65.

A blind woman

A woman from Narni who had been struck blind was found worthy of receiving the longed-for light immediately on the blessed Francis' make the sign of the cross over her eyes.

A woman's contracted hands

At Gubbio there was a woman both whose hands were contracted

so that she could do nothing with them. As soon as she knew that
St Francis had entered the city she ran to him, and with miserable
and woe-begone face showed him her deformed hands and began
to pray that he would deign to touch them. He was moved with
compassion, touched her hands and healed them. And straightway
the woman returned joyfully to her house, made a cheesecake with
her own hands and offered it to the holy man; he took a little in
token of kindness, and bade her and her household eat the rest.

A cripple at Toscanella

Once when Francis the saint of God was making a long circuit
through various regions to preach the gospel of God's kingdom he
came to a city called Toscanella. Here, while he was sowing the
seed of life, as he was wont, he was entertained by a knight of that
same city whose only son was a cripple and weak in all his body.
Though the child was of tender years, he had passed the age of
weaning; but he still remained in a cradle. But the boy's father,
seeing the man of God to be endued with such holiness, humbly
fell at his feet and besought him to heal his son. Francis, deeming
himself to be unprofitable and unworthy of such power and grace,
for a long time refused to do it. At last, conquered by the urgency
of the knight's entreaties, after offering up prayer he laid his hand
on the boy, blessed him, and lifted him up. And in the sight of all
the boy straightway arose whole in the name of our Lord Jesus
Christ, and began to walk hither and thither about the house.

A paralytic at Narni

Once when Francis the man of God had come to Narni and was
staying there several days, a man of that city named Peter was lying
in bed paralysed. For five months he had been so completely deprived of the use of all his limbs that he could in no wise lift himself
up or move at all; and thus, having lost all help from feet, hands
and head, he could only move his tongue and open his eyes. But
on hearing that St Francis was come to Narni he sent a messenger
to the bishop to ask that he would, for divine compassion's sake, be

pleased to send the servant of God Most High to him, for he trusted that he would be delivered, by the sight and presence of the saint, from the infirmity whereby he was holden. And so indeed it came to pass; for when the blessed Francis was come to him he made the sign of the cross over him from head to feet, and forthwith drove away all his sickness and restored him to his former health.

Deliverance from the falling sickness, or from a devil

There was a brother who often suffered from a grievous infirmity that was horrible to see; and I know not what name to give it; though some think it was caused by a malignant devil. For oftentimes he was dashed down and with a terrible look in his eyes he wallowed foaming; sometimes his limbs were contracted, sometimes extended, sometimes they were folded and twisted together, and sometimes they became hard and rigid. Sometimes, tense and rigid all over, with his feet touching his head, he would be lifted up in the air to the height of a man's stature and would then suddenly spring back to the earth. The holy father Francis pitying his grievous sickness went to him and after offering up prayer signed him with the cross and blessed him. And suddenly he was made whole, and never afterwards suffered from this distressing infirmity.

A demon-possessed woman delivered at the fortress of St Gemini

One day when the most blessed father Francis was passing through the diocese of Narni he reached a fortress known as that of St Gemini, and while he was there preaching the gospel of God's kingdom, he with three brethren were entertained by a man who feared and worshipped God and was very well reported of in that town. But his wife, as was known to all the inhabitants of the place, was vexed with a devil; and so her husband besought the blessed Francis for her, trusting that by his merits she might be delivered. But St Francis, desiring in his simplicity rather to be had in contempt than through ostentation of sanctity to be uplifted by the favour of this world, altogether refused to do this thing. At length, since God was concerned in the case, he yielded too the prayers of the many who were entreating him. So he called the three brethren who were with him, and setting each one in a corner of the house, he said to them, 'Brethren, let us pray to the Lord for this woman, that God may break off from her the devil's yoke, to his praise and glory. Stand we apart, he added, in the corners of the house, that this evil spirit may not be able to escape us delude us by trying to sneak into the corners.'

Accordingly, having finished his prayer blessed Francis went in the power of the Spirit to the woman who was being miserably tormented and crying horribly; and he said, 'In the name of our Lord Jesus Christ, I charge thee, devil, on obedience, to go out of her nor dare to impede her any more.' Hardly had he finished speaking when the devil with furious roaring rushed out so swiftly that the holy father thought himself under some illusion, because of the sudden healing of the woman and the prompt obedience of the devil. And forthwith he departed from that place shamefacedly, for God's providence had so wrought in the matter that there might be no place for vainglory on his part.

The Lives of S. Francis of Assisi, Brother Thomas of Celano, translated by A. G. Ferrers Howell (London: Methuen, 1908), pp. 64–8.

Waldensians

Founded by Waldes (d. 1210), a wealthy merchant in Lyons, the group tried to live according to the teaching of Matthew chapter 10.

Therefore, concerning this anointing of the sick, we hold it as an article of faith, and profess sincerely from the heart that sick people, when they ask for it, may lawfully be anointed with the anointing oil by one who joins them in praying that it may be efficacious to the healing of the body according to the design and end and effect mentioned by the apostles; and we profess that such an anointing performed according to the apostolic design and practice will be healing and profitable.

A. J. Gordon, *The Ministry of Healing* (Harrisburg: Christian Publications, 1902), p. 65.

Thomas Aquinas
(1225–75)

Dominican philosopher, theologian and prolific writer.

Aquinas' revelation

Towards the end of his life, in the winter of 1273, Aquinas had a mystical experience that moved him so much that he never wrote or dictated another word, even though he had spent a great deal of his life writing over 16,000 pages in his numerous writings. One of his secretaries tried to encourage him to start writing again, but he replied, 'I am unable to do that. Everything that I have written now seems to be to be like straw, in comparison with what I have seen and what has been revealed to me.'

Angela of Foligno
(1248–1309)

The Italian mystic, Angela of Foligno, in the thirteenth century passed through an experience as soul-shaking as those of George Fox and Boehme. She felt herself immersed in inward communion with the Holy Spirit, 'and wherever I turned my eyes he said to me, "Behold, that have I created," and I felt an inexpressible sweetness.' Another time, 'The eyes of my soul were opened for a moment and I saw the fulness of God, in which I saw the whole world. The sea also and the abyss and all things, but in all this I could see nothing save the divine power in a manner completely beyond expression. And in measureless astonishment my soul cried out and said: "Truly this world is full of God!" And I felt the whole world as something small. And I saw that the power of God surpasseth all things and filleth all things.'

Beatae Angelae de Fulginio, Visionum et Instructionum Liber (Cologne, 1851), chapter xx, p. 66. Quoted by N. S. Arsenev in *Mysticism and the Eastern Church* (London: SCM Press, 1926), pp. 71–2.

Julian of Norwich
(1342– ?)

English anchoress of Norwich whose Revelations of Divine Love *was the first book to be written in English by a woman.*

The hazelnut vision

The mystical glorification of the world during the Middle Ages perhaps found its highest expression in the experiences of the English mystic of the end of the fourteenth century, Lady Julian of Norwich, in her *Revelations of Divine Love*. The world is small and nothing worth. God showed her in a vision 'a little thing, the quantity of a hazel not, lying the palm of my hand; and, to my understanding, it was round as any ball.' And it was said to her: '"It is all that is made." I marvelled how it might last, for methought it might fall suddenly to nought for littleness.' It cannot satisfy the cravings of the soul: 'all that is beneath God, suffices not to us.' In order to find real satisfaction in God we must free the soul of all that is made: 'No soul is rested, till it be noughted of all that is made.' And yet God loves this world which, in comparison with him, is infinitely small and mean: 'It lasts and ever shall, for God loves it. And so all-thing hath its being through the love of God.'

'In this little thing,' i.e., the universe, Julian continues, 'I saw three parts: the first is that God made it. The second is that he loves it. The third is that God keeps it.' And in this light of God's love the world assumes for this mystic a new meaning, a new nobility, a new worth. 'I saw all-thing God had made. It is great and fair and large and good. But the cause why it showed so little too my sight was because I saw it in the presence of him that is its Maker. For to a soul that sees the Maker of all-thing, all that is made seems full little.' The great worth and highest merit of the universe lies in this, that it is a fruit of the divine love and also has love as its goal. God 'made all-thing that is made for love, and through the same love it is kept and ever shall be without end.' For 'God is all-thing that is good, and the goodness that all-thing has is he.' Therefore 'he is in all-thing.' 'God doth all-thing, be it never so little. And nothing is done by hap nor by chance, but by the endless foresight of the wisdom of God.' But this is not pantheism: the foundation of all that exists and also of our being is God; real, actual being belongs to God only, and yet the being of us his creatures is in itself not God, although it is in God.

Comfortable Words for Christ's Lovers, being the visions vouchsafed to Lady Julian, recluse at Norwich in 1373, ed. Rev Dundas Harford (London, 1912), ch. iv, v, viii.

Agnes Blannbekin of Vienna

A German visionary, at the end of the fourteenth century.

She was swept away into an indescribable light, and in this divine light she saw the elements and the creatures and the things which are made from them, both small and great, stand out in such brilliance, that each of them, however small, appeared a hundred times more brilliant than the sun – even the smallest grain of corn or pebble. And the light of the present world compared with this brilliance would have seemed dark like the moon when she is covered by a dark cloud. And created things appeared so clearly in this radiance that each could be distinguished by its quality; a green grain, a red rose, etc. But among all the elements and created things the earth was the most splendid. And this because God took his body from the earth; and because during the Lord's Passion the earth was drenched with the blood of the Saviour. All this was in the Man, i.e., in Christ.

Agnetis Blannbekin, Vita et Revelationes, chapter I. Quoted by N. S. Arsenev in *Mysticism of the Eastern Church* (London: SCM Press, 1926), p. 104.

Man, i.e., in Christ.

Agnetis Blannbekin, Vita et Revelationes, chapter I. Quoted by N. S. Arsenev in *Mysticism of the Eastern Church* (London: SCM Press, 1926), p. 104.

15TH CENTURY

Desiderius Erasmus
(1467–1536)

Dutch scholar who prepared an accurate edition of the Greek New Testament.

The purpose of miracles

It belongs to magicians and wonder-workers to effect or simulate marvellous deeds for mere ostentation, or to tickle the idle curiosity of spectators, where there is no praise about God's glory, nor any usefulness for one's neighbour. Jesus never performed any miracle, except when it glorified God's power, and was beneficial to men, or challenged human incredulity.

Paraphrases, commenting on Matthew 4:4.

Martin Luther
(1483–1546)

German monk and theologian who led the Protestant Reformation and translated the Bible into German.

Luther and prophecy

One may prophesy new things but not things that go beyond the bounds of faith. If you wish to prophesy, do it in such a way that it does not go beyond faith so that your prophesying can be in harmony with the peculiar quality of faith.

Laying hands on the sick: 'We cured him by prayer in Christ's name'

The tax collector in Torgau and the counsellor in Belgern have written me to ask that I offer good advice and help for Mrs John Korner's afflicted husband. I know of no worldly help to give. If the doctors are at a loss to find a remedy, you can be sure that it is not a case of ordinary melancholy. It must, rather, be an affliction that comes from the devil, and this must be counteracted by the power of Christ with the prayer of faith. This is what we do, and what we have been accustomed to do, for a cabinet maker here was similarly afflicted with madness and we cured him by prayer in Christ's name.

Accordingly you should proceed as follows: Go to him with the deacon and two or three good men. Confident that you, as pastor of the place, are clothed with the authority of the ministerial office, lay your hands upon him and say, 'Peace be with you, dear brother, from God our Father and from our Lord Jesus Christ'. Thereupon repeat the Creed and the Lord's Prayer over him in a clear voice, and close with these words: 'O God, almighty Father, who has told us through your Son, "Truly, truly, I say to you, Whatever you ask the Father in my name, he will give it you"; who have commanded and encouraged us to pray in his name, "Ask, and you will receive," and who in like manner has said, "Call on me in the day of trouble: I will deliver you, and you will glorify me"; we unworthy sinners, relying on these your words and commands, pray for your mercy with such faith as we can muster. Graciously deign to free this man from all evil, and defeat the work that Satan has done in him, to the honour of your name and the strengthening of the faith of believers; through the same Jesus Christ, your Son, our Lord, who lives and reigns with you, world without end. Amen.'

Then, when you leave, lay your hands on the man again and say,

'These signs will follow them that believe; they shall lay hands on the sick, and they shall recover'. Do this three times, once on each of three successive days.

Letters of Spiritual Counsel, 18:52.

Nobody can receive anything from the Holy Spirit unless he experiences it

No one can understand God or God's word unless he has it revealed immediately by the Holy Spirit; but nobody can receive anything from the Holy Spirit unless he experiences it.

Preface to the Magnificat.

Thomas Münzer
(c.1489–1525)

German mystic.

Prophets, men of the Spirit

My dear brethren, do your best to become prophets, men of the Spirit; otherwise, your theology will not avail you one groat. Contemplate your God from close to, not from a distance.

Philip Melanchthon
(1497–1560)

German theologian, Greek expert, and friend of Martin Luther.

Melanchthon and the Anabaptists

Melanchthon writes: 'I have given them a hearing, and it is astonishing what they tell of themselves; namely that they are positively sent by God to teach; that they have familiar conferences with God, that they can foretell events; and, to be brief, that they are on a footing with prophets and apostles. I cannot describe how I am moved by these lofty pretensions. I see strong reasons for not despising the men; for it is clear to me that there is in them something more than a mere human spirit; but whether the spirit be God or not none, except Martin, can easily be judged.

Spalatinus, quoted in Joseph Milner, *The History of the Church,* v. viii.

16TH CENTURY

John Calvin
(1509–64)

Leading Reformation theologian who settled in Geneva as religious leader.

Complete submission to the Holy Spirit

The philosophers of old made reason the sole ruler of man and listened only to her, as the arbiter of conduct. But Christian philosophy makes her move aside and give complete submission to the Holy Spirit, so that the individual no longer lives, but Christ lives and reigns in him (see Galatians 2:20).

The Institutes of Christian Religion, 3.7.1

Distinguish between the natural and the supernatural work of the Holy Spirit

In reading profane authors the admirable light of truth displayed in them should remind us that the human mind, however much fallen and perverted from its original integrity, is still adorned and invested with admirable gifts from its creator. If we reflect that the Spirit of God is the only fountain of truth, we shall be careful, as we would avoid offering insult to him, not to reject or condemn truth wherever it appears. In despising the gifts, we insult the Giver.

The Institutes of Christian Religion, 1.13.14.

Miraculous powers lasted 'only for a time'

Without doubt, the Holy Spirit is still present amidst God's people, for the Holy Spirit has to be its guide and director if it is to stand . . . But those miraculous powers and manifest workings, which were given through the laying on of hands, have ceased. They have lasted only for a time. It was fitting that the new preaching of the gospel, and Christ's new kingdom should be illumined and magnified by extraordinary and unusual miracles. The Lord did not leave his church when these miracles ceased, but he proclaimed that the magnificence of his kingdom and the dignity of his Word had been excellently enough disclosed.

The Institutes of Christian Religion, 4.19.6

Commentary on John 7:37–39

'If a man is thirsty, let him come to me and drink.'
Throughout this clause Christ exhorts everyone to share his blessings, so long as they are aware of their own poverty and want to be helped. Indeed, we are all poor, empty, and destitute of all blessings, although s sense of poverty does not convict everyone to search for the remedy. This is why many people do not make any move but waste away in a wretched decline. There are also many people who even remain unaffected by their own emptiness until the fire of God's Spirit kindles hunger and thirst in their hearts. Therefore, it is the work of the Spirit to give us an appetite for his grace.

As far as the present passage in concerned, the first thing to be understood is that no one is called to receive the riches of the Spirit except he who burns with a desire for them. We know how acutely painful thirst can be. It can make the strongest of men, who can endure any amount of labour, feel faint. Christ invites the thirsty, rather than the hungry, so that he can keep this metaphor when later on he uses the words 'water' and 'drink'. In this way the different parts of his teaching are consistent with each other. I am sure that Christ is alluding to the passage in Isaiah which says, 'Come, all you who are thirsty, come to the waters' (Isaiah 55:1), for what the prophet there attributes to GOd had eventually to be fulfilled in Christ. It is also like the blessed Virgin Mary's song: 'He has . . . sent the rich away empty' (Luke 1:53). Therefore, Christ tells us to go straight to him, as if he is saying only he can fully satisfy everyone's thirst and that everyone who seeks even the slightest relief from their thirst elsewhere is cheated and works in vain.

'Let him come to me and drink'
A promise is added to the exhortation. Christ declares that he is not a dry and empty cistern but an inexhaustible spring plentifully and abundantly supplying everyone who comes to drink. From this it follows that if we ask Christ for what we want, our wishes will not be disappointed.

'Whoever believes in me . . .'
Christ now points out how we come. We come not on foot but by faith. Or rather, to come is simply to believe – that is, if you define the word 'believe' properly. We believe in Christ when we welcome him as he is shown to us in the gospel – full of power, wisdom, righteousness, purity, life, and all the gifts of the Spirit. Further, Christ emphasises here even more clearly the promise we have just spoken about, for he says that he has a rich abundance with which he will fully satisfy us.

'Streams of living water will flow from within him'
At first sight this metaphor seems definitely uncouth. But Christ's meaning is quite straightforward. People who believe in him will never lack any spiritual blessings. Christ calls it 'living water' whose spring never grows dry and whose flow never ceases. 'Streams', in the plural, I interpret as the many diverse graces of the Spirit which are necessary for the spiritual life of the soul. In summary, there are promised here, for ever, the abundance of the gifts of the Spirit. Some people interpret the saying that 'water will flow' from believers to mean that he to whom the Spirit has been given passes on some of the 'water' to his brother, since we should give to each other. But the meaning seems simpler than this to me. Who-

ever believes in Christ will have a spring of life welling up in him, as it were. This will be as Christ said before: 'Whoever drinks the water I give him will never thirst' (John 4:14). For whereas ordinary drinking only quenches the thirst for a short time, Christ says that by faith we draw on the Spirit, who is the spring of water, welling up to eternal life.

However, he does not say that believers are so filled with Christ on the first day that they neither hunger nor thirst afterwards, but rather that the enjoyment of Christ kindles a new desire for him. This means that the Holy Spirit is like a living and constantly flowing spring in believers, just as Paul says that he 'lives in you' (Romans 8:11), although we still carry about the cause of death in the remnants of sin. And, indeed, just as everyone shares the gifts of the Spirit according to the amount of faith they have, so there cannot be complete fullness in them in this life. But as believers progress in the faith, they continually aspire to new increases of the Spirit, so that the firstfruits which they have tasted are enough for the continuance of eternal life. This is also a warning for us about the small capacity of our faith, since the graces of the Spirit come to us by drops, whereas they would flow like rivers if we gave due place to Christ – that is, if faith made us capable of receiving him.

'As the Scripture has said . . .'
Some commentators restrict this to the former clause, others to the latter. I extend it to cover the whole discourse. Indeed, I think that Christ is not referring to any one scriptural passage but takes a testimony from the common teaching of the prophets. For whenever the Lord promises an abundance of his Spirit, he refers mainly to Christ's kingdom and focuses the minds of the believers on that. Therefore all the predictions about living waters are fulfilled in Christ, who alone has opened and revealed God's hidden treasures. The graces of the Spirit are poured out on him, so that we may all draw from his fullness. Therefore people who are so kindly and graciously called by Christ and yet wander off in every direction deserve to perish miserably.

'By this he meant the Spirit'

The word 'water' is sometimes used for the Spirit because of its purity, for it is his role to cleanse away our pollutions. But in this and similar passages the expression has a different meaning, which is that we are destitute of all the sap and moisture of life except when the Spirit of God gives us life and waters us, as it were, by a secret power. This is an expression in which one part if included under the whole, for under the one word 'water' he includes all the parts of life. From this we also infer that everyone who has not been brought to life by Christ's Spirit is to be thought of as being dead, no matter how much they pretend to be alive.

'Up to that time the Spirit had not been given'

As we know, the Spirit is eternal. But the evangelist is saying that so long as Christ lives in the world in the humble form of a servant, that grace of the Spirit which was poured out on mankind after Christ's resurrection had not yet come about openly. Christ is speaking comparatively, just as when the New Testament is compared with the Old. God promises his Spirit to believers as if he had never given him to the fathers. By that time the disciples had undoubtedly already received the firstfruits of the Spirit, for where does faith come from if it does not come from the Spirit? So the evangelist is not just denying that the grace of the Spirit was revealed to believers before Christ's death, but that it was not yet so bright and illustrious as it would be later. The main glory of Christ's kingdom is that he governs the church by his Spirit. But he entered into the lawful and, as it was, ceremonial possession of his kingdom when he was exalted to the right hand of the Father. So there is nothing surprising in his delaying the full manifestation of the Spirit until then.

There is one outstanding question. Is Christ referring here to the visible graces of the Spirit, or to being given new life. which is the fruit of adoption? My reply is: the Spirit, who had been promised at the coming of Christ, appeared in those visible gifts like mirrors. Here, however, Christ is just referring to the power of the Spirit, through whom we are born again in Christ and become new creatures. That we lie on earth poor and hungry and almost destitute of the Father, clothed with the highest majesty, must be put down to our slothfulness and to our tiny faith.

John (Wheaton (IL): Crossway Books, 1994), pp. 195–8.

Commentary on Acts 2:1–4

'When the day of Pentecost came'
The miracle described in this chapter was performed on the festival day in order to make it better known, because during the festival very large numbers of people converged on Jerusalem. Similarly, Christ often went up to Jerusalem on the holy days (John 2:13; 5:1; 7:2, 10; 10:22–3; 12:1), so that many people might see his miracles, and because in the larger crowds there might be more fruit from his teaching.

'A sound . . . came from heaven . . . they saw . . .'
The gift had to be visible, so that the disciples might be roused through their physical senses. We are so slow to think about the gifts of God that unless he wakes up all our senses, his power passes away without our noticing. These physical signs prepared the disciples to understand more clearly that the Spirit Christ had promised had now come. Even so, God did not have to use an outward sign when he gave the apostles the ability to preach the gospel. They would have understood that they had not suddenly changed as a result of some accident or through their own hard work. So the tongues of fire were more for our benefit and the benefit of the whole church. Throughout the ages Christians have been helped by these signs.

The violence of the wind made the disciples afraid. We are not ready to receive the grace of God if our cocksure natures have not been tamed. Just as access to him comes by faith, so humility and fearfulness open the gate for him to come into us. He has nothing to do with those who are proud and unconcerned.

The Spirit is often symbolised by wind (Ezekiel 4). Indeed, the word 'Spirit' is itself a figure of speech. The *hupostasis* of Person of the divine being who is called Spirit is beyond our ability to comprehend. To refer to him, the Scriptures borrow the word for wind, because the Spirit is the personal power that God pours into all his creatures, as it were, by breathing into them.

'What seemed to be tongues of fire'

Only here does the Spirit take the shape of tongues. Just as the Spirit took the shape of a dove coming down on Christ (John 1:32) because a dove was a good symbol of the work and nature of Christ, so now God chose a sign that suited the Holy Spirit's work in the apostles. The different languages were an obstacle threatening the spread of the gospel; yet if the preachers had spoken in only one tongue, everyone would have thought that Christ was confined to a small corner of Judea. But God invented a way of allowing the gospel to break out. He divided the language of the apostles, so that they could tell everyone what had been told them.

This reveals the very great goodness of God. Something that had plagued men and women and had been a punishment for human pride was now turned into a source of blessing, for how did this diversity of languages come about if not to thwart the evil and godless plans of humankind (see Genesis 11:7)? But now God equipped the disciples with many tongues, so that they might call home men and women who were wandering aimlessly here and there and bring them into a unity made happy by God. These languages made everyone speak the language of Canaan, just as Isaiah had prophesied (Isaiah 19:18). Whatever language they spoke, with one mouth and one spirit they called to one Father in heaven (Romans 15:6).

As I said, all this was done for our sakes, and not only because we received its fruit, but because it shows that the gospel did not come by accident but was planned by God. He gave the disciples different languages so that no nation would miss out on their teaching. This proves, first, that God has called the Gentiles, and, second, that the disciples' teaching was not man-made, for the Spirit lived in their tongues.

As for the fire, there is no doubt that it symbolised the effectiveness of the disciples' words. Otherwise, even if their voices had been heard in the remotest parts of the world, they would only have been beating the air, without doing any good at all. So the Lord showed that his fire would inflame the hearts of their listeners, consuming the emptiness of the world and cleansing and renewing all things. They would never have dared take on such a hard task if the Lord had not assured them that their preaching would be powerful. Nor was this power restricted to the time of the apostles. It is still seen every day.

Finally, the Lord gave the Holy Spirit a visible shape so that we may be certain that the church will never lack his invisible and hidden grace.

'All of them were filled with the Holy Spirit'

When Luke says that everyone received the fullness of the Spirit, he does not mean that they were all filled to the same extent with the gifts, but that each one received what was best for him to fulfil his own calling.

'And began to preach'

Luke shows the immediate result of the gift, and the use to which they put their gift of tongues. Some people think Luke does not mean that the apostles spoke different languages, but that they spoke one language that all the foreigners could understand as well as they could understand their own language. A further view is that since Peter only spoke one sermon, and everyone understood it, the voice that came to their ears was not Peter's.

But we must notice, first, that the disciples really did speak in strange languages. If not, the miracle would not have been in the disciples at all, but in the hearers, and the imagery of wind and flames would have been false, since the Spirit would have been given to those listening. Later, Paul thanked God that he spoke in other tongues (1 Corinthians 14:18) that he claimed he could both understand and use. He did not acquire this ability by his own study and hard work, but it was a gift of the Spirit. In the same passage, Paul maintains that this is a special gift that is not given to everyone. From all this it is clear that the apostles were given various languages and the ability to understand them, so that they might speak in Greek to the Greeks and in Latin to the Italians, and so true communication would take place.

A question I have left unresolved is whether there was a second miracle, enabling the Egyptians and Elamites to hear Peter speaking in Chaldean as if he were speaking in different languages. Some arguments lead me to think this, but they can all be refuted. It may be that the apostles spoke in different languages one after another, to one person in one language, to the next person in another, the miracle then being that they were able to speak in different languages. Regarding Peter's sermon, most of those listening may have been able to understand it wherever they came from, for it is thought that many of those who came to Jerusalem were familiar with Chaldean. But it does not matter if we maintain that he spoke in other languages, either way I do not mind, as long as it is agreed that the apostles changed their language.

Acts (Wheaton (IL): Crossway Books, 1995), pp. 29–31.

Commentary on Acts 2:17–21

'I will pour out my Spirit'
Peter wanted to show that the only way for the church to be restored is through the gift of the Holy Spirit. So, although they all looked forward to this restoration, they were sluggish, because they never thought about how it would occur. Peter followed the Greek translation of the Hebrew word for 'from': 'I will pour out my Spirit from.' Some people, trying to be clever and playing with words, attempt to alter the meaning here, which is not possible; the prophet's meaning must be retained. Nevertheless, when the text says God will pour out his Spirit, it must be understood that he is bestowing a variety of gifts to people from his Spirit. They flow, as it were, from a fountain that never runs dry. Paul writes: 'There are different kinds of gifts, but the same Spirit' (1 Corinthians 12:4). From this we learn that nothing more excellent can be given us than the grace of the Spirit. Without the Spirit, everything else is valueless. When God promises his people salvation, he says he will give them his Spirit. From this it follows that we can obtain nothing of any worth until the Spirit has been given to us. This key

unlocks the door to a spiritual treasury, through which we enter into the kingdom of God.

'On all people'
From what follows, the strength of this generality is clear. The prophet starts with a general phrase, 'all people'. He goes on to show that age or type of person makes no difference, as God welcomes everyone to receive his grace. 'All people' signifies the young and the old, men and women. But this raises a question: why does God promise his people some new, good thing that he had been giving them down through the ages since the beginning of time? For no age has been without the grace of the Spirit. The answer to this question is contained in the two phrases: 'I will pour out' and 'on all people'. There is a double antithesis between Old Testament times and New Testament times. The pouring out of the Spirit signifies a great outpouring, but under the law the Spirit's distribution was scarce. So John says that the Holy Spirit was not given until Christ ascended into heaven. 'All people' signifies a limitless supply, whereas in the past God only occasionally bestowed his Spirit in this way.

All godly people, since the beginning of the world, have been endued with the same spirit of understanding, righteousness, and sanctification as the Lord regenerates us with today. But only a few people were illumined with this knowledge in comparison with the multitudes of faithful people whom Christ suddenly collected at his coming. In the same way, their knowledge was slight and, as it were, obscured by a veil, in comparison with those people who live today with the gospel, in which Christ, the Sun of Righteousness, shines like the noonday sun. However, the former state did not harm those who had a strong faith, the strength of which is hardly equalled today. But their understanding was still under the law. Godly kings and prophets had not heard or seen what Christ revealed at his coming. In order to emphasise the brilliance of the New Testament, Joel prophesied that the grace of the Spirit would be more available then, and that more people would receive it (see Matthew 13:17; Luke 10:24).

'Your sons and daughters will prophesy'
The word 'prophesy' means the special gift of understanding. It is as if Joel were saying: in Christ's kingdom there will not be just a few prophets to whom God reveals his secrets, but everyone will be given this spiritual wisdom, so that they can make excellent prophecies (see Jeremiah 31:34). Peter invited his audience of Jews to receive this same grace. It is as if he were saying, the Lord is ready to pour out that Spirit far and wide whom he has poured on us; so you can receive this fullness of Spirit with us, unless you put up some barrier. The message is the same for us today as it was then for those Jews. For although those visible graces have ceased, God has not withdrawn his Spirit from his church. Each day he offers the Spirit to us all. So if we are poor and in need, it is due to our own indolence. There are also evil and sacrilegious enemies of the Spirit who prevent ordinary Christians from receiving God's knowledge. But God not only welcome men and women, young and old, to himself, he also calls them individually by name.

'Even on my servants'
These words show that God's promise is restricted to those who worship him. God does not profane his Spirit. He would be doing this if he made no distinction between his followers and unbelievers. We know for certain that we become God's servants through the Spirit, and until this happens we are not God's servants. Once we are adopted into God's family and given the Spirit, we subsequently receive his gifts. This grace was only for the church. So long as the church was among the Jews, they were called God's servants. But once God called people to himself from everywhere into his church, the wall of separation was pulled down, and all members of the covenant were given the same name. So remember, the Spirit is given only to true members of the church.

'I will show wonders . . . before the coming of the great and glorious day of the Lord'
This great and glorious day started on the day the gospel was first preached and will continue until the day of resurrection. Joel speaks about these things as they begin to occur, but these things

will continue until the end of the world. The sun being turned into darkness and the moon into blood (verse 20) is only figurative language indicating that God reveals his anger through all of the created world, which should make people despair. The sun and the moon are tokens of God's fatherly care of us, giving light to the earth, although Joel says they can also be messengers of God's anger and displeasure.

This is the second part of the prophecy. The world will be in turmoil and very afraid (see Matthew 24 and Luke 21).

This only served to highlight God's grace all the more. People who were threatened with disaster now call on the name of the Lord and are sure to be saved. In this we see God's goodness as well as man's ingratitude in rejecting God. Peter quoted this passage to the Jews in order to show them the miserable state they were in while they refused to accept the grace of the Spirit.

We may ask why Christ's revelation produced such a sea of miseries. Firstly, we note in reply that if people are too silly to receive Christ, they must be encouraged to do so by various afflictions, as if they were being whipped into faith. Secondly, although Christ calls the burdened (Matthew 11:28), people must first of all learn humility from miseries. Men erect great horns of pride in prosperity. Anybody who is content in himself cannot help despising Christ. Thirdly, because we are so earthbound that we tie Christ's grace to this present life, we must become used to thinking that Christ's kingdom is spiritual. So that we may learn that Christ's good things are heavenly, God visits us with many miseries in this life, so that we do not seek our happiness in this world. In addition to this, people bring disasters upon themselves because of their ingratitude (see Luke 12:47). The day of Christ's coming will only be frightening if we have lived in contempt of God's grace.

'And everyone who calls on the name of the Lord'
God treats us like donkeys, with terrifying events, to drive us into the path of salvation. Once we have experienced the darkness of heaven and earth God's salvation is displayed, shining in front of our eyes. If God just promised us salvation, it would be wonderful; but it is even more wonderful that he gives us this promise in the

middle of dungeons of death. As we lie in this chaos, fearful of destruction, God says, 'Call on me and you will be saved.' So no matter what miseries we are in, God offers a way of escape. Notice that the universal word 'everyone' is used. God invites everyone to himself for salvation, without exception (see Romans 10:13 and Psalm 65:2).

Acts (Wheaton (IL): Crossway Books, 1995), pp. 33–6.

Teresa of Avila
(1515–82)

Spanish Carmelite mystic, who wrote The Interior Castle.

The prayer of union

In the prayer of union our souls are deeply asleep to the things of this world and to ourselves. In fact, for the brief period this state lasts, the soul is without consciousness, and without power to think even if it wanted to. At last, there is no need for the soul to struggle to stop thinking. Even if it loves, it cannot understand how or what it is that it loves, it cannot understand how or what it is that it loves, nor what it desires. In fact, it has completely died to the world so that it may live more completely to God.

This is a delicious death. It is a withdrawing from all bodily activity; it is a death full of delight, for truly the soul appears to have left the body in order to draw near to God. I don't even know if the body still has life enough in it to breathe. On reflection, I believe it has not; or at least if it does breathe, then it does so without realising it.

Now the mind wishes to bend all its powers to understanding what is happening – but it does not have the strength. It is so astounded that even if consciousness is not completely lost, no movement is possible. In this state a person may be compared to someone who has fallen into a dead faint.

So let us now turn, to this sign that proves whether or not the prayer of union has been genuinely with God. As you have seen, God has made the soul look utterly foolish, in order that he may more clearly imprint his true wisdom on it. It loses all its senses; it cannot see, hear, or understand anything while this state lasts. It is always a short time, and to the soul may appear even shorter than it really is, but while it lasts God impresses himself within the soul in a way that removes all doubt. When the soul returns to itself it is absolutely certain that it dwelt in God, and God in it. That truth is so firmly fixed that though years may pass before this favour recurs, the soul can never forget it or doubt it. This certainty within the soul is the significant point.

But now you will ask me: how can someone incapable of seeing or understanding anything, see and understand these things? I'm not saying she realises it at the time, but that when it is over she clearly sees it, not because of a vision but because of a certainty which stays within the soul and which can only have been put there by God. I know of someone who had not learned that God is in all things by presence, power and essence, but then God granted her a favour of this kind which firmly convinced her. She was so sure that although one of those half-learned priests of whom I spoke, and whom she asked in what way God was in us, replied that he was only present in us by grace, she did not believe him. The priests was as ignorant on the subject as she had been before our Lord revealed the truth to her. She questioned other spiritual people on this matter and to her joy they confirmed the truth of her understanding.

You may well ask: if we do not see anything, how can we become so convinced of something? I don't know. It is the work of God. But I do know I'm speaking the truth. If the experience leaves anyone in doubt, I can only say it was not complete union of the soul with God, but union of one of the faculties, or it was one of the many favours which God grants the soul.

The Interior Castle, edited by Halcyon Backhouse (London: Hodder & Stoughton, 1988), pp. 58–62.

St John of the Cross
(1542–91)

Spanish Carmelite mystic, who wrote The Dark Night of the Soul.

The deity compenetrates the soul in dark contemplation

This dark contemplation is described as 'secret'. Mystical theology
has been called secret wisdom by theologians. St Thomas says that
this comes into the soul by means of love. The soul's understanding and other faculties are unaware of this because it happens sec-
retly and in darkness. The soul receives it by means of the Holy
Spirit and the soul's faculties do not acquire it. The Bride in the
Song of Songs correctly says that this happens without the soul's
knowledge or understanding and that is why it is called a secret. In
addition to the soul's not understanding it nobody else understands it, not even the devil himself, for the master who teaches it
to the soul lives within it.

This isn't the only reason it is called secret. It is also called secret
because of what it does in the soul. It is secret in the darknesses
and the distressful time of purification when the soul is purified by
this wisdom of love. While this is happening, the soul cannot talk
about it and in the same way after the soul has been illumined the
soul still remains silent. Apart from not wanting to talk about it,
the soul cannot find the words to express such an exquisite
spiritual experience. So it would still remain secret and hidden,
even if the soul did want to talk about it and find the correct words
for this. This inner wisdom is so single-minded and so all-
embracing and so spiritual that it doesn't enter the soul's mind in
disguise. Therefore the soul's sense and imagination know that it
is experiencing something most unusual and delightful but does
not know what. It is like somebody who sees something that he has
never seen before and like nothing else he has ever seen. Although
he may take pleasure in it, he may not be able to give it a name. He
would not be able to say what it was no matter how much he tried,
even though he had observed it with his senses. How much less

would he be able to describe something that he had not received with his senses. One of the characteristics of God's way of communicating is that it is very intimate and spiritual in its relationship to the soul. It goes beyond all the senses which immediately stand before it in silence.

The Dark Night of the Soul, edited by Halcyon Backhouse (London: Hodder & Stoughton, 1989), pp. 94–5.

The Huguenots
(French Protestants of the sixteenth century.)

Respecting the physical manifestations, there is little discrepancy between the accounts of friend and foe. The people affected were men and women, young and old. Many were children, aged nine or ten. They were taken from people, their enemies said, from the dregs of society, ignorant and uncultured; for the most part unable to read or write, and speaking in everyday life the patois of the province with which alone they were conversant.

Such people would suddenly fall backward, and, while extended at full length on the ground, undergo strange and apparently involuntary contortions; their chests would seem to heave, their stomachs to inflate. On coming gradually out of this condition, they appeared instantly to regain the power of speech. Beginning often in a voice interrupted by sobs, they soon poured forth a torrent of words – cries for mercy, calls to repentance, exhortations to the bystanders to cease frequenting the mass, denunciations of the church of Rome, prophecies of coming judgement. From the mouths of those who were little more than babes came texts of Scripture, and discourse in good and intelligent French, such as they never used in their conscious hours. When the trance ceased, they declared that they remembered nothing of what had occurred, or of what they had said. In rare cases they retained a general and vague impression, but nothing more. There was no appearance of deceit or collusion, and no indication that in uttering their predictions respecting coming events they had any thought of prudence, or doubt as to the truth of what they foretold. Brueys, their most inveterate opponent, is not less positive on this point than are the witnesses who are most favourable to them. 'These poor madmen,' he said, 'believed that they were indeed inspired by the Holy Ghost. They prophesied without any (ulterior) design, without evil intent, and with so little reserve, that they always boldly marked the day, the place and people of whom they spoke in their predictions'.

Henry Baird, *The Huguenots* (New York: Charles Scribner, 1885), vol. 2, pp. 186–7.

Book of Homilies
(1547)

A book of prescribed homilies, first published on 31st July 1547, which disaffected and unlearned clergy were obliged to read out to their congregations.

It is not the duty and part of any Christian, under the pretence of the Holy Ghost, to bring in his own dreams and fantasies into the church; but he must diligently provide that his doctrine and decrees be agreeable to Christ's Holy Testament; otherwise, in making the Holy Ghost the Author thereof, he doth blaspheme and belie the Holy Ghost to his own condemnation.

Homily on Whitsunday.

Anabaptists

A generic title for different groups of sixteenth-century continental Christians who refused to have their children baptised.

The Anabaptists in perfectly consistent accordance with their biblical-Christian theory of things, would admit no break in the conditions of revelation between biblical and primitive times and the year of grace in which they found themselves. Prophets were as possible in the third and fourth decades of the sixteenth century as they had been in the first century of the Christian era.

Belfort Bax, *The Rise and Fall of the Anabaptists*, p. 165.

Ecstasy among the Anabaptists

Bullinger writes: 'They claimed to see visions and dream dreams, and generally to be the recipients of divine revelations. When under the influence of the Spirit, their countenances were contorted, they made deprecatory gestures, fell on the ground as if in a fit, and finally lay stretched out as if they were dead.'

Quoted by Belfort Bax, *The Rise and Fall of the Anabaptists*, chapter 2.

Jacob Boehme
(1575–1624)

A leader of mystical spiritualism in the Lutheran tradition.

'My spirit . . . saw God'

After much wrestling and 'severe storms,' his spirit forced a way, 'not without God's help,' through the gates of hell into the very heart of the Deity. 'But the triumph that was in my spirit I cannot write or speak, nor can it be compared with anything save with the birth of life in the midst of death, with the resurrection of the dead. In this light my spirit straightway looked through all things and saw God in all created things, even in the herbs and the grass.'

Aurora, xix. 11–13.

Such joy that the whole body trembles

From the Son, who is the heart of the Father rises the eternal heavenly joy, that eye has not seen, nor ear heard, nor has ever risen in the heart of man, as St Paul says. But when a man here on earth is illumined by the Holy Spirit from the spring of Jesus Christ, there enters into his heart and into all his veins such joy that the whole body trembles and the animal spirit triumphs, as though it were in the Holy Trinity, which they alone understand who have been its guests.

Aurora, i. 102.

Augustine Baker
(1575–1641)

English spiritual writer and Benedictine monk.

Conversion affected different parts of my body

[And this exercise] that I said to have been in hands, arms, feet, and legs [was not] altogether without motion; for at times the exercise was with much movement. For half a year together his evening's exercise had those movements in them, and certain senseless aspirations were joined with these movements, and the movements were very strong and violent, but yet passed and were acted with great readiness and facility, and no manner of harm or peril by them to physical health or strength. For their invitation and enablement began and proceeded from the spirit and not from the sensuality. Our scholar [writes Baker, using an obvious reference to himself] living alone was and might be loud enough in his voice, uttering and venting forth his foresaid senseless aspirations, yet not so but that he was sometimes in peril to have been heard by others; and if he had been heard or seen he would doubtless have been taken for a man who was out of his mind. But those who live in communities do often lack such commodity of privateness and therefore must refrain from such seemingly mad exercises when they are in company, or, otherwise, they are in danger of being seen and heard by others.

The Confessions of Venerable Father Augustine Baker (London: Burns & Oates, 1922), pp. 101–2.

John of St Thomas
(1589–644)

A Spanish Dominican who devoted his life to expounding St Thomas Aquinas.

The gifts of the Holy Spirit do not override our freedom

When a man is inwardly disposed by the gifts of the Holy Spirit – and this is, in fact, a way of telling whether a man is spiritual or not – he feels himself remarkably free in all he does. He is unconstrained and unimpeded, without confusion, obstacles or inhibitions, for 'where the Spirit of the Lord is, there is freedom.'

In case we make the mistake of thinking that people born of the Spirit are being driven by some kind of raving mad urge, like those whom some evil spirit has got hold of, the first thing the Lord requires on the way of the Spirit is that he should 'blow where he wills', to show that birth from the Spirit enhances rather than destroys freedom of choice.'

Cursus Theologicus, q. 70, disp. 18, art. 1,5.

17TH CENTURY

John Preston
(1587–1628)

English Puritan preacher.

The Seal of the Spirit is subsequent to conversion

You will say, what is the seal or witness of the Spirit? My beloved, it is a thing that we cannot express ... a certain inexpressible assurance that we are the sons of God, a certain secret manifestation, that God hath received us, and put away our sins: I say, it is such a thing, that no man knows, but they that have it.

The New Covenant (London, 1634), pp. 400–1; quoted by J. I. Packer, *Among God's Giants* (Eastbourne: Kingsway, 1991), p. 249, footnote 28.

Richard Baxter
(1615–91)

English Puritan minister and religious writer.

The prayer of faith saves the sick

I know men's atheism and infidelity will never lack somewhat to say against the most eminent providences, though they were miracles, but when mercies of healing are granted in the very time of prayer, and when, to reason, there is no hope, and without the use of help of any other means is not this as plain as if God from heaven should say to us: I am fulfilling to thee the true word of my promise in Christ my Son? How many times have I known the prayer of faith to save the sick when all physicians have given them up as dead!

Works, vol. I, p. 224.

The Holy Spirit then, the Holy Spirit now

The Holy Spirit, by immediate inspiration, revealed to the apostles the teaching of Christ and caused them infallibly to indite the Scriptures. But this is not the way of ordinary illumination now.

Works, vol. II, p. 104.

John Owen
(1616–83)

English Puritan theologian, chaplain and adviser to Oliver Cromwell.

The Holy Spirit works immediately

God works immediately by his Spirit in and on the wills of his saints.

'That dispensation of the Spirit has long since ceased'

Gifts which in their nature exceed the power of all our faculties [tongues, prophecies and healings] that dispensation of the Spirit has long since ceased, and where it is now pretended unto by any, it may justly be suspected as an enthusiastical delusion.

Works, vol. 4, p. 518; quoted by J. I. Packer, *Among God's Giants* (Eastbourne: Kingsway, 1991), p. 290.

Comment on 'encourage one another and build each other up' (1 Thessalonians 5:11)

It is the loss of those spiritual gifts which hath introduced among many an utter neglect of these duties, so as that they are scarce heard of among the generality of them that are called Christians. But, blessed be God, we have large and full experience of the continuance of this dispensation of the Spirit, in the eminent abilities of a multitude of private Christians.

By some, I confess gifts have been abused: some have presumed on them beyond the line and measure which they have received; some have been puffed up with them; some have used them disorderly in churches and to their hurt; some have boasted of what they have not received; – all which miscarriages also befell the primitive churches. And I had rather have the order, rule, spirit, and practice of those churches that were planted by the apostles, with all their troubles and disadvantages, than the carnal peace of others in their open degeneracy from all those things.

Works, vol. 4, p. 518; quoted by J. I. Packer, *Among God's Giants* (Eastbourne: Kingsway, 1991), pp. 292–3.

No authentic church life without the exercise of spiritual gifts

That profession which renders a Church visible according to the mind of Christ, is the orderly exercise of the spiritual gifts bestowed on it, in a conversation evidencing the invisible principle of saving grace.

. . . It is inquired what power the Lord Christ did employ for the erecting of that kingdom I say, it was these gifts of the Holy Spirit. By them it was, or in their exercise, that the Lord Christ erected his empire over the souls and consciences of men, destroying both the work and kingdom of the devil. It is true, it is the word of the gospel itself that is the rod of his strength which is sent out of Sion to erect and dispense his rule: but that hidden power which made the word effectual in the dispensation of it, consisted in these gifts of the Holy Spirit . . . By these gifts does the Lord Christ demonstrate his power, and exercise his rule.

. . . [Speaking of the early church] All gospel administrations were in those days avowedly executed by virtue of spiritual gifts.

. . . Gospel ordinances are found to be fruitless and unsatisfactory, without the attaining and exercising of gospel gifts.

. . . As the neglect of saving grace, wherein the power of godliness does consist, has been the bane of Christian profession as to obedience, so the neglect of these gifts has been the ruin of the same profession as to worship and order, which has thereon issued in fond superstitions.

. . . A ministry devoid of spiritual gifts is sufficient evidence of a church under a degenerating apostasy.

Works, vol. 4, pp. 428, 479, 426, 471, 421, 421, 482; quoted by J. I. Packer, *Among God's Giants* (Eastbourne: Kingsway, 1991), pp. 294–5.

Prophets in the New Testament

1. In Ephesians 4:11 and 1 Corinthians 12:28 extraordinary gifts are intended. Two things are ascribed to them: Firstly, they are received immediate revelations and directions for the Holy Spirit (see Acts 13:2); secondly, they are foretold things to come (see Acts 11:28ff.; 21:10f.).

2. Sometimes an extraordinary gift without office is intended (see Acts 21:9; 19:6; 1 Corinthians 14:29–33).

3. Again, an ordinary office with ordinary gifts is intended by this expression. Hence also those who are not called to office, who have yet received a gift enabling them to declare the mind of God in the Scripture to the edification of others, may also be said to 'prophecy'.

Works, vol. 4, pp. 451–2; quoted by J. I. Packer, *Among God's Giants* (Eastbourne: Kingsway, 1991), p.305, footnote 31.

Ministers need spiritual gifts

The church has no power to call any to office of the ministry, where the Lord Christ has not gone before it in the designation of him by an endowment of spiritual gifts.

Works, vol. 4, p. 495.

Prayer is a principal means for their attainment. This the apostle directs unto when he enjoins us earnestly to desire the best gifts; for this desire is to be acted by prayer, and no otherwise.

Of Spiritual Gifts.

The complementary nature of gifts and graces

Where saving graces and spiritual gifts are bestowed on the same people they are exceedingly helpful to each other. A soul sanctified by saving grace, is the only proper soil for gifts to flourish in. Grace influences gifts to a due exercise, prevents their abuse, stirs them up to proper occasions, keeps them from being a matter of pride or contention, and subordinates them to all things unto the glory of God. When the actings of grace and gifts are inseparable, as when in prayer the Spirit is a spirit of grace and supplication, the grace and gift of it working together, when utterance in other duties is always accompanied with faith and love, then is God glorified, and our own salvation promoted. Then have edifying gifts a beauty and lustre on them, and generally are must successful, when they are clothed and adorned with humility, meekness, a reverence of God, and compassion for the souls of men. Gifts excite and stir up grace unto its proper exercise and operation. How often is faith, love, and delight in God, excited and drawn forth unto especial exercise in believers by the use of their own gifts.

Works, vol. 4, p. 438.

Blaise Pascal
(1623–62)

French mathematician, inventor and philosopher. Converted in Rouen in 1646, he had a 'second conversion' on 23rd November 1654, a spiritual revival encountering the Holy Spirit that lasted from 10.30 p.m. to 12.30 a.m. He recorded this on parchment in a 'Memorial' which he sewed into the lining of his doublet and so kept with him to his death.

The Memorial
In the Year of Grace 1654,
On Monday, 23 November, Feast of Saint Clement,
Pope and Martyr,
and of others in the Martyrology,
and Eve of Saint Chrysogonus and other Martyrs,
From about half past ten at night until about half past twelve.

Fire
'God of Abraham, God of Isaac, God of Jacob' (Exodus 6:3),
not of the philosophers and scientists.
Certitude. Certitude. Feeling. Joy. Peace.
God of Jesus Christ.
God of Jesus Christ.

'My God and your God' (John 20:17).

'You shall be my God' (Ruth 1:16).

Forgetting the world and all things, except only God.
He is to be found only by the ways taught in the Gospel.
Greatness of the human soul.

'Righteous Father, the world has not known Thee, but I have
known Thee' (John 17:25).

Joy, joy, joy, tears of joy.
I have fallen away from Him.
'They have forsaken me, the fountain of living water'
(Jeremiah 2:13).
'My God, wilt thou forsake me?' (see Matthew 27:46).
May I not be separated from Him in all eternity.
'Now this is eternal life, that they may know Thee, the only true
God, and Jesus Christ, whom Thou hast sent' (John 17:3).

Jesus Christ.
Jesus Christ.

I have fallen away from Him; I have fled from Him, denied him,
crucified Him.
May I not be separated from Him for eternity.
We hold him only by the ways taught in the Gospel.
Renunciation total and sweet.
Total submission to Jesus Christ and to my director.
Eternally in joy for one day of trial upon earth.
'I will not forget thy Word' (Psalm 119:16). Amen.

John Bunyan
(1628–88)

English non-conformist minister and writer; author of The Pilgrim's
Progress.

A voice did suddenly dart from heaven into my soul

There are some natures to whom the great spiritual world of the
unseen is always present as the background of life. It was so with
Shakespeare. It was so also with Bunyan, though in a different
way. Even when he was a child, the wrong things of the day were
followed by the remorse, and fears, and dread dreams of the
night. But the real struggle began later, when after his marriage
and the reading of his wife's books, he was seen 'going to church
twice a day, and with the foremost'. He had not done this long
before there arose a fight with his conscience about Sunday sports,
in the course of which there came the weird voices that seemed to
be shouted into his ear on Elstow Green.

Somewhere on the sward round the broken pillar of the old
Market Cross he was one Sunday in the middle of a game of cat [a
forerunner of cricket]. He had struck it one blow from the hole
and was about to strike it the second time, when, as he says, 'A
voice did suddenly dart from heaven into my soul, which said, Wilt
thou leave thy sins and go to heaven, or have thy sins and go to
hell? At this I was put to an exceeding maze. Wherefore, leaving

my cat upon the ground, I looked up to heaven, and was as if I had with the eyes of my understanding, seen the Lord Jesus looking down upon me, as being very hotly displeased with me.'

Thus conscience-stricken he afterwards made a desperate fling to be rid of conscience altogether, only to find, as other men have, that its grip was tighter than he thought . . .

His wonderful power of dreaming waking dreams

Then blossomed into shape his wonderful power of dreaming waking dreams. There were these good people at Bedford sitting on the sunny side of a mountain, while he was separated from them by a wall all about, and shivering in the cold. Round and round that wall he goes to see if there be no opening, be it ever so narrow, and at last he finds one. But it is narrow, indeed so narrow that none can get through but those who are in downright earnest, and who leave the wicked world behind them. There is just room for body and soul, but not for body and soul and sin. It must be a strait gate through which a man gets rid of self; but by dint of sidling and striving he first gets in his head, then his shoulders, and then his whole body, at which he is exceeding glad, for now too he is in the sunshine and is comforted. But as yet this is only in a dream, and dreams tarry not . . .

Methought I saw with the eye of my soul, Jesus Christ at God's right hand

One day as he was passing into the field, still with some fears in his heart, suddenly this sentence fell into his soul, '"Thy righteousness is in heaven': and methought withal I saw with the eye of my soul, Jesus Christ at God's right hand. I saw, moreover, that it was not my good frame of heart that made my righteousness better, not yet my bad frame that made my righteousness worse; for my righteousness was Jesus Christ Himself, the same yesterday, today, and for ever. Now did my chains fall from my legs indeed; I was loosed from my afflictions and irons. Oh, methought, Christ! Christ! there was nothing but Christ that was before my eyes! I could look from myself to Him and should reckon that all those graces of God that now were green on me, were yet like those crack-groats and fourpence halfpennies that rich men carry in their purses, when their gold is in their trunks at home! Oh, I saw my gold was in my trunk at home! Oh, I saw my gold was in my trunk at home! In Christ my Lord and Saviour! Now Christ was all; all my wisdom, all my righteousness, all my sanctification, and all my redemption!'

John Brown, *John Bunyan* (London: Isbister, 1885), pp. 62–8.

The holiness of the Spirit of God

Some think that the love of the Father and blood of the Son will do, without the holiness of the Spirit of God; but they are deceived. There is a sort that think that holiness of the Spirit is sufficient in itself; but they (if they had it) are deceived also; for it must be the grace of the Father, the grace of the Son, and the grace of the Spirit, jointly, that must save them.

Bunyan, quoted by H. Watkin-Jones in *The Holy Spirit in the Medieval Church* (London: Epworth Press, 1922), p. 172.

Philipp Jakob Spener
(1635–1705)

Founder of German Pietism.

Resignation

Examples of people resigning themselves to follow the Holy Spirit are found in Judges 14:6, 19; 15:14; 1 Samuel 10:6; 11:6; 16:13. See also 2 Peter 1:21; Romans 15:18 and 2 Corinthians 11:3. Such people who directly impelled give us examples of resignation. They resign themselves to the Spirit. They do not hinder the Spirit. They do the deeds the Spirit desires. All Christians should be resigned in this way to the Holy Spirit. Then, the Holy Spirit will work in and through them what pleases him. They will say the words the Spirit tells them to say in every situation they find themselves in. We must give ourselves to the Holy Spirit as a new canvas on which he can paint.

Sermon on Matthew 12:2.

George Fox
(1642–91)

English preacher; founder of the Quakers.

Fox's spiritual awakening

[A new world appeared after the spiritual awakening to the eyes of the great Puritan mystic, George Fox. Passing through the sword of flame, he came 'in spirit' into the 'Paradise of God'.] All things were new and all the creation gave another smell unto me than before, beyond what words can utter.

The Journal of George Fox (London, 1852), vol i, p. 17.

Power to work miracles and discern spirits

There is no doubt Fox was perfectly earnest in believing that he had power both to work miracles and to discern spirits. As the discerning of spirits was a gift claimed by many of the Anabaptists, Fox's pretensions excited no surprise.

Bickley, *The Independents against the Quakers*, p. 104.

'Cry, "Woe to the bloody city of Lichfield!"'

As I was walking with several friends, I lifted up my head, and saw three steeple-house spires, and they struck at my life. I asked them what place that was? They said, Lichfield. Immediately the word of the Lord came to me, that I must go there. Being come to the house we were going to, I wished the friends to walk into the house, saying nothing to them of whither I was to go. As soon as they were gone I stept away, and went by my eye over hedge and ditch till I cam within a mile of Lichfield; where, in a great field, shepherds were keeping their sheep.

'I pulled off my shoes'

Then was I commanded by the Lord to pull of my shoes. I stood still, for it was winter: but the word of the Lord was like a fire in me. So I put off my shoes and left them with the shepherds; and the poor shepherds trembled, and were astonished. Then I walked on about a mile, and as soon as I was got within the city, the word of the Lord came to me again, saying: Cry, 'Woe to the bloody city of Lichfield!' So I went up and down the streets, crying with a loud voice, Woe to the bloody city of Lichfield! It being market day, I went into the market-place, and to and fro in the several parts of it, and made stands, crying as before, Woe to the bloody city of Lichfield!

'A channel of blood running down the streets'

And no one laid hands on me. As I went thus crying through the streets, there seemed to me to be a channel of blood running down the streets, and the market-place appeared like a pool of blood. When I had declared what was upon me, and felt myself clear, I went out of the town in peace; and returning to the shepherds gave them some money, and took my shoes of them again. But the first of the Lord was so on my feet, and all over me, that I did not matter to put on my shoes again, and was at a stand whether I should or no, till I felt freedom from the Lord so to do: then, after I had washed my feet, I put on my shoes again.

One thousand martyrs

After this a deep consideration came upon me, for what reason I should be sent to cry against that city, and call it The bloody city! For though the parliament had the minister one while, and the king another, and much blood had been shed in the town during the wars between them, yet there was not more than had befallen many other places. But afterwards I came to understand, that in the Emperor Diocletian's time a thousand Christians were martyred in Lichfield. So I was to go, without my shoes, through the channel of their blood, and into the pool of their blood in the market-place, that I might raise up the memorial of the blood of those martyrs, which had been shed above a thousand years before, and lay cold in their streets. So the sense of this blood was upon me, and I obeyed the word of the Lord.

The Journal of George Fox (London, 1852), vol. I, pp. 100–1

Anointing teaches believers

I brought them Scriptures, and told them there was an anointing within man to teach him, and that the Lord would teach his people himself.

. . . So mind the faith of Christ, and the anointing which is in you, to be taught by it, which will discover all workings in you; and as he teaches you, so obey and forsake; else you will not grow up in the faith, nor in the life of Christ, where the love of God is received.

. . . You, who deny the light, which lights every man who comes into the world, are seduced from the anointing which should teach you; and if you would be taught by it, you would not need anyone to teach you. But those who are taught by anointing, which abides in them, and deny man's teaching, these you call seducers, quite contrary to John's teaching (2 John 2).

. . . The work of the Lord is beginning again, as it was in the apostles' days; people shall come to receive an unction in them again from the Holy One, by which they shall know all things, and shall not need any man to teach them, but as the anointing teaches them.

Knowing God through the Spirit

Now the Lord God opened to me by his invisible power, 'that every man was enlightened by the divine light of Christ;' and I saw it shine through all; and that they that believed in it came out of condemnation to the light of life, and became the children of it; but they that hated it, and did not believe in it, were condemned by it, though they made profession of Christ. This I saw in the pure openings of the light, without the help of any man; neither did I then know where to find it in Scriptures, though afterwards, searching the Scriptures, I found it. For I saw in the Light and Spirit which was before the Scriptures were given forth, and which led the holy men of God to give them forth, that all must come to that Spirit, if they would know God, or Christ, or the Scriptures aright, which they that gave them forth were led and taught by.

The Journal of George Fox (London, 1852), vol. I, p. 70.

Prophecy

As I was walking by the steeple-house [church], in Mansfield, the Lord said to me, 'That which the people trample on must be thy food.' And as the Lord spoke he opened it to me, that people and professors trampled on the life, even the life of Christ; they fed on words, and fed one another with words; but they trampled on the life; trampled underfoot the blood of the Son of God, which blood was my life, and lived in their airy notions, talking of him. It seemed strange to me at first, that I should feed on that which the high professors trampled down; but the Lord opened it clearly to me by his eternal Spirit and Power.

The Journal of George Fox (London, 1852), vol I, pp. 60–1.

A discerning given me by the Lord

There was one Brown, who had great prophecies and sights on his death-bed of me. He spoke only of what I should be made instrumental by the Lord to bring forth. And of others he spoke, that they should come to nothing, which was fulfilled on some, who then were something in show. When this man was buried, a great work of the Lord fell on me, to the admiration of many, who thought I had been dead; and many came to see me for about fourteen days. I was very much altered in countenance and person, as if my body had been new moulded or changed. While I was in that condition, I had a sense and discerning given me by the Lord, through which I saw plainly, that when many people talked of God and of Christ, etc., the serpent spoke in them.

The Journal of George Fox (London, 1852), vol I, p. 61.

Discerning an unclean spirit

After this I went to a village, and many people accompanied me. As I was sitting in a house full of people, declaring the word of life unto them, I cast mine eye on a woman, and discerned an unclean spirit in her. And I was moved by the Lord to speak sharply to her, and told her she was under the influence of an unclean spirit; whereupon she went out of the room. Now, I being a stranger there, and knowing nothing of the woman outwardly, the people wondered at it, and told me afterwards that I had discovered a great thing; for all the country looked on her to be a wicked person.

The Lord had given me a spirit of discerning, through which I many times saw the states and conditions of people, and could try their spirits. For not long before, as I was going to a meeting, I saw some women in a field, and I discerned an evil spirit in them; and I was moved to go out of my way into the field to them; and to declare to them their conditions.

At another time there came one into Swarthmore Hall in the meeting time; and I was moved to speak sharply to her, and told her she was under the power of an evil spirit; and the people said afterwards she was generally accounted so. There came also at another time another woman, and stood at a distance from me, and I cast mine eye on her, and said, 'You have been a harlot'; for I perfectly saw the condition and life of the woman. The woman answered and said, many could tell her of her outward sins, but none could tell her of her inward. Then I told her her heart was not right before the Lord, and that from the inward came the outward. This woman came afterwards to be convinced of God's truth, and became a Friend.

The Journal of George Fox (London, 1852), vol I, p. 157.

Trembling

Being set at liberty I went to the inn again, where Captain Drury had at first lodged me. This Captain Drury, though he sometimes carried fairly, was an enemy to me and to truth, and opposed it; and when professors came to me (while I was under his custody) and he was by, he would scoff at trembling, and call us Quakers, as the Independents and Presbyterians had nick-named us before. But afterwards he once came to me, and told me, that, as he was lying on his bed to rest himself in the day-time, a sudden trembling seized him, so that his joints knocked together, and his body shook so that he could not rise from his bed; he was so shaken, that he had not strength enough left to rise. But he felt the power of the Lord was upon him, and fell off his bed, and cried to the Lord, and said, he never would speak against the Quakers more, or such as trembled at the word of God.

The Journal of George Fox (London, 1852), vol I, pp. 186–7.

Dreams

Removing to another place, I came among a people who relied much on dreams. I told them, except they could distinguish between dream and dream, they would confound all together; for there were three sorts of dreams; multitude of business sometimes caused dreams; and there were whisperings of Satan in man in the night-season; and there were speakings of God to man in dreams. But these people came out of these things, and at last became Friends.

Groans: true and false

After this, a pure fire appeared in me; than I saw how he sat as a refiner's fire and as fullers' soap; then the spiritual discerning came into me, by which I did discern my own thoughts, groans, and sighs; and what it was that so veiled me, that I could not be patient in all trials, troubles, and perplexities; – could not give up self to die by the cross, the power of God, that the living and quickened might follow him; and that that which would cloud and veil from the presence of God – that which the sword of the Spirit cuts down, and which must die, might not be kept alive. I discerned also the groans of the Spirit, which opened me, and made intercession to God; in which Spirit is the true waiting upon God, for the redemption of the body and of the whole creation. By this Spirit, in which the true sighing is, I saw over the false sighings and groanings. By this invisible Spirit I discerned all the false hearing, the false seeing, and the false smelling which was above the Spirit, quenching and grieving it; and that all they that were there, were in confusion and deceit, where the false asking and praying is, in deceit, in that nature and tongue that takes God's holy name in vain, wallows in the Egyptian sea, and asks, but has not; for they hate his light and resist the Holy Spirit; turn grace into wantonness, and rebel against the Spirit; and are erred from the faith they should ask in, and from the Spirit they should pray by.

The Journal of George Fox (London, 1852), vol I, pp. 57–8.

Mysteries revealed

For though I read the Scriptures that spoke of Christ and of God; yet I knew him not, but by revelation, as he who hath the key did open, and as the Father of Life drew me to his Son by his Spirit.
    . . . At another time, I saw the great love of God, and I was filled with admiration at the infinitude of it; I saw what was cast out from God, and what entered into God's kingdom; and how by Jesus, the opener of the door, with his heavenly key, the entrance was given; and I saw death, how it had passed on all men, and oppressed the seed of God in man, and in me; and how I in the seed came forth, and what the promise was to. Yet it was so with me, that there seemed to be two pleading in me; questioning arose in my mind about gifts and prophecies; and I was tempted again to despair, as if I had sinned against the Holy Spirit.

The Journal of George Fox (London, 1852), vol. I, pp. 56–7.

Shaking needed in hearts

In 1648, as I was sitting in a friend's house in Nottinghamshire (for by this time the power of God had opened the hearts of some to receive the word of life and reconciliation), I saw there was a great crack to go throughout the earth, and a great smoke to go as the crack went; and that after the crack there should be a great shaking: this was the earth in people's hearts, which was to be shaken before the seen of God was raised out of the earth. And it was so; for the Lord's power began to shake them, and great meetings were begun to have, and a mighty power and work of God there was among people, to the astonishment of both people and priests.

The Journal of George Fox (London, 1852), vol. I, p. 63.

Shaking and prayer

After this I went again to Mansfield, where was a great meeting of professors and people; here I was moved to pray; and the Lord's power was so great, that the house seemed to be shaken. When I had done, some of the professors said it was now as in the days of the apostles, when the house was shaken where they were. After I had prayed, one of the professors would pray, which brought deadness and a veil over them; and other professors were grieved at him and told him, it was a temptation on him. Then he came to me, and desired that I would pray again; but I could not pray in man's will.

The Journal of George Fox (London, 1852), vol. I, p. 63.

A smell

Now was I come up in Spirit through the flaming sword, into the paradise of God. All things were new; and all the creation gave another smell unto me than before, beyond what word can utter. I knew nothing put pureness, and innocency and righteousness, being renewed into the image of God by Christ Jesus, to the state of Adam, which he was in before he fell. The creation was opened to me; and it was showed me how all things had their names given them, according to their nature and virtue. I was at a stand in my mind, whether I should practice physic for the good of mankind, seeing the nature and virtues of things were so opened to me by the Lord. But I was immediately taken up in Spirit, to see into another or more steadfast state than Adam's innocency, even into a state in Christ Jesus, that should never fall. And the Lord showed me that such as were faithful to him, in the power and light of Christ, should come up into that state in which Adam was before he fell; in which the admirable works of creation, and the virtues thereof, may be known, through the openings of that divine Word of wisdom and power, by which they were made. Great things did the Lord lead me into, and wonderful depths were opened to me, beyond what can by words be declared; but as people come into subjection to the Spirit of God, and grow up in the image and power of the Almighty, they may receive the word of wisdom, that opens all things, and come to know the hidden unity in the eternal Being.

The Journal of George Fox (London, 1852), vol I, p. 66.

Sighs and groans

And Friends, 'quench not the Spirit, nor despise prophesying,' where it moves; neither hinder the babes and sucklings from crying Hosanna; for out of their mouths will God ordain strength. There were some in Christ's day that were against such, whom he reproved; and there were some in Moses' day, who would have stopped the prophets in the camp, whom Moses reproved, and said, by way of encouragement to them, 'Would God, that all the Lord's people were prophets!' So I say now to you. Therefore you, who stop it in yourselves, do not quench it in others, neither in babe nor suckling; for the Lord hears the cries of the needy, and the sighs and groans of the poor. Judge not that, nor the sighs and groans of the Spirit, which cannot be uttered, lest you judge prayer; for prayer as well lies in sighs and groans to the Lord as otherwise. Let not the sons and daughters, nor the hand-maidens be stopped in their prophesyings, nor the young men in their visions, nor the old men in their dreams; but let the Lord be glorified in and through all, who is over all, God blessed for ever! So every one may improve his talents, every one exercise his gifts, and every one speak as the Spirit gives him utterance. Thus every one may minister as he has received grace, as a good steward to him that has given it him; so that all plants may bud and bring forth fruit to the glory of God; 'for the manifestation of the Spirit is given to every one to profit withal.'

The Journal of George Fox (London, 1852), vol. I, pp. 311–12.

Praying and singing in the Spirit

I was to bring them off from all the world's fellowships, and prayings, and singings, which stood in forms without power; that their fellowship might be in the Holy Spirit, and in the eternal Spirit of God; that they might pray in the Holy Spirit, and sing in the Spirit, and with the grace that comes from Jesus.

The Journal of George Fox (London, 1852), vol. I, pp. 71–2.

Miracle of healing

After some time I went to a meeting at Arn-side, where Richard Myer was, who had been long lame of one of his arms. I was moved of the Lord to say unto him, among all the people, 'Stand up on your legs' (for he was sitting down): and he stood up, and stretched out his arm that had been lame a long time, and said, 'Be it known to you, all people, that this day I am healed.' Yet his parents could hardly believe it; but after the meeting was done, they had him aside, took off his doublet, and then saw it was true. He came soon after to Swarthmore meeting, and then declared how that the Lord had healed him. Yet after this the Lord commanded him to go to York with a message from him, but he disobeyed the Lord; and the Lord struck him again, so that he died about three-quarters of a year after.

The Journal of George Fox (London, 1852), vol I, pp. 152–3.

A distracted woman healed: 1649

Now, after I was released from Nottingham jail, where I had been kept prisoner some time, I travelled as before, in the work of the Lord. Coming to Manfield-Woodhouse, there was a distracted woman under a doctor's hand, with her hair loose all about her ears. He was about to bleed her, she being first bound, and many people being about her, holding her by force; but he could get no blood from her. I desired them to unbind her, and let her alone, for they could not touch the spirit in her, by which she was tormented. So they unbound her, and I was moved to speak to her, and in the name of the Lord to bid her be quiet and still; and she was so. The Lord's power settled her mind, and she mended; and afterwards she received the truth, and continued in it to her death. The Lord's name was honoured; to whom the glory of all his works belongs. Many and great wonderful things were wrought by the heavenly power in those days.

The Journal of George Fox (London, 1852), vol. I, p. 77.

A great man lain sick: 1694

As I travelled through markets, fairs, and divers places, I saw death and darkness in all people, where the power of the Lord God had not shaken them. As I was passing on in Leicestershire, I came to Twycross, where there were excise men. I was moved by the Lord to go to them, and warn them not to oppress the poor; as many poor people were afflicted by them. There was in that town a great man, that had long lain sick, and was given up by the doctors; and some Friends in the town wanted me to go to see him. I went up to him in his bedroom, and spoke the word of life to him, and was moved to pray by him; and the Lord was entreated, and restored him to health.

But when I was come downstairs, into a lower room, and was speaking to the servants, and to some people that were there, a serving-man of his came raving out of another room, with a naked rapier in his hand, and set it just to my side. I looked steadfastly on him, and said, 'Alack for you, poor creature! What will you do with your carnal weapon? It is no more to me than a straw.' The by-standers were much troubled, and he went away in a rage, and full of wrath. But when the news of it came to his master, he turned him out of his service. Thus the Lord's power preserved me, and raised up the weak man, who afterwards was very loving to Friends; and when I came to that town again, both he and his wife came to see me.

The Journal of George Fox (London, 1852), vol. I, p. 79.

The Quakers trembling

I came to Carlisle and went into the steeple-house; and after the priest had done, I preached the truth to the people, and declared the word of life among them. The priest got away, and the magistrates desired me to go out of the steeple-house. But I still declared the way of the Lord to them, and told them, 'I came to speak the word of life and salvation from the Lord among you.'

The power of the Lord was dreadful among them in the steeple-house, so that the people trembled and shook, and they thought the steeple-house shook; and some of them feared it would fall down on their heads.

The Journal of George Fox (London, 1852), vol, I, p. 158.

To those who scorn trembling and quaking

Among other services for the Lord, which then lay on me in the city of London, I was moved to give a paper to those who scorned trembling and quaking, as follows:

'The Lord of the Lord to all you that scorn trembling, and quaking; who scoff at, scorn, stone, and belch forth oaths against, those who are trembling and quaking; threatening them, and beating them. Strangers you are to all the apostles and prophets; and are of the generation that stoned them, and mocked them in those ages. You are the scoffers whom they spoke against, that are come in the last times. Be ye witnesses against yourselves. To the light in all your consciences I speak, that with it you will see yourselves to be out of the life of the holy men of God.

'. . . The prophet Jeremiah trembled, he shook, his bones quaked, he reeled to and fro, like a drunken man, when he saw the deceits of the priests and prophets, who had turned away from the Lord.

'Isaiah said, "Hear the word of the Lord, you that tremble at his word." And, "to this man will I look, even to him that is poor, and of contrite spirit, and trembles at my word."

'. . . Habakkuk, the prophet of the Lord, trembled. And Joel said, "Blow the trumpet in Zion, and let all the inhabitants of the earth tremble: the people shall tremble." And now this trembling is witnessed by the power of the Lord. This power of the Lord is come; the trumpet is sounding; the dead are arising, and the living are praising God; the world is raging, and the scoffers are scorning; and those who witness trembling and quaking in themselves by the power of the Lord, can hardly pass up and down the streets, but with stones and blows, fists and sticks, or dogs set at them; or they are pursued with mockings and reproaches.

'. . . Paul, a minister of God, said, when he came to the Corinthians, that he was with them in weakness, and in fear, and in much trembling, that their faith might not stand on man's wisdom, but on God's power; in that power which made him tremble . . .

'Take warning, all you powers of the earth, how you persecute those whom the world nickname and call Quakers, who dwell in the eternal power of God; let the hand of the Lord be turned against you, and you be all cut off. We exalt and honour God's power, that makes the devils tremble, shakes the earth, and throws down the loftiness and haughtiness of man, which makes the beasts of the field tremble, and the earth reel to and fro.'

The Journal of George Fox (London, 1852), vol. I, pp. 190–1.

Discerning false prophets

I declared to them the marks of the false prophets, and showed that they had already come; and set the true prophets, and Christ, and his apostles over them. I directed the people to their inward teacher, to Christ Jesus, who would turn them from darkness to light. And having opened divers Scriptures to them, I directed them to the Spirit of God in themselves, by which they might come to him, and by which they might also come to know who the false prophets were. So having had a large opportunity among them, I departed in peace.

The Journal of George Fox (London, 1852), vol. I, pp. 108–9.

Spiritual hearing is inward

Christ told the saints that the Spirit of truth, the Holy Spirit, should be their leader into all truth; and Jude exhorts the church to 'pray in the Holy Spirit.' Christ, by his servant John, exhorted the seven churches to hear what the Spirit said to the churches, and this was an inward, spiritual hearing.

The Journal of George Fox (London, 1852), vol. I, p. 274.

Spiritual hearing is known in silence

The mayor of Norwich, having to previous notice of the meeting I intended to have there, granted a warrant to apprehend me. Among the priests at the meetings one shouted, 'Error, blasphemy, and an ungodly meeting!' He said, my error and blasphemy was, in that I said, that people must wait upon God by his power and Spirit, and feel his presence when they did not speak words. I asked him them whether the apostles and holy men of God did not hear God speak to them in their silence, before they spoke forth the Scripture, and before it was written? He replied, Yes, David and the prophets heard God, before they penned the Scriptures, and felt his presence in silence, before they spoke them forth.

The Journal of George Fox (London, 1852), vol. I, p. 352.

A vision of a desperate creature: 1657

The night before I had a vision of a desperate creature, that was coming to destroy me, but I got victory over it. And the next day in meeting-time came one Otway, with some rude fellows. He round about the meeting with his sword or rapier, and would fain have got in through the Friends to me; but the meeting being great, the Friends stood close, so that he could not easily come at me. When he had rode about several times raging, and found he could not get in, being limited by the Lord's power, he went away.

The Journal of George Fox (London, 1852), vol. I, p. 312.

A drawn sword vision: 1664

As I was walking in my chambers, with my eye to the Lord, 'I saw the angel of the Lord with a glittering drawn sword stretched southward, as though the court had been all on fire.' Not long afterwards the wars broke out with Holland, the sickness broke forth, and later the fire of London; so the Lord's sword was drawn indeed.

The Journal of George Fox (London, 1852), vol. II, p. 35.

Quakerism

Swell in their bellies

Men, women and little children at their meetings are strangely wrought upon in their bodies, and brought to fall, foam at the mouth, roar and swell in their bellies.

William Charles Braithwaite, *Beginnings of Quakerism* (1912), p. 73.

Some foamed at the mouth

Two Quakers, Audland and Camm, preaching at Bristol, September, 1654, . . . opened the way of life in the mighty power of God with such effect that the congregation were seized in the soul and pricked at the heart; and some fell to the ground and foamed at the mouth, while others cried out, while the sense of their states of sin was opened to them.

The Journal of George Fox, 23rd May 1676.

Violent Tremblings and sometimes Vomitings in their meetings

At first they did use too fall into violent Tremblings and sometimes Vomitings in their meetings, and pretended to be violently acted by the Spirit; but now that is ceased, they only meet, and he that pretendeth to be moved by the Spirit speaketh; and sometimes they say nothing, but sit an hour or more in silence, and then depart.

Richard Baxter, *Reliquiae Baxterianae* (1696).

Ranters

Exaggerated inner-light theology

One Ranter said: 'Have not I the Spirit, and why may not I write the Scripture as well as Paul, and what I write be as binding and infallible as that which Paul writ?'

Robert Barclay, *Inner Life of the Religious Societies* (London: Hodder & Stoughton, 1912), p. 418.

Madame Guyon
(1648–1717)

French quietist author.

'I felt, even in my sleep, a singular possession of God'

It was my practice to arise at midnight for the purposes of devotion. It seemed to me that God came at the precise time and woke me from sleep in order that I might enjoy him. When I was out of health or greatly fatigued, he did not awaken, but at such times I felt, even in my sleep, a singular possession of God. He loved me so much that he seemed to pervade my being, at a time when I could be only imperfectly conscious of his presence. My sleep is sometimes broken – a sort of half sleep; but my soul seems to be awake enough to know God, when it is hardly capable of knowing anything else.

T.C. Upham, *The Life and Religious Experiences of Madame de la Mothe Guyon* (New York, 1877), vol. i, p. 260.

August Hermann Franke
(1663–1727)

German theologian, influenced by Spener's Pietism.

Distinguish between extraordinary gifts and ordinary gifts

One must make a distinction between extraordinary and ordinary gifts. In a certain book, the extraordinary gives are those for which we must wait. The ordinary gifts, which are essential for salvation, such as genuine humility, mortification, crucifixion of the flesh and of sinful lusts and desires, meekness, patience, long-suffering, goodness, are common. God gives us these gifts when we ask him for them. However, if we ask for the extraordinary gifts of grace, especially if we desire great sweetness, taste, experience and such things, our natural pride and self-will quickly becomes mixed up with such requests. Satan delights to show himself to us as an angel of light, and this happens even more easily when one does not stay in a state of resignation, but tries to force God's hand into giving us what we pray for.

Sermon on Matthew 17:1–9.

Spiritual transfiguration

A foretaste of eternal life, a transfiguration which occurs through the Holy Spirit in the heart by faith in a spiritual way, is of much more use that the transfiguration of Jesus, which Peter, James and John witnessed. Once the disciples had seen the transfiguration they carried on with their old way of life (Matthew 18 and 20). This shows us that the spiritual transfiguration of Christ is some-

thing far more glorious and greater than the external transfiguration of Christ. We are not considering the transfiguration of the
Lord before the physical eyes of the disciples as something paltry
but as something great and glorious, because in it God himself witnessed about his Son. If we want to concentrate on what is helpful
for our spiritual health, blessedness and salvation, we must place
more emphasis on the Holy Spirit transfiguring Christ spiritually
in our hearts, than on what our physical eyes might have observed
about Christ's physical transfiguration.

Take note of this, then, you who pride yourself greatly that you
are with the Lord Christ, who speak a great deal about him in your
life, who read many prayers about him and often sing, 'Jesus My
Joy, My Heart's Desire,' and so on, but yet have little experience of
him in your heart. Take note of this – if you know Jesus as your
joy, as your heart's desire, as your treasure, as your richness, as
your honour, and as everything that you desire, if you love him
and truly taste him, then you will enjoy a foretaste of eternal life
and experience the first drop of living water which will then
become a fountain springing up into eternal life in you. Then you
will be filled with the Spirit and words from Matthew 17:2 will be
true for you, 'his face was shining like the sun.'

Sermon on Matthew 17:1–9.

18TH CENTURY

Howel Harris
(1714–73)

Leader of revival in Wales.

Harris' conversion: 18th June 1735, 'I felt suddenly my heart melting'

I felt suddenly my heart melting within me, like wax before the fire, with love to God my Saviour. I felt not only love and peace, but also a longing to be dissolved and to be with Christ; and there was a cry in my inmost soul, with which I was totally unacquainted before, it was this – 'Abba, Father; Abba, Father!' I could not help calling God MY Father; I know that I was his child, and that he loved me; my soul being filled and satiated, crying, 'It is enough – I am satisfied; give me strength, and I will follow thee through fire and water.'

Quoted by Eifion Evans in *The Welsh Revival of 1904* (Port Talbot: Evangelical Movement of Wales, 1969), p. 65.

Like a drunken man

Sealed by the Spirit of adoption and feeling that I loved God with all my heart, that I was in God and he in me. In private society till two in the morning like a drunken man. Could say nothing but 'glory', 'glory' for a long time.

Quoted by Eifion Evans in *The Welsh Revival of 1904* (Port Talbot: Evangelical Movement of Wales, 1969), p. 67.

Drunk in the Spirit

Howell Harris called on me and said he had been much dissuaded from either hearing me or seeing me by many who said all manner of evil of me. 'But as soon as I heard you preach,' he stated, 'I quickly found of what spirit you were. Before you were done, I was so overpowered with joy and love that I had much trouble walking home.

John Wesley, *Journals*, 5th June 1747.

Camisards

*According to J. I. Packer (*Among God's Giants *(Eastbourne: Kingsway, 1991), p. 304), 'The only Protestant tongue-speakers in the seventeenth century appear to have been the Camisards, Huguenot refugees who fled to the Cevennes after the Edict of Nantes was revoked in 1685.'*

A follower of the Camisards, in 1717

J. P. was for a long time under violent agitations, and laboured greatly with struggles in his throat and organs of speech, almost as if he were choking, and uttered some inarticulate sounds. Here the Spirit threw him violently upon the floor, where he lay stretched out as dead, without motion or breathing. After some time, there came a trembling motion into every part of him at once, his feet, legs, arms and shoulders; after which there appeared some breathing, which grew still louder and stronger in him.

Edward Smedley, *History of the Reformed Religion in France* (1832–4), vol. 3, p. 312, note.

Charles Wesley and a Camisard

[Charles Wesley shared a bedroom with a Camisard follower and was alarmed that while he undressed this man] 'fell into violent agitations, and gobbled like a turkey-cock'.

Robert Southey, *Life of Wesley*, ch. 8.

A Camisard prophetess

She came in, and soon after leaned back in her chair, and seemed to have strong workings in her breast, with deep sighings. Her head and hands, and by turns every part of her body, seemed also to be in a kind of convulsive motion. She spoke much, all in the person of God, and mostly in Scripture words, of the fulfilling of the prophecies, the coming of Christ at hand, and the spreading of the gospel all over the earth.

John Wesley, *Journal*, vol. 28, chapter 1, section 39.

The French prophets (Camisards)

The Shakings of their Heads, Crawling on the Knees, Quakings and Tremblings; their Whistlings, Drummings, Trumpetings; their thunderings, their Snuffling; Blowing as with a Horn; Panting, and Difficulty of Breathing; Sighing and Groaning; Hissing; Smiling; Laughing; Pointing with the Finger; Shaking the Hand; Striking; Threshing; as likewise their perpetual Hesitations; Childish Repetitions; unintelligible Stuff; gross Contradictions; manifold Lies; Conjectures turn'd into Predictions; their Howling in their Assemblies like a Dog, and being in all manner of Disorder.

Nathaniel Spinkes, in *The Spirit of Enthusiasm Exorcis'd*, (London: Richard Sare, 1709).

Camisards at Oxford

About a week since came to Oxford, and put up at the Greyhound, six of the pretended prophets, called Camisards; namely, two men, three women, and a girl. They continued three or four days in the town without any discovery; but at last the woman had agitations, and abundance of people went to see them.

Reliquiae Hernianae, vol. i, p. 147, quoted by R. A. Knox, *Enthusiasm* (Oxford: Clarendon Press, 1950), pp. 370–1.

Jansenists

Cornelius Jansen, born 28th October 1585 in the province of Utrecht, gave his name to the Jansenists, a spiritual movement of the seventeenth and eighteenth centuries, which did not break away from the Catholic church.

The Dance of the Convulsionaries

[This took place in the cemetery of Saint-Medard, in Paris.]
Men falling like epileptics, others swallowing pebbles, glass, and even live coals, women walking feet in the air. You heard nothing but groaning, singing, shrieking, whistling, declaiming, prophesying, caterwauling.

L. Figuier, quoted in P. F. Mathieu, *Histoire des miracles et des convulsionaries de Saint-Medard*, p. 217, quoted in R. A. Knox, *Enthusiasm* (Oxford: Clarendon Press, 1950), p. 377.

The convulsionaries of Saint-Medard

Violent convulsions or contortions of the whole body, rolling on the ground, leaping about on the pavement, rigours, tumultuous shakings of the arms, the legs, the head, and all the limbs, resulting in a difficulty of breathing, a quickening and an irregularity of the pulse.

P. F. Mathieu, *Histoire des miracles et des convulsionaries de Saint-Medard*, p. 271, quoted in R. A. Knox, *Enthusiasm* (Oxford: Clarendon Press, 1950), p. 378.

Mennonites

Protestant followers of the old Anabaptist tradition.

1749: 'Like falling sickness'

They would sigh, groan, and bawl. They made the strangest contortions, and wrung their hands with violence. A cold sweat overspread their faces. They were dying with drought and could hardly drink. They breathed with difficulty; their whole body was convulsed. They were exactly in the situation of a person afflicted with the falling sickness, for they could neither walk nor support themselves.

J. Stinstra, *Essay on Fanaticism* (Dublin: Ewing, 1774), pp. cxxvi–cxxvii; quoted by R. A. Knox, *Enthusiasm* (Oxford: Clarendon Press, 1950), p. 389.

Jonathan Edwards
(1703–58)

Jonathan Edwards was a scholar, a Calvinist preacher, a pastor and revival leader, a metaphysician and a theologian. He saw a remarkable movement of the Spirit of God in his congregation in 1734–5, and throughout all New England in 1740–2.

A new experience for Edwards

The first instance that I remember of that sort of inward, sweet delight of God and divine things, that I have lived in much since, was on reading those words, in 1 Timothy 1:17: 'Now unto the King eternal, immortal, invisible, the only wise God, be honour and glory for ever and ever.' As I read the words, there came into my soul, and was as it were diffused through it, a sense of the glory of the Divine being; a new sense, quite different from anything I ever experienced before.

Personal Narrative, in *The Works of Jonathan Edwards*, I.xiii.a.

A sense of the glory of the Third Person of the Trinity

I have, many times, had a sense of the glory of the Third Person of the Trinity, and His office as Sanctifier; in His holy operations, communicating divine light and life to the soul. God in the communications of His Holy Spirit, has appeared as an infinite fountain of divine glory and sweetness.

Personal Narrative, in *The Works of Jonathan Edwards* (Edinburgh: Banner of Truth, 1974), I.xlvii.b.

Isaac Watts and John Guyse

Never did we hear or read, since the first ages of Christianity, any event of this kind so surprising as the present Narrative hath set before us.

Narrative (London, 1737), Preface.

Assessment of the revival at Northampton

For a long period, revivals of religion had been chiefly unknown, both in Great Britain and on the continent of Europe. The church at large had grievously ceased to expect events of this nature; and appears to have entertained very imperfect views of their causes, their nature, and the manner in which they ought to be regarded. In no previous publication had these important subjects been adequately explained.

By the astonishing work of grace at Northampton, an impulse had been given to the churches of this whole western world, which could not soon be lost. The history of that event, having been extensively circulated, produced a general conviction in the minds of Christians, that the preaching of the gospel might be attended by effects, not less surprising than those which followed it in apostolic times. This conviction produced an important change in the views, and conduct, both of ministers and churches.

S. E. Dwight, *The Life of President Edwards* (New York, 1830), p. 138; quoted in A. Skevington Wood, *The Inextinguishable Blaze* (London: Paternoster, 1960), p. 62.

Best preacher . . . best divine

John Newton was once asked: Who do you think is the greatest preacher you have ever heard?'

Without hesitating, Newton replied: 'Whitefield.'

Then Newton was asked: 'Who do you think is the greatest divine of our time?'

Newton answered, even more speedily, 'Edwards. There is as much in his little finger as in Whitefield altogether.'

Studying phenomena linked with revivals

And it has been very observable, that people of the greatest understanding, and who had studied most about things of this nature, have been more confounded than others. Some such people declare, that all their former wisdom is brought to nought, and that they appear to have been babes, who knew nothing.

A Faithful Narrative of a Surprising Work of God, in *The Works of Jonathan Edwards,* ed. Henry Hickman (Edinburgh: Banner of Truth, 1974), vol. 1, p. 354.

False affections, true affections ('the moving springs of all the affairs of life'; the emotions)

Though there are false affections in religion, and in some respects raised high: yet undoubtedly there are also true, holy, and solid affections; and the higher these are raised, the better. And when they are raised to an extremely great height, they are not to be suspected merely because of their degree, but on the contrary to be esteemed.

The Works of Jonathan Edwards, ed. Henry Hickman (Edinburgh: Banner of Truth, 1974), vol. 1, p. 367.

Laughter in New Hampshire

Their joyful surprise has caused their hearts as it were to leap, so that they have been ready to break forth into laughter, tears often at the same time issuing like a flood, and intermingling a loud weeping.

The Works of Jonathan Edwards, ed. Henry Hickman (Edinburgh: Banner of Truth, 1974), vol. 1, p. 354.

A sweet and humble melting

[This extract is taken from Edwards' catechism class of 1.3.47 in Crossweeksung, New Jersey.]
Toward the close of my discourse, divine truths made considerable impressions upon the audience, and produced tears and sobs in some under concern; and more especially a sweet and humble melting in sundry that, I have reason to hope, were truly gracious.

The Works of Jonathan Edwards, ed. Henry Hickman (Edinburgh: Banner of Truth, 1974), vol. 2, p. 407.

The nature of true religion and its distinguishing marks

In times of great revivals, as it is with the fruit-trees in the spring, there are multitudes of blossoms, which appear fair and beautiful, and there is a promising appearance of young fruit; but many of them are of short continuance; they soon fall off, and never come to maturity.

Preface to *A Treatise Concerning Religious Affections*, in *The Works of Jonathan Edwards*, ed. Henry Hickman (Edinburgh: Banner of Truth, 1974), vol. 1, p. 235.

Holy affections [emotions]

Holy affections . . . are a very great part of [true] religion. And as true religion is practical, and God has so constituted the human nature, that the affections are very much the springs of men's actions, this also shows, that true religion must consist very much in the affections.

The Works of Jonathan Edwards, ed. Henry Hickman (Edinburgh: Banner of Truth, 1974), vol. 1, pp. 237–8.

Enthusiasm

If such things are enthusiasm or the fruit of a distempered brain, let my brain be evermore possessed of that happy distemper! If this be distraction, I pray God that the world of mankind may be seized with this benign, meek, beneficent, glorious distraction.

Edwards' conversion

After this my sense of divine things gradually increased, and became more and more lively, and had more of that inward sweetness. The appearance of everything was altered; there seemed to be, as it were, a calm, sweet cast, or appearance of divine glory, in almost everything. God's excellency, his wisdom, his purity and love, seemed to appear in everything; in the sun, moon, and stars; in the clouds and blue sky; in the grass, flowers, and trees; in the water and all nature; which used greatly to fix my mind. And scarce anything, among all the works of nature, was so sweet to me as thunder and lightning; formerly nothing had been so terrible to me. Before, I used to be uncommonly terrified with thunder, and to be struck with terror when I saw a thunderstorm rising; but now, on the contrary, it rejoices me.

S. E. Dwight, *The Life of President Edwards* (New York, 1830), p. 61.

Conversion: God's most glorious work

I am bold to say that the work of God in the conversion of one soul, considered together with the source, foundation, and purchase of it, and also the benefit, end, and eternal issue of it, is a more glorious work of God than the creation of the whole material universe.

Devotional reading

Christian devotional reading helps us find intimate union with God, its motivation being to love God with all our heart, mind, and will.
Concerning the Religious Affections.

Satan's strategy in revival

When Satan finds that he can keep men quiet and secure no longer, then he drives them to excesses and extravagances. He holds them back as long as he can; but when he can do it no longer, then he will push them on, and, if possible, run them upon their heads.

The Works of Jonathan Edwards, ed. Henry Hickman (Edinburgh: Banner of Truth, 1974), vol. 1, p. 397.

Their bodies in convulsions

There have been several instances here [in America during the Great Awakening] of people waxing cold and benumbed, with their hands clinched, yes, and their bodies in convulsions.

Thoughts on Revival, I, ii.

Whitefield in Northampton, USA, 1741

The whole room was full of nothing but outcries, faintings and the like. The children there were very generally and greatly affected with the warnings and counsels that were given them, and many exceedingly overcome. When they were dismissed, they almost all of them went home crying aloud through the streets.

Memoir, ch. 10.

Revival grows in Northampton

The revival at first chiefly appeared among professors and those that had entertained the hope that they were in a state of grace, to whom Mr Whitefield chiefly addressed himself; but in a very short time there appeared an awakening and deep concern among some young persons that looked upon themselves as in a Christless state; and there were some hopeful appearances of conversion, and some professors were greatly revived. In about a month or six weeks there was a great alteration in the town, both as to the revivals of professors, and awakenings of others. By the middle of

December a very considerable work of God appeared among those that were very young; and the revival of religion continued to increase; so that in the spring, an engagedness of spirit about things of religion was become very general among young people and children, and religious subjects almost wholly took up their conversation when they were together.

Tyerman, *Whitefield*, vol. 1, p. 429; quoted in A. Skevington Wood, *The Inextinguishable Blaze* (London: Paternoster, 1960), pp. 63–4.

Continuous commotion at Northampton

The town seemed to be in a great and continued commotion, day and night.

T. Prince, *Christian History*, No. 46; quoted in A. Skevington Wood, *The Inextinguishable Blaze* (London: Paternoster, 1960), p. 64.

Praying for revival

It is God's will through his wonderful grace, that the prayers of his saints should be one great principal means of carrying on the designs of Christ's kingdom in the world. When God has something very great to accomplish for his church, it is his will that there should precede it the extraordinary prayers of his people; as is manifest by Ezekiel 36:37. And it is revealed that, when God is about to accomplish great things for his church, he will begin by remarkably pouring out the spirit of grace and supplication (see Zechariah 12:10).

The Works of Jonathan Edwards, ed. Henry Hickman (Edinburgh: Banner of Truth, 1974), vol. 1, p. 426.

Mrs Edwards experiencing 'enveloping friendliness'

Last night was the sweetest night I ever had in my life. I never before, for so long a time together, enjoyed so much of the light and rest and sweetness of heaven in my soul, but without the least agitation of body during the whole time. Part of the night I lay awake, sometimes asleep, and sometimes between sleeping and waking. But all night I continued in a constant, clear, and lively sense of the heavenly sweetness of Christ's excellent love, of his nearness to me, and of my dearness to him; with an inexpressibly sweet calmness of soul in an entire rest in him. I seemed to myself to perceive a glow of divine love come down from the heart of Christ in heaven into my heart in a constant stream, like a stream or pencil of sweet light. At the same time my heart and soul all flowed out in love to Christ, so that there seemed to be a constant flowing and reflowing of heavenly love, and I appeared to myself to float or swim, in these bright, sweet beams, like the motes swimming in the beams of the sun, or the streams of his light which come in at the window. I think that what I felt each minute was worth more than all the outward comfort and pleasure which I had enjoyed in my whole life put together. It was pleasure, without the least sting, or any interruption. It was a sweetness, which my soul was lost in; it seemed to be all that my feeble frame could sustain. There was but little difference, the sweetness was greatest while I was asleep. As I awoke early the next morning, it seemed to me that I had no more to do with any outward interest of my own than with that of a person whom I never say. The glory of God seemed to swallow up every wish and desire of my heart.

And it seemed to me that I found a perfect willingness, quietness, and alacrity of soul in consenting that it should be so, if it were most for the glory of God, so that there was no hesitation, doubt, or darkness in my mind. The glory of God seemed to overcome me and swallow me up, and every conceivable suffering, and everything that was terrible to my nature, seemed to shrink to nothing before it. This resignation continued in its clearness and brightness the rest of the night, and all the next day and the night following, and on Monday in the forenoon, without interruption or abatement.

Narrative of the Revival in New England.

Jonathan Edwards' comments on his wife's experiences

I have been particularly acquainted with many persons who have been the subject of the high and extraordinary transports of the present day. But in the highest transports I have been acquainted with, and where the affections of admiration, love and joy, so far as another could judge, have been raised to the highest pitch, the following things have been united: a very frequent dwelling for some considerable time together, in views of the glory of the divine perfections and Christ's excellencies, so that the soul has been as it were perfectly overwhelmed, and swallowed up with light and live, a sweet solace, and a rest and joy of soul altogether unspeakable, sometimes for five or six hours together, without interruption.

Thoughts on Revival.

A test to expose the mercenary spirit among revivalist experiences

By this you may examine your love to God, and to Jesus Christ, and to the Word of God, and your joy in them, and also your love to the people of God, and your desires after heaven; whether they be from a supreme delight in this sort of beauty, without being primarily moved from your own imagined interest in them, or expectations from them.

. . . What they are principally taken and elevated with, is not the glory of God, or beauty of Christ, but the beauty of their experiences. They keep thinking of themselves, what a good experience is this. They put their experiences in the place of Christ, and his beauty and fulness; and instead of rejoicing in Christ Jesus, they rejoice in their admirable experiences.

Original Sin, ed. C. A. Holbrook (New Haven, 1970), pp. 240, 251.

Edwards' reply to those critical of those who made much of cries, faintings and other bodily effects

When I see a great crying out in a congregation, in the manner that I have seen it, when those things are held forth to them which are worthy of their being greatly affected by them, I rejoice in it.

To rejoice that the work of God is carried on calmly, without much ado, is in effect to rejoice that it is carried on with less power, or that there is not so much of the influence of God's Spirit. For though the degree of the influence of the Spirit of God on particular people, is by no means to be judged by the degree of external appearances, because of the different constitutions, tempers and circumstances of people; yet, if there is a very powerful influence of the Spirit of God on a mixed multitude, it will cause some way or other a great visible commotion.

Thoughts on the Present Revival, in *The Works of Jonathan Edwards,* ed. Henry Hickman (Edinburgh: Banner of Truth, 1974), vol. 1, p. 394b.

Assessing 'effects'

We are to observe the effect wrought; and if, upon examination of that, it is found to be agreeable to the word of God, we are bound to rest in it as God's work; and we shall be rebuked for our arrogance if we refuse to acknowledge it until God explains to us how he has brought this effect to pass, or why he has made use of such and such means in doing it.

It seems to me that the great God has poured contempt on all that human strength, wisdom, prudence and sufficiency which people have been wont to trust and glory in so that the Lord alone shall be exalted.

Thoughts on the Present Revival, in *The Works of Jonathan Edwards,* ed. Henry Hickman (Edinburgh: Banner of Truth, 1974), vol. 1, p. 366 a, b.

Jonathan Edwards: Distinguishing Marks of a Work of the Spirit of God

PART 1

Beloved, believe not every spirit, but try the spirits whether they are of God: because many false prophets are gone out into the world (1 John 4:1).

Judging between the true and the false

In the apostolic age, there was the greatest outpouring of the Spirit of God that ever was, both as to his extraordinary influences and gifts, and his ordinary operations, in convincing, converting, enlightening, and sanctifying the souls of men. But as the influences of the true Spirit abounded, so counterfeits did also abound: the devil was abundant in mimicking, both the ordinary and extraordinary influences of the Spirit of God, as is manifest by innumerable passages of the apostles' writings. This made it very necessary that the church of Christ should be furnished with some certain rules, distinguishing and clear marks, by which she might proceed safely in judging of the true from the false without danger of being imposed upon. The giving of such rules is the plain design of this chapter, where we have this matter more expressly and fully treated of than anywhere else in the Bible. The apostle, of set purpose, undertakes to supply the church of God with such marks of the true Spirit as may be plain and safe, and well accommodated to use and practice; and that the subject might be clearly and sufficiently handled, he insists upon it throughout the chapter, which makes it wonderful that what is said here is no more taken notice of in this extraordinary day, when there is such an uncommon and extensive operation on the minds of people, such a variety of opinions concerning it, and so much talk about the work of the Spirit.

The indwelling of the Spirit

The apostle's discourse on this subject is introduced by an occasional mention of the indwelling of the Spirit, as the sure evidence of an interest in Christ. 'And he that keepeth his commandments dwelleth in him, and he in him; and hereby we know that he abideth in us, by the Spirit which he hath given us.' From this we may infer that the apostle's purpose is not only to give marks by which to distinguish the true Spirit from the false, in his extraordinary gifts of prophecy and miracles, but also in his ordinary influences on the minds of his people, in order that they may be united to Christ, and be built up in him. This is also manifest from the marks themselves that are given, which we shall consider later.

Credulity and counterfeits

The words of the text are an introduction to this discourse of the distinguishing signs of the true and false Spirit. Before the apostle proceeds to lay down these signs, he exhorts Christians, first, against being over-credulous, and forward to admit every specious appearance as a work of a true Spirit. 'Beloved, believe not every spirit, but try the spirits whether they are of God.' And, second, he shows that there were many counterfeits, 'because many false prophets are gone out into the world'. These not only claimed to have the Spirit of God in his extraordinary gifts of inspiration, but also to be the great friends and favourites of heaven, to be eminently holy persons, and to have much of the ordinary saving, sanctifying influences of the Spirit of God on their hearts. Hence we are to look upon these words as a direction to examine and try their claims to the Spirit of God in both these respects.

The Scripture is our guide

My purpose therefore at this time is to show what are the true, certain, and distinguishing evidences of a work of the Spirit of God, by which we may safely proceed in judging any operation we find in ourselves, or see in others. And here I would observe that we are to take the *Scriptures* as our guide in such cases. This is the great and standing rule which God has given to his church, in order to guide them in things relating to the great concerns of their souls; and it is an infallible and sufficient rule. There are undoubtedly sufficient marks given to guide the church of God in this great affair of judging of spirits, without which it would lie open to woeful delusion, and would be remedilessly exposed to be imposed on and devoured by its enemies. And we need not be afraid to trust these rules. Doubtless that Spirit who indited the Scriptures knew how to give us good rules, by which to distinguish his operations from all that is falsely claimed to be from him. And this, as I observed before, the Spirit of God has here done of set purpose, and done it more particularly and fully than anywhere else; so that in my present discourse I shall go nowhere else for rules or marks for the trial of spirits, but shall confine myself to those that I find in this chapter.

But before I proceed to speak about these particularly, I would prepare my way by first observing *negatively*, in some instances, what are *not* signs or evidences of a work of the Spirit of God.

Nine Negative signs

1. The very unusual and extraordinary character of a work

What the church has been used to is not a rule by which we are to judge. Nothing can be certainly concluded from a work being carried on in a very unusual and extraordinary way, provided the variety or difference is such as may still be included within the limits of scriptural rules. What the church has been used to is not a rule by which we are to judge, because there may be new and extraordinary works of God, and he has hitherto evidently worked in an extraordinary manner. He has brought to pass new things, strange works; and has worked in such a manner as to surprise both men and angels. And as God has done thus in times past, so we have no reason to think but that he will still do so. The prophecies of Scripture give us reason to think that God has things to accomplish which have never yet been seen. No deviation from what has hitherto been usual, let it be never so great, is an argument that a work is not from the Spirit of God, if it is no deviation from his prescribed rule. The Holy Spirit is sovereign in his operation; and we know that he uses a great variety; and we cannot tell how great a variety he may use, within the compass of the rules he himself has fixed. We ought not to limit God where he has not limited himself.

Therefore it is not reasonable to determine that a work is not from God's Holy Spirit because of the extraordinary degree in which the minds of persons are influenced. If they seem to have an extraordinary conviction of the dreadful nature of sin, and a very uncommon sense of the misery of a Christless condition – or extraordinary views of the certainty and glory of divine things – and are proportionably moved with very extraordinary affections of fear and sorrow, desire, love, or joy; or if the apparent change is very sudden, and the work carried on with very unusual swiftness – and the persons affected are very numerous, and many of them are very young, with other unusual circumstances, not infringing upon scriptural marks of a work of the Spirit – these things are no argument that the work is not of the Spirit of God. The extraordinary and unusual degree of influence, and power of operation, if in its nature it fits the rules and marks given in Scripture, is rather an argument in its favour; for by how much higher the degree which in its nature is agreeable to the rule, so much the more is there of conformity to the rule; and so much the more evident that conformity. When things are in small degrees, though they may really follow the rule, it is not so easily seen whether their nature agrees with the rule.

People are very apt to have doubts about things that are strange
People are very apt to have doubts about things that are strange; especially elderly persons, who doubt that things are right which they have never been used to in their day, and have not heard of in the days of their fathers. But if it is a good argument that a work is not from the Spirit of God if it is very unusual, then it was so in the apostles' days. The work of the Spirit then was carried on in a manner that, in very many respects, was altogether new – such as had never been seen or heard since the world stood. The work was then carried on with more visible and remarkable power than ever; nor had there been seen before such mighty and wonderful effects of the Spirit of God in sudden changes and such great engagedness and zeal in great multitudes – such a sudden alteration in towns, cities, and countries; such a swift progress, and vast extent of the work – and many other extraordinary circumstances might be mentioned. The great unusualness of the work surprised the Jews; they knew not what to make of it, but could not believe it to be the work of God; many looked upon the persons that were the subjects of it as bereft of reason; as you may see in Acts 2:13 and 26:24, and in 1 Corinthians 4:10.

And we have reason from Scripture prophecy to suppose that at the commencement of that last and greatest outpouring of the

Spirit of God that is to come in the latter ages of the world, the manner of the work will be very extraordinary, and such as has never yet been seen; so that there shall be occasion to say, as in Isaiah 56:8, 'Who hath heard such a thing? Who hath seen such things? Shall the earth be made to bring forth in one day? Shall a nation be born at once? for as soon as Zion travailed, she brought forth her children.' It may be reasonably expected that the extraordinary manner of the work then will bear some proportion to the very extraordinary events, and that glorious change in the state of the world, which God will bring to pass by it.

2. How the body is affected

A work is not to be judged by tears, trembling, groans, loud outcries, agonies of body, or the failing of bodily strength
The influence people are under is not to be judged of one way or the other by such effects on the body; and the reason is, because the Scripture nowhere gives us any such rule. We cannot conclude that people are under the influence of the Spirit because we see such effects upon their bodies, because this is not given as a mark of the true Spirit; nor on the other hand have we any reason to conclude from any such outward appearances that persons are not under the influence of the Spirit of God, because there is no rule of Scripture given us to judge of spirits by, that does either expressly or indirectly exclude such effects on the body, nor does reason exclude them.

It is easily accounted for from the consideration of the nature of divine and eternal things, and the nature of man, and the laws of the union between soul and body, how a right influence, a true and proper sense of things, should have such effects on the body, even those that are of the most extraordinary kind, such as taking away the bodily strength, or throwing the body into great agonies, and extorting loud outcries. None of us does not suppose that the misery of hell is doubtless so dreadful, and eternity so vast, that if a person should have a clear apprehension of that misery as it is, it would be more than his feeble frame could bear, and especially if at the same time he saw himself in great danger of it, and to be utterly uncertain whether he would be delivered from it, and have no security from it one day or hour. If we consider human nature, we must not wonder that when person have a great sense of that which is so amazingly dreadful, and also have a great view of their own wickedness and God's anger, that things seem to them to forebode speedy and immediate destruction. We see the nature of man to be such that when he is in danger of some terrible calamity to which he is greatly exposed, he is ready upon every occasion to think that it is coming *now*.

The manifestation of God's wrath overwhelms human strength
When people's hearts are full of fear, in time of war, they are ready to tremble at the shaking of a leaf, and to expect the enemy every minute, and to say within themselves, '*Now* I shall be slain.' If we should suppose that a person saw himself hanging over a great pit, full of fierce and glowing flames, by a thread that he knew to be very weak, and not sufficient to bear his weight, and knew that multitudes had been in such circumstances before, and that most of them had fallen and perished, and saw nothing within reach that he could take hold of to save him, what distress would he be in! How ready to think that *now* the thread was breaking, that now, *this minute*, he would be swallowed up in those dreadful flames! And would he not be ready to cry out in such circumstances? How much more those that see themselves in this manner hanging over an infinitely more dreadful pit, or held over it in the hand of God, who at the same time they see to be exceedingly provoked! No wonder that the wrath of God, when manifested only a little to the soul, overbears human strength.

So it may easily be accounted for, that a true sense of the glorious excellence of the Lord Jesus Christ, and of his wonderful dying, love, and the exercise of a truly spiritual love and joy, should be such as very much to overcome the bodily strength. We are all ready to admit that no one can see God and live, and that it is only a very small part of that apprehension of the glory and love of Christ, which the saints enjoy in heaven, that our present frame can bear; therefore it is not at all strange that God should sometimes give his saints such foretastes of heaven as to diminish their bodily strength.

Some extraordinary things are not mentioned in the New Testament

Some people object against such extraordinary appearances, that we have no instances of them recorded in the New Testament, under the extraordinary effusions of the Spirit. Were this allowed, I can see no force in the objection, if neither reason nor any rule of Scripture exclude such things – especially considering what was observed under the last heading. I do not know that we have any express mention in the New Testament of any person's weeping, or groaning, or sighing through fear of hell, or a sense of God's anger; but is there anybody so foolish as to argue from this, that anyone in whom these things appear is not being convicted by the Spirit of God? And the reason why we do not argue thus is because these are easily accounted for from what we know of the nature of man, and from what the Scripture informs us in general concerning the nature of eternal things, and the nature of the convictions of God's Spirit; so that there is no need that anything should be said in particular concerning these external, circumstantial effects. Nobody supposes that there is any need of express scripture for every external, accidental manifestation of the inward motion of the mind: and though such circumstances are not particularly recorded in sacred history, there is a great deal of reason to think, from the general accounts we have, that it could not be otherwise than that such things must be in those days.

The jailer fell down and trembled

And there is also reason to think that such great outpouring of the Spirit was not wholly without those more extraordinary effects on people's bodies. The jailer in particular seems to have been an instance of that nature, when he, in the utmost distress and amazement, came trembling, and fell down before Paul and Silas. His falling down at that time does not seem to be intentionally putting himself into a posture of supplication, or humble address to Paul and Silas; for he seems not to have said anything to them then; but he first brought them out, and then he says to them, 'Sirs, what must I do to be saved?' (Acts 16:29–30). But his falling down seems to be from the same cause as his trembling.

The example of the Psalmist
The psalmist gives an account of his crying out aloud, and a great weakening of his body under convictions of conscience, and a sense of the guilt of sin: 'When I kept silence my bones waxed old, through my roaring all the day long; for day and night thy hand was heavy upon me: my moisture is turned into the drought of summer' (Ps. 32:3–4). We may at least argue so much from it, that such an effect of conviction of sin may well in some cases be supposed; for the psalmist would not represent his case by what would be absurd, and to which no degree of that exercise of mind he spoke of would have any tendency.

The disciples cried out for fear
We read of the disciples that when they saw Christ coming to them in the storm, and took him for some terrible enemy, threatening their destruction in that storm, 'they cried out for fear' (Matt. 14:26). Why then should it be thought strange that people should cry out for fear when God appears to them as a terrible enemy, and they see themselves in great danger of being swallowed up in the bottomless gulf of eternal misery?

The Song of Songs
The spouse, once and again, speaks of herself as overpowered with the love of Christ, so as to weaken her body, and make her faint: 'Stay me with flagons, comfort me with apples; for I am sick of love . . . I charge you, O ye daughters of Jerusalem, if ye find my Beloved, that ye tell him that I am sick of love' (S. of S. 2:5, 8). From this we may at least argue that such an effect may well be supposed to arise from such a cause in the saints in some cases, and that such an effect will sometimes be seen in the church of Christ.

It is a weak objection to say that the impressions of enthusiasts have a great effect on their bodies. That the Quakers used to tremble is no argument that Saul, afterwards called Paul, and the jailer did not tremble from real convictions of conscience. Indeed, all such objections from effects on the body, whether greater or less, seem to be exceedingly frivolous. Those who argue from them proceed in the dark – they do not know what ground they go upon, nor by what rule they judge. The root and course of things is to be looked at, and the nature of the operations and affections are to be inquired into, and examined by the rule of God's word, and not the motions of the blood and animal spirits.

3. 'A great deal of noise about religion'

It is no argument that an operation on people's minds is not the work of the Spirit of God, that it occasions a great deal of noise about religion.

For though true religion is contrary to that of the Pharisees – which was ostentatious, and delighted to set itself forth to the view of men for their applause – yet such is human nature that it is morally impossible for there to be a great concern, strong affection, and a general engagedness of mind among a people, without causing a notable, visible, and open commotion and alteration among that people. – Surely, it is no argument that people's minds are not under the influence of God's Spirit, that they are very much moved; for indeed spiritual and eternal things are so great, and of such infinite concern, that there is a great absurdity in men's being only moderately moved and affected by them; and surely it is no argument that they are affected with these things in some measure as they deserve, or in some proportion to their importance. And when was there ever any such thing since the world, stood, as a people in general being greatly affected in any affair whatsoever, without noise or stir? The nature of man will not allow it.

They turned the world upside down
Indeed, Christ says: 'The kingdom of God cometh not with observation' (Luke 17:20). That is, it will not consist in what is outward and visible; it will not be like earthly kingdoms, set up with outward pomp, in some particular place which will be the special royal city and seat of the kingdom. As Christ explains in the words

which come next: 'Neither shall they say, Lo here, or lo there; for behold the kingdom of God is within you.' ' Not that the kingdom of God will be set up in the world on the ruin of Satan's kingdom, without a very observable great effect: a mighty change in the state of things, to the observation and astonishment of the whole world. Just such an effect as this is foretold in the prophecies of Scripture, and by Christ himself in this very passage, and indeed in his own explanation of these words: 'For as the lightning that lightneth out of one part under heaven, shineth unto another part under heaven, so shall also the Son of man be in his day' (verse 24). This is to distinguish Christ's coming to set up his kingdom from the coming of false Christs, which he tells us will be in a private manner in the deserts and in the secret chambers; whereas this event of setting up the kingdom of God would be open and public in the sight of the whole world with clear manifestation, like lightning that cannot be hidden but glares in everyone's eyes and shines from one side of heaven to the other. And we find that when Christ's kingdom came, by that remarkable outpouring of the Spirit in the apostles' days, it occasioned a great stir everywhere. What a mighty opposition was there in Jerusalem on occasion of that great effusion of the Spirit! And so in Samaria, Antioch, Ephesus, Corinth, and other places! News of the affair filled the world, and caused some people to say of the apostles that they had turned the world upside down (Acts 17:6).

4. People's imaginations are affected

It is no argument that an operation on people's minds is not the work of the Spirit of God, that many who are subject to it have great impressions made on their imaginations. That people have many impressions on their imaginations does not prove that they have nothing else.

It is easy to account for there being much of this nature among a people, where a great many, of all kinds, have their minds engaged with intense thought and strong feelings about invisible things. Indeed, it would be strange if this did not happen. Such is our nature that we cannot think about invisible things without a degree of imagination. I dare appeal to any man, of the greatest powers of mind, whether he is able to fix his thoughts on God or Christ, or the things of another world, without imaginary ideas attending his meditations? And the more engaged the mind is, and the more intense the contemplation and affection, still the more lively and strong the imaginary idea will ordinarily be; especially when attended with surprise. And this is the case when the mental prospect is very new, and takes strong hold of the passions, such as fear or joy; and when the state and views of the mind suddenly changes from a contrary extreme, such as from that which was extremely dreadful to that which is extremely delightful. And it is no wonder that many people do not easily distinguish between that which is imaginary and that which is intellectual and spiritual; and that they are apt to lay too much weight on the imaginary part, and are most ready to speak of that in the account they give of their experiences, especially people of less understanding and distinguishing capacity.

The imagination is a God-given faculty
As God has given us such a faculty as the imagination, and so made us that we cannot think of things spiritual and invisible without some exercise of this faculty; so it appears to me that such is our state and nature that this faculty is really subservient and helpful to the other faculties of the mind, when a proper use is made of it; though often, when the imagination is too strong, and the other faculties weak, it overbears, and disturbs them in their exercise. It seems clear to me, in many instances with which I have been acquainted, that God has really made use of this faculty to truly divine purposes; especially in some that are more ignorant. God seems to condescend to their circumstances, and deal with them as babes; as of old he instructed his church, whilst in a state of ignorance and minority, by types and outward representations. I can see nothing unreasonable in such a position. Let others who have much occasion to deal with souls in spiritual concerns, judge whether experience does not confirm it.

It is no argument that a work is not of the Spirit of God, that some who are the subjects of it have been in a kind of ecstasy, in which they have had their minds transported into a train of strong and pleasing imaginations, and a kind of visions, as though they were rapt up to heaven, and there saw glorious sights. I have been acquainted with some such instances, and I see no need of bringing in the help of the devil into the account that we give of these things, nor yet of supposing them to be of the same nature as the visions of the prophets, or St Paul's rapture into paradise. Human nature, under these intense exercises and affections, is all that need be brought into the account.

The whole soul is ravished
If it may be well accounted for, that people under a true sense of the glorious and wonderful greatness and excellence of divine things, and soul-ravishing views of the beauty and love of Christ, should have the strength of nature overpowered, as I have already shown that it may; then I think it is not at all strange that amongst great numbers that are thus affected and overborne, there should be some persons of particular constitutions that have their imaginations effected like this. The effect is no other than what bears a proportion and analogy to other effects of the strong exercise of their minds. It is no wonder, when the thoughts are so fixed, and the affections so strong – and the whole soul so engaged, ravished, and swallowed up – that all other parts of the body are so affected as to be deprived of their strength, and the whole frame ready to dissolve. Is it any wonder that, in such a case, the brain in particular (especially in some constitutions), which we know is most especially affected by intense contemplations and exercises of mind, should be so affected that its strength and spirits should be diverted for a while, and taken off from impressions made on the organs of external sense, and wholly employed in a train of pleasing delightful imaginations, corresponding with the present frame of the mind? Some people are ready to interpret such things wrongly, and to lay too much weight on them, as prophetic visions, divine revelations, and sometimes indications from heaven of what is to happen (which, in some instances I have known, have been disproved in the event). But yet it appears to me that such things are evidently sometimes from the Spirit of God, though indirectly;

that is, their extraordinary frame of mind, and that strong and lively sense of divine things which is the occasion of them, is from his Spirit; and also as the mind continues in its holy frame, and retains a divine sense of the excellence of spiritual things even in its rapture; which holy frame and sense is from the Spirit of God, though the imaginations that attend it are only accidental, and therefore there is commonly something or other in them that is confused, improper, and false.

5. The influence of example

It is no sign that a work is not from the Spirit of God that example is a great means of it.

It is surely no argument that an effect is nor from God, that means are used in producing it; for we know that it is God's manner to make use of means in carrying on his work in the world, and it is no more an argument against the divinity of an effect, that this means is made use of, than if it was by any other means. It is agreeable to Scripture that people should be influenced by one another's good example. The Scripture directs us to set good examples to that end (Matt. 5:16; 1 Pet. 3:1; 1 Tim. 4:12; Titus 2:7), and also directs us to be influenced by the good examples of others, and to follow them (2 Cor. 8:1–7; Heb. 6:12; Phil. 3:17; 1 Cor. 4:16 and 11:1; 2 Thess. 3:9–11; 1 Thess. 1:7). By this it appears that example is one of God's means; and certainly it is no argument that a work is not of God, that his own means are made use of to effect it.

And as it is a *scriptural* way of carrying on God's work, by example, so it is a *reasonable* way. It is no argument that men are not influenced by reason, that they are influenced by example. This way of people holding forth truth to one another has a tendency to enlighten the mind, and to convince reason. None will deny but that for people to communicate things to one another by words may rationally be supposed to tend to enlighten each other's minds; but the same thing may be communicated by actions, and much more fully and effectually. Words are of no use unless they convey our own ideas to others; but actions, in some cases, may do it much more fully.

There is a language in actions; and in some cases it is much more clear and convincing than in words. It is therefore no argument against the goodness of the effect, that people are greatly affected by seeing others so; indeed, though the impression may be made only by seeing the tokens of great and extraordinary affection in others in their behaviour, taking for granted what they are affected with, without hearing them say one word. There may be language sufficient in such a case in their behaviour alone, to convey their minds to others, and to communicate their sense of things more than can possibly be done by words alone. If a person should see another under extreme bodily torment, he might receive much clearer ideas, and more convincing evidence of what he suffered by his actions in his misery, than he could do only by the words of an unaffected, indifferent relater. In like manner he might receive a greater idea of anything that is excellent and very delightful, from the behaviour of one that is in actual enjoyment, than by the dull narration of one who is inexperienced and insensible himself.

I desire that this matter may be examined by the strictest reason. Is it not manifest that effects produced in people's minds are rational, since not only weak and ignorant people are much influenced by example, but also those who make the greatest boast of strength of reason, are more influenced by reason held forth in this way than almost any other way? Indeed, the religious affections of many when raised by this means (such as by hearing the word preached, or any other means) may prove flashy, and soon vanish, as Christ represents the stony-ground hearers; but the affections of some thus moved by example are abiding, and prove to result in salvation.

There never yet was a time of remarkable pouring out of the Spirit, and great revival of religion, but that example had a main hand. So it was at the reformation, and in the apostles' days in Jerusalem and Samaria and Ephesus, and other parts of the world, as will be most manifest to anyone who attends to the accounts we have in the Acts of the Apostles. As in those days one person was moved by another, so one city or town was influenced by the example of another: 'So that ye were ensamples to all that believe in Macedonia and Achaia, for from you sounded out the word of the Lord, not only in Macedonia and Achaia, but also in every place your faith to God-ward is spread abroad' (1 Thess. 1:7–8).

The word of God applied by example

It is no valid objection against example being so much used, that the Scripture speaks of the words as the principal means of carrying on God's work; for the word of God is the principal means, nevertheless, by which other means operate and are made effectual. Even the sacraments have no effect except by the word; and so it is that example becomes effectual; for all that is visible to the eye is unintelligible and vain without the word of God to instruct and guide the mind. It is the word of God that is indeed held forth and applied by example, as the word of the Lord sounded forth to other towns in Macedonia and Achaia by the example of those who believed in Thessalonica.

That example should be a great means of propagating the church of God seems to be indicated in Scripture in several ways: it is indicated by Ruth's following Naomi out of the land of Moab, into the land of Israel, when she resolved that she would not leave her, but would go wherever she went, and would lodge where she lodged; and that Naomi's people would be her people, and Naomi's God, her God. Ruth, who was the ancestral mother of David, and of Christ, was undoubtedly a great type of the church; and for this reason her story is inserted in the canon of Scripture. In her leaving the land of Moab, and its gods, to come and put her trust under the shadow of the wings of the God of Israel, we have a type of the conversion not only of the Gentile church but of every sinner, that is naturally an alien and stranger, but in his conversion forgets his own people, and father's house, and becomes a fellow-citizen with the saints and a true Israelite.

The same seems to be indicated in the effect which the example of the love-sick spouse has on the daughters of Jerusalem, i.e., visible Christians, who are first awakened by seeing the spouse in such extraordinary circumstances, and then converted (see Song of Songs 5:8–9 and 6:1). And this is undoubtedly one way that 'the Spirit and the bride say, come' (Rev. 22:17) – i.e., the Spirit in the bride. It is foretold that the work of God will be very much carried on by this means in the last great outpouring of the Spirit that will introduce the glorious day of the church, so often spoken of in Scripture: 'And the inhabitants of one city shall go to another, saying, Let us go speedily to pray before the Lord, and to seek the Lord of hosts: I will go also. Yea, many people, and strong nations, shall come to seek the Lord of hosts in Jerusalem, and to pray before the Lord. Thus saith the Lord of hosts, In those days it shall come to pass, that ten men shall take hold of the skirt of him that is a Jew, saying, We will go with you for we have heard that God is with you' (Zech. 8:21–3).

6. Serious mistakes

It is no sign that a work is not from the Spirit of God, that many people who seem to be the subjects of it are guilty of great imprudences and irregularities in their conduct.

We are to consider that the end for which God pours out his Spirit is to make men holy, and not to make them politic. It is no wonder that, in a mixed multitude of all sorts – wise and unwise, young and old, of weak and strong natural abilities, under strong impressions of mind – there are many who behave imprudently. There are but few who know how to conduct themselves under strong feelings of any kind, whether of a temporal or spiritual nature; to do so requires a great deal of discretion, strength, and steadiness of mind. A thousand imprudences will not prove a work to be not of the Spirit of God; indeed, if there are not only imprudences but many things prevailing that are irregular, and really contrary to the rule of God's holy word. That it should be like this may be accounted for by the exceeding weakness of human nature, together with the remaining darkness and corruption of those that are the subjects of the saving influence of God's Spirit, and have a real zeal for God.

The church at Corinth
We have a remarkable instance, in the New Testament, of a people who partook largely of that great effusion of the Spirit in the

apostles' days, among whom there nevertheless abounded imprudence and great irregularities; namely, the church at Corinth. There is scarcely any church more celebrated in the New Testament for being blessed with large measures of the Spirit of God, both in his ordinary influences, in convincing and converting sinners, and also in his extraordinary and miraculous gifts; yet what manifold imprudences, great and sinful irregularities, and strange confusion did they run into, at the Lord's supper, and in the exercise of church discipline! To which may be added their indecent manner of attending other parts of public worship, their jarring and contention about their teachers, and even the exercise of their extraordinary gifts of prophecy, speaking with tongues, and the like, in which they spoke and acted by the immediate inspiration of the Spirit of God.

The apostle Peter was guilty of a great and sinful error
And if we see great imprudences, and even sinful irregularities, in some who are great instruments to carry on the work, it will not prove it not to be the work of God. The apostle Peter himself, who was a great, eminently holy, and inspired apostle – and one of the chief instruments of setting up the Christian church in the world – when he was actually engaged in this work was guilty of a great and sinful error in his conduct; of which the apostle Paul speaks in Galatians 2:11–13: 'But when Peter was come to Antioch, I withstood him to the face, because he was to be blamed; for before that certain men came from James, he did eat with the Gentiles, but when they were come, he withdrew, and separated himself, fearing them that were of the circumcision; and the other Jews dissembled likewise with him; insomuch, that Barnabas also was carried away with their dissimulation.' If a great pillar of the Christian church – one of the chief of those who are the very foundation son which, next to Christ, the whole church is said to be built – was guilty of such an irregularity, is it any wonder if other lesser instruments, who have not that extraordinary conduct of the divine Spirit he had, should be guilty of many irregularities?

Censuring others

And in particular, it is no evidence that a work is not of God, if many who are either the subjects or the instruments of it are guilty of too great forwardness to censure others as unconverted. For this may be through mistakes they have embraced concerning the marks by which they are to judge of the hypocrisy and carnality of others; or from not duly apprehending the latitude the Spirit of God uses in the methods of his operations; or, from not making due allowance for that infirmity and corruption that may be left in the hearts of the saints; as well as through lack of a due sense of their own blindness and weakness, and remaining corruption, by which spiritual pride may have a secret vent this way, under some disguise, and not be discovered. If we admit that truly pious men may have a great deal of remaining blindness and corruption, and may be liable to mistakes about the marks of hypocrisy, as undoubtedly all will agree, then it is not unaccountable that they should sometimes run into such errors as these. It is easy, and upon some accounts more easy to be accounted for, why the remaining corruption of good men should sometimes have an unobserved vent like this, than in most other ways; and without doubt (however lamentable) many holy men have erred in this way.

Zeal needs to be strictly watched and searched

Lukewarmness in religion is abominable, and zeal an excellent grace; yet above all other Christian virtues, this needs to be strictly watched and searched; for it is that with which corruption, and particularly pride and human passion, is exceedingly apt to mix unobserved. And it is observable that there never was a time of great reformation, to cause a revival of zeal in the church of God, that has not been attended in some notable instances with irregularity, and undue severity in one way or another. Thus in the apostles' days, a great deal of zeal was spent about unclean foods, with heat of spirit in Christians against one another, both parties condemning and censuring one another as not true Christians; when the apostle had charity for both, as influenced by a spirit of real piety: 'he that eats,' he says, 'to the Lord he eats, and giveth God thanks; and he that eateth not, to the Lord he eateth not, and giveth God thanks.' So in the church of Corinth, they had got into a way of extolling some ministers, and censuring others, and were puffed up against one another: but yet these things were no sign that the work then so wonderfully carried on was not the work of God. And after this, when religion was still greatly flourishing in the world, and a spirit of eminent holiness and zeal prevailed in the Christian church, the zeal of Christians ran out into a very improper and undue severity, in the exercise of church discipline towards delinquents. In some cases they would by no means admit them into their charity and communion though they appeared never so humble and penitent. And in the days of Constantine the Great, the zeal of Christians against heathenism overflowed into a degree of persecution. Similarly in that glorious revival of religion, at the reformation, zeal in many instances appeared in a very improper severity, and even a degree of persecution; indeed, in some of the most eminent reformers, such as the great Calvin in particular. And many in those days of the flourishing of vital religion were guilty of severely censuring others who differed from them in opinion in some points of divinity.

7. Errors of judgment and delusions

Nor are many errors of judgment, and some delusions of Satan intermixed with the work, any argument that the work in general is not of the Spirit of God.

However great a spiritual influence may be, it is not to be expected that the Spirit of God should be given now in the same manner as to the apostles, infallibly to guide them in points of Christian doctrine, so that what they taught might be relied on as a rule to the Christian church. And if many delusions of Satan appear at the same time that a great religious concern prevails, it is not an argument that the work in general is not the work of God, any more than it was an argument in Egypt that there were no true miracles wrought there by the hand of God, because Jannes and Jambres wrought false miracles at the same time by the hand of the devil. Indeed, the same persons may be the subjects of much of the influences of the Spirit of God, and yet in some things be led away by the delusions of Satan, and this be no more of paradox than many other things that are true of real saints, in the present state, where grace dwells with so much corruption, and the new man and the old man subsist together in the same person; and the kingdom of God and the kingdom of the devil remain for a while together in the same heart. Many godly persons have undoubtedly in this and other ages exposed themselves to woeful delusions by an aptness to lay too much weight on impulses and impressions, as if they were immediate revelations from God, to signify something future, or to direct them where to go, and what to do.

8. Some counterfeits

If some who were thought to be wrought upon fall away into gross errors, or scandalous practices, it is no argument that the work in general is not the work of the Spirit of God.

That there are some counterfeits is no argument that nothing is true: such things are always expected in a time of reformation. If we look into church history, we shall find no instance of any great revival of religion but what has been attended with many such things. INstances of this nature in the apostles' days were innumerable; some fell away into gross heresies, others into vile practices, though they seemed to be the subjects of a work of the Spirit – and were accepted for a while amongst those that were truly so as their brethren and companions – and were not suspected till they went out from them. And some of these were teachers and officers – and eminent persons in the Christian church – whom God had endowed with miraculous gifts of the Holy Spirit; as appears from the beginning of Hebrews 6.

Judas

An instance of these was Judas, who was one of the twelve apostles, and had long been constantly united to, and intimately conversant with, a company of disciples of true experience, without being discovered or suspected, till he revealed himself by his scandalous practice. He had been treated by Jesus himself, in all external things, as if he had truly been a disciple, even investing him with the character of apostle, sending him out to preach the gospel, and enduing him with miraculous gifts of the Spirit. For though Christ knew him, yet he did not then clothe himself with the character of omniscient Judge and searcher of hearts, but acted the part of a minister of the visible church (for he was his Father's minister); and therefore did not reject him till he had revealed himself by his scandalous practice; thereby giving an example to guides and rulers of the visible church, not to take it upon themselves to act the part of searcher of hearts, but to be influenced in their administrations by what is visible and open.

There were some instances then of such apostates, who were esteemed eminently full of the grace of God's Spirit. An instance of this nature probably was Nicolas, one of the seven deacons, who was looked upon by the Christians in Jerusalem, in the time of that extraordinary outpouring of the Spirit, as a man full of the Holy Spirit, and was chosen out of the multitude of Christians for that office for that reason (Acts 6:3, 5); yet he afterwards fell away and became the head of a sect of vile heretics, of gross practices, called from his name the sect of the Nicolaitans (Revelation 2:6, 15).

Reformation apostates

So in the time of the reformation, how great was the number of those who for a while seemed to join with the reformers, yet fell away into the grossest and most absurd errors, and abominable practices. And it is particularly observable that in times of great pouring out of the Spirit to revive religion in the world, a number of those who for a while seemed to partake in it, have fallen off into whimsical and extravagant errors, and gross enthusiasm, boasting of high degrees of spirituality and perfection, censuring and condemning others as carnal. Thus it was with the Gnostics in the apostles' times; and thus it was with several sects at the reformation, as Anthony Burgess observes:

The first worthy reformers, and glorious instruments of God, found a bitter conflict herein, so that they were exercised not only with formalists, and traditionary papists on the one side, but men that pretended themselves to be more enlightened than the reformers were, on the other side: hence they called those that did adhere to the Scripture, and would try revelations by it, Literists and Vowelists, as men acquainted with the words and vowels of Scripture, having nothing of the Spirit of God: and wheresoever in any town, the true doctrine of the gospel brake forth to the displacing of popery, presently such opinions arose, like tares that came up among the good wheat; whereby great divisions were raised, and the reformation made abominable and odious to the world; s if that had been the sun to give heat and warmth to those worms and serpents to crawl out of the ground. Hence they inveighed against Luther, and said he had only promulgated a carnal gospel. (*Spiritual Refinings* I.23, p. 132)

Some of the leaders of those wild enthusiasts had been for a while highly esteemed by the first reformers, and peculiarly dear to them.

Thus also in England, at the time when vital religion much prevailed in the days of King Charles I, the interregnum, and Oliver Cromwell, such things as these abounded. And so in New England in her purest days, when vital piety flourished, such kind of things as these broke out. Therefore the devil's sowing such tares is no proof that a true work of the Spirit of God is not gloriously carried on.

Making people aware of hell

It is no argument that a work is not from the Spirit of God, that it seems to be promoted by ministers insisting very much on the terrors of God's holy law, and that with a great deal of pathos and earnestness.

If there really is a hell of such dreadful and never-ending torments as is generally supposed, of which multitudes are in great danger – and into which the greater part of men in Christian countries do actually from generation to generation fall, for lack of a sense of its terribleness, and so for lack of taking due care to avoid it – then why is it not proper for those who have the care of souls to take great pains to make men aware of it? Why should they not be told as much of the truth as can be? If I am in danger of going to hell, I should be glad to know as much as I possibly can of the dreadfulness of it. If I am very prone to neglect due care to avoid it, the person who does me the best kindness is he who does most to represent to me the truth of the case, setting forth my misery and danger in the liveliest manner.

I ask everyone whether this is not the very course they would take in case of exposure to any great temporal calamity. If any of you who are heads of families saw your children in a house all on fire, and in imminent danger of soon being consumed in the flames, yet seemed to be very unaware of its danger, and neglected to escape after you had often called them – would you go on to speak only in a cold and indifferent manner? Would you not cry aloud, and call earnestly, and tell them the danger they were in, and their folly in delaying, in the most lively manner of which you were capable? Would not nature itself teach this, and oblige you to do so? If you continued to speak only in a cold manner, as you usually do in ordinary conversation about indifferent matters, would not those about you begin to think that you were bereft of reason yourself? This is not the way of mankind in temporal affairs of great moment, that require earnest heed and great haste, and about which they are greatly concerned. They do not usually speak to others of their danger, and warn them just a little, or in a cold and indifferent manner. Nature teaches men otherwise. If we who have the care of souls knew what hell was, had seen the state of the damned or by any other means had become aware how dreadful their case was – and at the same time knew that most people went there, and saw our hearers not aware of their danger – it would be morally impossible for us to avoid most earnestly setting before them the dreadfulness of that misery, and their great exposedness to it, and even to cry aloud to them.

Preaching about hell in a cold manner
When ministers preach about hell, and warn sinners to avoid it, in a cold manner – though they may say in words that it is infinitely terrible – they contradict themselves. For actions, as I observed

before, have a language as well as words. If a preacher's words represent the sinner's state as infinitely dreadful, while his behaviour and manner of speaking contradict it – showing that the preacher does not think so – he defeats his own purpose; for the language of his actions in such a case is much more effectual than the bare meaning of his words. Not that I think that the law only should be preached: ministers may preach other things too little. The gospel is to be preached as well as the law, and the law is to be preached only to make way for the gospel, and in order that it may be preached more effectually. The main work of ministers is to preach the gospel: 'Christ is the end of the law for righteousness'. So a minister would miss it very much if he should insist so much on the terrors of the law as to forget his Lord, and neglect to preach the gospel; but the law is still very much to be insisted on, and the preaching of the gospel will probably be in vain without it.

And certainly such earnestness and affection in speaking is beautiful, as becomes the nature and importance of the subject. Not but that there may be such a thing as an indecent boisterousness in a preacher, something besides which the matter and manner do not well agree together. Some people talk of it as an unreasonable thing to frighten people to heaven; but I think it is a reasonable thing to endeavour to frighten people away from hell. They stand upon its brink, and are just ready to fall into it, and are unaware of their danger. Is it not a reasonable thing to frighten a person out of a house on fire? The word 'fright' is commonly used for sudden, causeless fear, or groundless surprise; but surely a fear for which there is good reason is not to be criticised by any such name.

PART 2

Evidence in Scripture

Having given some examples of things that are not evidence that a work wrought among a people is not a work of the Spirit of God, I now proceed to show positively what are the sure, distinguishing scripture evidences and marks of a work of the Spirit of God, by

which we may proceed in judging any operation we find in ourselves, or see among a people, without danger of being misled.
And in this, as I said before, I shall confine myself to those marks
which are given us by the apostle in 1 John 4, where this matter is
dealt with particularly, and more plainly and fully than anywhere
else in the Bible. And in speaking about these marks, I shall take
them in the order in which I find them in the chapter.

1. Jesus is seen to be the Son of God

When the operation is such as to raise their esteem of that Jesus
who was born of the Virgin, and was crucified outside the gates of
Jerusalem; and seems more to confirm and establish their minds in
the truth of what the gospel declares to us of his being the Son of
God, and the Saviour of men, this is a sure sign that it is from the
Spirit of God. The apostle gives us this sign in verses 2 and 3:
'Hereby know ye the Spirit of God; and every spirit that confesseth
that Jesus Christ is come in the flesh is of God; and every spirit that
confesseth not that Jesus Christ is come in the flesh is not of God.'
This implies a confessing not only that there was such a person
who appeared in Palestine and did and suffered those things that
are recorded of him, but that he was the Christ, i.e. the Son of
God, anointed to be Lord and Saviour, as the name Jesus Christ
implies.

Confessing that Jesus is the Son of God
That thus much is implied in the apostle's meaning is confirmed by
verse 15, where the apostle is still on the same subject of signs of
the true Spirit: 'Whosoever shall confess that Jesus is the Son of
God, God dwelleth in him, and he in God.' And it is to be observed
that the word *confess*, as it is often used in the New Testament, signifies more than merely *allowing*: it implies an establishing and
confirming of a thing by testimony, and declaring it with manifestation of esteem and affection. 'Whosoever therefore shall *confess* me before men, him will I *confess* also before my Father which
is in heaven' (Matt. 10:32). 'I will *confess* to thee among the Gentiles, and sing unto thy name' (Rom. 15:9). 'That every tongue

shall *confess* that Jesus Christ is Lord, to the glory of God the Father' (Phil. 2:11). And that this is the force of the expression as the apostle John uses it in this passage is confirmed in the next chapter, verse 1: 'Whosoever believeth that Jesus is the Christ, is born of God, and every one that loveth him that begat, loveth him also that is begotten of him.' And by that parallel passage of the apostle Paul, where we have the same rule given to distinguish the true Spirit from all counterfeits: 'Wherefore I give you to understand that no man speaking by the Spirit of God, calleth Jesus accursed [or will show an ill or mean esteem of him]; and that no man can say that Jesus is the Lord, but by the Holy Ghost' (1 Cor. 21:3).

So if the spirit that is at work among a people is plainly observed to work so as to convince them of Christ, and lead them to him – to confirm their minds in the belief of the history of Christ as he appeared in the flesh – and that he is the Son of God, and was sent by God to save sinners; that he is the only Saviour, and that they stand in great need of him; and if he seems to beget in them higher and more honourable thoughts of him than they used to have and to incline their affections more to him; it is a sure sign that it is the true and right Spirit; however incapable we may be of determining whether that conviction and affection is in that manner, or to that degree, as to be saving or not.

But the words of the apostle are remarkable; the person to whom the Spirit gives testimony, and for whom he raises their esteem, must be that Jesus who appeared in the flesh, and not another Christ in his stead; nor any mystical, fantastical Christ, such as the light within. The spirit of Quakers extols this, while it diminishes their esteem of and dependence upon an outward Christ – or Jesus as he came in the flesh – and leads them off form him; but the spirit that gives testimony for that Jesus, and leads to him, can be no other than the Spirit of God. The devil has the most bitter and implacable enmity against that person, especially in his character of the Saviour of men; he mortally hates the story and doctrine of his redemption; he never would go about to beget in men more honourable thoughts of him, and lay greater weight on his instructions and commands. The Spirit that inclines men's hearts to the seed of the woman is not the spirit of the serpent that has such an irreconcilable enmity against him. He that heightens men's esteem of the glorious Michael, that prince of the angels, is not the spirit of the dragon that is at war with him.

Working against Satan's kingdom

When the spirit that is at work operates against the interests of Satan's kingdom, which lies in encouraging and establishing sin, and cherishing men's worldly lusts; this is a sure sign that it is a true, and not a false spirit.

This sign we have given us in verses 4 and 5: 'Ye are of God, little children, and have overcome them; because greater is he that is in you, than he that is in the world. They are of the world, therefore speak they of the world, and the world heareth them.' Here is a plain antithesis: it is evident that the apostle is still comparing those that are influenced by the two opposite kinds of spirits, the true and the false, and showing the difference; the one is of God, and overcomes the spirit of the world; the other is of the world, and speaks and savours the things of the world. The spirit of the devil is here called 'he that is in the world'. Christ says, 'My kingdom is not of this world'. But it is otherwise with Satan's kingdom; he is 'the god of this world'.

What the apostle means by *the world,* or 'the things that are of the world', we learn by his own words in 1 John 2:15–16: 'Love not the world, neither the things that are in the world: if any man love the world, the love of the Father is not in him: for all that is in the world, the lust of the flesh, and the lust of the eyes, and the pride of life, is not of the Father, but is of the world.' So by the world the apostle evidently means everything that appertains to the interest of sin, and comprehends all the corruptions and lusts of men, and all those acts and objects by which they are gratified.

So we may safely determine from what the apostle says that the spirit that is at work among a people, after such a manner as to lessen their esteem of the pleasures, profits, and honours of the world, and to take off their hearts from an eager pursuit after these things; and to engage them in a deep concern about a future state and eternal happiness which the gospel reveals — and puts them upon earnestly seeking the kingdom of God and his right-eousness; and the spirit that convinces them of the dreadfulness of sin, the guilt it brings, and the misery to which it exposes — this must be the Spirit of God.

Waking up the conscience

It is not to be supposed that Satan would convince men of sin, and awaken the conscience; it can no way serve his end to make that candle of the Lord shine the brighter, and to open the mouth of that vicegerent of God in the soul. It is for his interest, whatever he does, to lull conscience asleep, and keep it quiet. To have that, with its eyes and mouth open in the soul, will tend to clog and hinder all his desires of darkness, and evermore to disturb his affairs, to cross his interest, and disquiet him, so that he can achieve nothing he wants without being molested. Would the devil, when he is try-ing to establish men in sin, take such a course, in the first place, to enlighten and awaken the conscience to see the dreadfulness of sin, and make them exceedingly afraid of it, and aware of their misery by reason of their past sins, and their great need of deliver-ance from their guilt? Would he make them more careful, inquisi-tive, and watchful to discern what is sinful, and to avoid future sins, and so be more afraid of the devil's temptations, and more careful to guard against them? What do those men do with their reason, who suppose that the Spirit that operates thus is the spirit of the devil?

Possibly some may say that the devil may even awaken men's consciences to deceive them, and make them think they have been the subject of a saving work of the Spirit of God, while they are indeed still in the gall of bitterness. But to this it may be replied that the man who has an awakened conscience is the least likely to be deceived by anyone in the world; it is the drowsy, unaware, stupid conscience that is most easily blinded. The more aware con-science is in a diseased soul, the less easily is it quieted without a real healing. The more aware conscience is made of the dreadful-ness of sin, and of the greatness of a man's own guilt, the less likely he is to rest in his own righteousness, or to be pacified with nothing but shadows. A man that has been thoroughly terrified with a sense of his own danger and misery is not easily flattered and made to believe himself safe, without any good grounds. To awaken conscience, and convince it of the evil of sin, cannot tend to establish it, but certainly tends to make way for sin and Satan's being cut out.

The spirit of the devil

Therefore this is a good argument that the Spirit that operates in this way cannot but the spirit of the devil – unless we suppose that Christ did not know how to argue, when he told the Pharisees (who supposed that the Spirit by which he worked was the spirit of the devil) that Satan would not cast out Satan (Matt. 12:25–6). And therefore, if we see people made aware of the dreadful nature of sin, and of the displeasure of God against it; of their own miserable condition as they are in themselves, by reason of sin, and earnestly concerned for their eternal salvation – and aware of their need of God's pity and help, and committed to seek it in the use of the means that God has appointed – we may certainly conclude that it is from the Spirit of God, whatever effects this concern has on their bodies – even if it causes them to cry out aloud, or to shriek, or to faint; or if it throws them into convulsions, or whatever other way the blood and spirits are moved.

The influence of the Spirit of God is yet more abundantly manifest if people have their hearts drawn away from the world, and weaned from the objects of their worldly lusts, and away from worldly pursuits, by the feelings they have for those spiritual enjoyments of another world, that are promised in the gospel.

Greater regard for the Scriptures

The spirit that operates in such a manner as to cause in men a greater regard for the Holy Scriptures, and establishes them more in their truth and divinity, is certainly the Spirit of God.

The apostle gives us this rule in verse 6: 'We are of God; he that knoweth God heareth us; he that is not of God heareth not us: hereby know we the spirit of truth, and the spirit of error.' *We are of God;* that is, 'We the apostles are sent forth by God, and appointed by him to teach the world, and to deliver those doctrines and instructions which are to be their rule; *he that knoweth God, heareth us . . .'*

The apostle's argument here equally reaches all that in the same sense are *of God;* that is, all those that God has appointed and inspired to deliver to his church its rule of faith and practice; all the prophets and apostles, whose doctrine God has made the foundation on which he has built his church, as in Ephesians 2:20 – in a word, all the penmen of the Holy Scriptures. The devil would never attempt to beget in people a regard for that divine word which God has given to be the great and standing rule for the direction of his church in all religious matters, and all concerns of their souls, in all ages. A spirit of delusion will not incline people to seek direction at the mouth of God. 'To the law and to the testimony' is never the cry of those evil spirits that have no light in them; for it is God's own direction to discover their delusions. 'And when they shall say unto you, Seek unto them that have familiar spirits, and unto wizards that peep and that mutter: should not a people seek unto their God? for the living to the dead? To the law and to the testimony; if they speak not according to this word, it is because there is no light in them' (Isa. 8:19–20). The devil does not say the same as Abraham did – 'They have Moses and the prophets, let them hear them' – nor the same as the voice from heaven did concerning Christ – 'Hear ye him'. Would the spirit of error, in order to deceive people, beget in them a high opinion of the infallible rule, and incline them to think a lot about it, and be very conversant with it? Would the prince of darkness, in order to promote his kingdom of darkness, lead men to the sun? The devil has always shown a mortal spite and hatred towards that holy book the Bible; he has done all in his power to extinguish that light, and to lead people away from it. He knows it to be that light by which his kingdom of darkness is to be overthrown. He has had for many ages experience of its power to defeat his purposes, and baffle his designs; it is his constant plague.

It is the main weapon which Michael uses in his war with him; it is the sword of the Spirit, that pierces him and conquers him. It is that great and strong word with which God punishes Leviathan, that crooked serpent. It is that sharp sword that we read of in Revelation 19:15, that proceeds out of the mouth of him that sat on the horse, with which he smites his enemies. Every text is a dart to torment the old serpent. He has felt the stinging dart thousands of times; therefore he is against the Bible, and hates every word in it; and we may be sure he will never attempt to raise people's esteem of it or feeling for it. And accordingly we see it common in enthusiasts, that they depreciate this written rule, and set up the light within or some other rule above it.

The Spirit of truth leading people to the truth

Another rule to judge spirits by may be drawn from the names given to the opposite spirits, in the last words of verse 6: 'the spirit of truth and the spirit of error'.

These words exhibit the two opposite characters of the Spirit of God, and other spirits that counterfeit his operations. And therefore, if by observing the manner of the operation of a spirit that is at work among a people, we see that it operates as a spirit of truth, leading people to truth, convincing them of those things that are true, we may safely determine that it is a right and true spirit. For instance, if we observe that the spirit at work makes people more aware than they used to be that there is a God, and that he is a great and a sin-hating God; that life is short, and very uncertain; and that there is another world; that they have immortal souls, and must give account of themselves to God, that they are exceedingly sinful by nature and practice; that they are helpless in themselves; and confirms them in other things that agree with some sound doctrine; the spirit that works in such a way operates as a spirit of truth; he represents things as they truly are. He brings people to the light; for whatever makes truth manifest is light; as the apostle Paul observes: 'But all things that are reproved [or discovered, as it is in the margin] are made manifest by the light; for whatsoever doth make manifest is light' (Ephesians 5:13).

And therefore we may conclude that it is not the spirit of darkness that thus reveals the truth and makes it clear. Christ tells us that Satan is a liar, and the father of lies; and his kingdom is a kingdom of darkness. It is upheld and promoted only by darkness and error. Satan has all his power and dominion by darkness. Hence we read of the power of darkness (Luke 22:53 and Col. 1:13). And devils are called 'the rulers of the darkness of this world'. Whatever spirit removes our darkness, and brings us to the light, undeceives us, and, by convincing us of the truth, does us a kindness. If I am brought to a sight of truth, and made aware of things as they really are, my duty is immediately to thank God for it, without stopping first to inquire by what means I have such a benefit.

A spirit of love for both God and man

If the spirit that is at work among a people operates as a spirit of love to God and man, it is a sure sign that it is the Spirit of God.

The apostle insist on this sign from verse 6 to the end of the chapter: 'Beloved, let us love on another; for love is of God, and every one that loveth is born of God, and knoweth God: he that loveth not, knoweth not God; for God is love . . .' Here it is evident that the apostle is still comparing those tow sorts of people that are influenced by the opposite kinds of spirits; and he mentioned love as a mark by which we may know who has the true spirit. This is especially evident from verses 12 and 13: 'If we love on another, God dwelleth in us, and his love is perfected in us: hereby know we that we dwell in him, and he in us, because he hath given us of his Spirit.'

In these verses love is spoken of as if it were that in which the very nature of the Holy Spirit consisted; or as if *divine love* dwelling in us, and the *Spirit of God* dwelling in us, were the same thing. It is the same in the last two verses of the previous chapter, and verse 16 of this chapter. Therefore this last mark which the apostle gives of the true Spirit he seems to speak of as the most eminent; and so insists much more largely upon it than upon all the rest; and speaks expressly of both love to God and love to men — of *love to men* in verses 7, 11, and 12; and of *love to God* in verses 17, 18, and 19; and of both together in the last two verses; and of love to men as arising from love to God, in these last two verses.

Therefore, when the spirit that is at work amongst the people tends this way, and brings many of them to high and exalting thoughts of the Divine Being, and his glorious perfections; and works in them an admiring, delightful sense of the excellence of Jesus Christ; representing him as the chief among ten thousand, and altogether lovely; and makes him precious to the soul, winning and drawing the heart with those motives and incitements to love, of which the apostle speaks in that passage of Scripture we are upon, namely the wonderful, free love of God in giving his only-begotten Son to die for us, and the wonderful love of Christ to us, who had no love to him, but were his enemies – this must be the Spirit of God. 'In this was manifested the love of God towards us, because God sent his only-begotten Son into the world, that we might live through him. Herein is love; not that we loved God, but that he loved us, and sent his Son to be the propitiation for our sins' (verses 9–10). 'And we have known, and believed, the love that God hath to us' (verse 16). 'We love him because he first loved us' (verse 19).

The spirit that excites people to love on these motives, and makes the attributes of God as revealed in the gospel, and manifested in Christ, delightful objects of contemplation; and makes the soul long after God and Christ – after their presence and communion, acquaintance with them, and conformity to them – and to live so as to please and honour them – the spirit that quells contentions among men, and gives a spirit of peace and good will, excites to acts of outward kindness, and earnest desires of the salvation of souls – and causes a delight in those that appears as the children of God, and followers of Christ; I say, when a spirit operates in this way among a people, there is the highest kind of evidence of the influence of a true and divine spirit.

Counterfeit love
Indeed there is a counterfeit love, that often appears among those who are led by a spirit of delusion. There is commonly in the wildest enthusiasts a kind of union and affection arising from self-love, occasioned by their agreeing in those things in which they

greatly differ from all others, and from which they are objects of the ridicule of all the rest of mankind. This naturally will cause them so much the more to prize those peculiarities that make them the objects of others' contempt. Thus the ancient Gnostics, and the wild fanatics that appeared at the beginning of the reformation, boasted of their great love to one another; one sect of them, in particular, calling themselves the *family of love*. But this is quite another thing than that Christian love I have just described: it is only the working of a natural self-love, and no true benevolence, any more than the union and friendship which may be among a company of pirates that are at war with all the rest of the world. There is enough said in this passage about the nature of a truly Christian love, thoroughly to distinguish it from all such counterfeits. It is love that arises from apprehension of the wonderful riches of the free grace and sovereignty of God's love to us, in Christ Jesus; being attended with a sense of our own utter unworthiness, as in ourselves the enemies and haters of God and Christ, and with a renunciation of all our own excellence and righteousness. See verses 9–11 and 19.

The Christian virtue of humility

The surest character of true divine supernatural love – distinguishing it from counterfeits that arise from a natural self-love – is that the Christian virtue of *humility* shine sin it; that which above all other renounces, abases, and annihilates what we term *self*. Christian love, or true charity, is a humble love. 'Charity vaunteth not itself, is not puffed up, doth not behave itself unseemly, seeketh not her own, is not easily provoked' (1 Cor. 13:4–5). When therefore we see love in people attended with a sense of their own littleness, vileness, weakness, and utter insufficiency; and so with self-diffidence, self-emptiness, self-renunciation, and poverty of spirit; these are the manifest tokens of the Spirit of God. He that thus dwells in love, dwells in God, and God in him. What the apostle speaks of as a great evidence of the true Spirit, is God's love or Christ's love: 'his love is perfected in us' (verse 12). What kind of love that is, we may see best in what appeared in Christ's example. The love that appeared in that Lamb of God was not only a love to friends, but to enemies, and a love attended with a meek and humble spirit. 'Learn of me,' he says, 'for I am meek and lowly in heart.'

Love and humility are two of the most contrary things in the world to the spirit of the devil, for the character of that evil spirit, above all things, consists in pride and malice.

Thus I have spoken particularly about the various marks the apostle gives us of a work of the true Spirit. There are some of these things which the devil *would not* do if he could: thus he would not awaken the conscience, and make people aware of their miserable state because of sin, and aware of their great need of a Saviour; and he would not confirm people in the belief that Jesus is the Son of God, and the Saviour of sinners, or raise people's value and esteem of him: he would not beget in men's minds an opinion of the necessity, usefulness, and truth of the Holy Scriptures, or incline them to make much use of them; nor would he show people the truth in things that concern their souls' interest; to undeceive them and lead them out of darkness into light, and give them a view of things as they really are. And there are other things that the devil *neither can nor will* do; he will not give people a spirit of divine love, or Christian humility and poverty of spirit; nor *could* he is he wanted to. He cannot give those things he does not himself have: these things are as contrary as possible to his nature. And therefore when there is an extraordinary influence or operation appearing on the minds of a people, if these things are found in it, we are safe in determining that it is the work of God, whatever other circumstances it may be attended with, whatever instruments are used, whatever methods are taken to promote it; whatever means a sovereign God, whose judgements are a great deep, employs to carry it on; and whatever motion there may be of the animal spirits, whatever effects may be wrought on men's bodies.

These marks that the apostle have given us are sufficient to stand alone, and support themselves. They plainly show the finger of God, and are sufficient to outweigh a thousand such little objections as many make from oddities, irregularities, errors in conduct, and the delusions and scandals of some who claim to believe.

But some people may raise as an objection to the sufficiency of the marks what the apostle Paul says in 2 Corinthians 11:13–14: 'For such are false apostles, deceitful workers, transforming themselves into the apostles of Christ; and no marvel, for Satan himself is transformed into an angel of light.'

False prophets, false apostles
To this, I answer that this can be no objection against the sufficiency of these marks to distinguish the true from the false spirit, in those false apostles and prophets in whom the devil was transformed into an angel of light, because it is principally with a view to them that the apostle gives these marks; as appears by the words of the text, 'Believe not every spirit, but try the spirits, whether they are of God'. This is the reason he gives – because many false prophets are gone out into the world: 'There are many gone out into the world who are the ministers of the devil, who transform themselves into the prophets of God, in whom the spirit of the devil is transformed into an angel of light; therefore try the spirits by these rules that I shall give you, that you may be able to distinguish the true spirit from the false, under such a crafty disguise.' Those *false prophets* the apostle John speaks of are doubtless the same sort of men as those *false apostles* and deceitful workers that the apostle Paul speaks of, in whom the devil was transformed into an angel of light; and therefore we may be sure that these marks are especially adapted to distinguish between the true Spirit, and the devil transformed into an angel of light, because they are given especially for that end; that is the apostle's declared purpose and design, to give marks by which the true Spirit may be distinguished from that sort of counterfeits.

And if we look over what is said about these false prophets, and false apostles (as there is much said about them in the New Testament), and take notice in what manner the devil was transformed into an angel of light in them, we shall not find anything that in the least injures the sufficiency of these marks to distinguish the true Spirit from such counterfeits. The devil transformed himself into an angel of light, as there was in them a show and great boast of extraordinary knowledge in divine things (Col. 2:8; 1 Tim. 1:6–7 and 6:3–5; 2 Tim. 2:14–18; Titus 1:10, 16). Hence their followers called themselves Gnostics, from their great pretended knowledge: and the devil in them mimicked the miraculous gifts of the Holy Spirit, in visions, prophecies, miracles, etc. Hence they are called false apostles, and false prophets (Matt. 24:24). Again, there was a false show of, and lying pretensions to, great holiness and devotion in words (Rom. 16:17–18; Eph. 4:14). Hence they are called deceitful workers, and wells and clouds without water (2 Cor. 11:13; 2 Pet. 2:17; Jude 12). There was also in them a show of extraordinary piety and righteousness in their superstitious worship (Col. 2:16–23). So they had a false, proud, and bitter zeal (Gal. 4:17–18; 1 Tim. 1:6 and 6:4–5). And likewise a false show of humility, in affecting an extraordinary outward meanness and dejection, when indeed they were 'vainly puffed up in their fleshly mind'; and made a righteousness of their humility, and were exceedingly lifted up with their eminent piety (Col. 2:18, 23). But how do such things as these in the least injure those things that have been mentioned as the distinguishing evidences of the true Spirit? Besides such vain shows which may be from the devil, there are common influences of the Spirit, which are often mistaken for saving grace; but these are out of the question, because though they are not saving, they are still the work of the true Spirit.

Having thus fulfilled what I at first proposed, in considering what are the certain, distinguishing marks by which we may safely proceed in judging whether any work that falls under our observation is the work of the Spirit of God or not, I now proceed to the application.

PART 3

Practical inferences

The recent revival comes from God
From what has been said, I will venture to draw this inference – that the extraordinary influence that has lately appeared, causing an uncommon concern and engagedness of mind about the things

of religion, is undoubtedly, in general, from the Spirit of God.

There are only two things that need to be known in order to judge such a work, namely *facts* and *rules*. The *rules* of the word of God we have had laid before us; and as to *facts*, there are only two ways that we can come at them, so as to be in a capacity to compare them with the rules, either by our own observation, or by information from others who have had opportunity to observe them.

The facts

As to this work, there are many things concerning it that are notorious, and which, unless the apostle John was out in his rules, are sufficient to determine it to be in general the work of God. The Spirit that is at work takes off person's minds from the vanities of the world, and engages them in a deep concern about eternal happiness, and sets them earnestly seeking their salvation, and convinces them of the dreadfulness of sin, and of their own guilty and miserable state as they are by nature. It awakens men's consciences, and makes them aware of the dreadfulness of God's anger, and causes in them a great desire and earnest care and endeavour to obtain his favour. It puts them upon a more diligent use of the means of grace which God has appointed; accompanied with a greater regard for the word of God, a desire of hearing and reading it, and of being more conversant with it than they used to be. And it is notoriously manifest that the spirit that is at work generally operates as a spirit of truth, making people more aware of their eternal salvation (e.g., that they must die, and that life is very short and uncertain; that there is a great sin-hating God, to whom they are accountable, and who will fix them in an eternal state in another world; and that they stand in great need of a Saviour).

It makes people more aware of the value of Jesus who was crucified, and their need of him; and that it sets them earnestly seeking an interest in him. These things must be apparent to people in general throughout the land; for these things are not done in a corner; the work has not been confined to a few towns in some remoter parts, but has been carried on in many places all over the land, and in most of the principal, populous, and public places in it. Christ in this respect has wrought amongst us, in the same manner that he wrought his miracles in Judea. It has now been continued for a considerable time; so that there has been a great opportunity to observe the manner of the work. And all such as have been very conversant with the subjects of it see a great deal more that, by the rules of the apostle, clearly and certainly shows it to be the work of God.

The widespread scope of the work

And here I would observe that the nature and tendency of a spirit that is at work may be determined with much greater certainty, and less danger of being imposed upon, when it is observed in a great multitude of people of all sorts, and in various places, than when it is only seen in a few, in some particular place, that have been much conversant with one another. A few particular persons may agree to cheat others by a false pretence, and professing things of which they never were conscious. But the work is spread out over great parts of a country, in places distant from one another, among people of all sorts and of all ages, and in multitudes possessed of a sound mind, good understanding, and known integrity. All that is heard and seen in them can be observed for many months together, and by those who are most intimate with them in these affairs, and have long been acquainted with them. There would therefore be the greatest absurdity in supposing that it still cannot be determined what kind of influence the operation they are under has upon people's minds. Can it not be determined whether it tends to awaken their consciences, or to stupefy them; whether it inclines them more to seek their salvation, or neglect it; whether it seems to confirm them in a belief in the Scriptures, or to lead them to deism; whether it makes them have more regard for the great truths of religion, or less?

And here it is to be observed that for people to profess that they are so convinced of certain divine truths as to esteem and love them in a *saving manner*, and for them to profess that they are *more convinced* or confirmed in the truth of them than they used to be, and find that they have a greater regard for them than they had before, are two very different things. People of honesty and common sense have much greater right to demand credit to be given to the latter profession than to the former. Indeed in the former it is less likely that a people in general should be deceived than some particular individuals. But whether people's convictions, and the alteration in their dispositions and affections, are in a degree and manner that is saving is beside the present question. If there are such effects on people's judgements, dispositions, and affections, as have been spoken of, whether they are in a degree and manner that is saving or not, it is nevertheless a sign of the influence of the Spirit of God. Scripture rules serve to distinguish the common influences of the Spirit of God, as well as those that are saving, from the influence of other causes.

By the providence of God, I have for some months past been much amongst those who have been the subjects of the work in question; and particularly, have been in the way of seeing and observing those extraordinary things with which many people have been offended – such as people's crying out aloud, shrieking, being put into great agonies of body, etc. I have seen the manner and result of such operations, and the fruits of them, for several months together. Many of them were people with whom I have been intimately acquainted in soul concerns, before and since. So I look upon myself as called on this occasion to give my testimony that – so far as the nature and tendency of such a work is capable of falling under the observation of a by-stander to whom those that have been the subjects of it have endeavoured to open their hearts, or can be come at by diligent and particular inquiry – this work has all those marks that have been pointed out. And this has been the case in very many instances, in *every article*; and in many others, all those marks have appeared in a very *great degree*.

Two kinds of people
The subjects of these uncommon experiences have been of two sorts: either those who have been in great distress from an apprehension of their sin and misery; or those who have been overcome with a sweet sense of the greatness, wonderfulness, and excellency of divine things. Of the multitude of those of the former sort, that I have had opportunity to observe, there have been very few whose distress has not arisen apparently from real

proper conviction, and being in a degree conscious of that which was the truth. And though I do not suppose, when such things were observed to be common, that people have laid themselves under those violent restraints to avoid outward manifestations of their distress, that perhaps they otherwise would have done; yet there have been very few in whom there has been any appearance of feigning or affecting such manifestations, and very many for whom it would have been undoubtedly utterly impossible for them to avoid them. Generally, in these agonies they have appeared to be in the perfect exercise of their reason; and those of them who could speak have been well able to give an account of the circumstances of their mind, and the cause of their distress, at the time, and were able to remember and give an account of it afterwards.

Never lastingly deprived of reason
I have known a very few instances of those who, in their great extremity, have for a short time been deprived in some measure of the use of reason; but among the many hundreds, and it may be thousands, that have recently been brought to such agonies, I never yet knew one lastingly deprived of their reason. Depression has evidently been part of the cause in some cases that I have known, and when it is so, the difference is very apparent; their distresses are of another kind, and operate in quite a different way from when their distress is from mere conviction. It is not only truth that distresses them, but many vain shadows and notions that will not yield either to Scripture or reason. Some in their great distress have not been well able to give an account of themselves, or to declare the cause of their trouble to others, yet I have had no reason to think they were not under proper convictions, and their state has ended up well. But this will not be at all wondered at by those who have had much to do with souls under spiritual difficulties: some things of which they are aware are altogether new to them; their ideas and inward sensations are new, and therefore they do not know how to express them in words. Some who, on first inquiry, said they did not know what was the matter with them have been able, on detailed examination and interrogation, to describe their case, though of them-

selves they could not find expressions and forms of speech to do it.

Very great fear, and needless fright

Some suppose that terrors producing such effects are only a fright. But certainly a distinction ought to be made between a very great fear, or extreme distress arising from an apprehension of some dreadful truth – a cause fully proportionable to such an effect – and a needless, causeless fright. The latter is of two kinds: either, first, when people are terrified with that which is not the truth (of which I have seen very few instances unless in case of depression); or, secondly, when they are in a fright from some terrible outward appearance and noise, and a general notion arising from that. These people apprehend that there is something or other terrible, they know not what; without having in their minds any particular truth whatever. I have seen very little of this kind of fright among either old or young people.

No way of escape seems possible

Those who are suffering so much often express a great sense of their exceeding wickedness, the multitude and aggravations of their actual sins; their dreadful pollution, enmity, and perverseness; their obstinacy and hardness of heart; a sense of their great guilt in the sight of God; and the dreadfulness of the punishment which sin deserves. Very often they have a lively idea of the horrible pit of eternal misery; and at the same time it appears to them that the great God who has them in his hands is exceedingly angry, and his wrath appears amazingly terrible to them. God appears to them so much provoked, and his great wrath so increased, that they are apprehensive of great danger, and that he will not bear with them any longer but will now cut them off straightaway, and send them down in the dreadful pit they have in view; and at the same time they see no refuge.

They see more and more of the vanity of everything they used to trust to, and with which they flattered themselves, till they are brought wholly to despair of all, and to see that they are at the disposal of the mere will of that God who is so angry with them. Very many, in the midst of their extremity, have been brought to an extraordinary sense of their fully deserving that wrath, and the destruction which was then before their eyes. They feared every moment that it would be executed upon them; they have been greatly convinced that this would be altogether just, and that God is indeed absolutely sovereign. Very often, some text of Scripture expressing God's sovereignty has been brought home to their minds, and has calmed them. They have been brought, as it were, to lie at God's feet; and after great agonies, a little before light has arisen, they have been composed and quiet, in submission to a just and sovereign God; but their bodily strength much spent. Sometimes it looked as though their lives were almost gone; and the light has appeared, and a glorious Redeemer, with his wonderful, all-sufficient grace, has been represented to them often, in some sweet invitation of Scripture. Sometimes the light comes in suddenly, sometimes more gradually, filling their souls with love, admiration, joy, and self-abasement; drawing out their hearts after the excellent, lovely Redeemer, and longings to lie in the dust before him; and that others might see, embrace, and be delivered by him. They had longings to live to his glory; but were aware that they can do nothing of themselves, appearing vile in their own hearts. And all the appearances of a real change of heart have followed; and grace has acted, from time to time, in the same way that it used to act in those who were converted formerly, with similar difficulties, temptations, buffetings, and comforts; except that in many, the light and comfort have been greater than usual. Many very young children have been affected like this. There have been some instances very much like those we read of in Mark 1:26 and 9:26, where 'when the devil had cried with a loud voice, and rent them sore, he came out of them'. And probably those instances were intended as a type of such things as these. Some have several turns of great agonies before they are actually delivered; and others have been in such distress, which has passed off, and no deliverance at all has followed.

Can great confusion be caused by God?
Some people object that when a number together are making a

noise in such circumstances, there is great confusion. They say that God cannot be the author of it because he is the God of order, not of confusion. But consider the proper meaning of confusion: it is breaking the order of things by which they are properly disposed, and duly directed to their end, so that the order and due connection of means is broken and they fail to achieve their end. Now the conviction of sinners for their conversion is achieving the end of religious means. Not but that I think the people thus extraordinarily moved should endeavour to refrain from such outward manifestations, as they well can do, and should refrain to their utmost at the time of their solemn worship. But if God chooses to convince people's consciences so that they cannot avoid great outward manifestations, even interrupting and breaking off those public means they were attending, I do not think this is confusion, or an unhappy interruption, any more than is a company met on the field to pray for rain, and were interrupted by a plentiful shower. Would to God that all the public assemblies in the land were interrupted with such confusion as this the next sabbath day! We need not be sorry for breaking the order of means by obtaining the end for which that order is made. He who is going to fetch a treasure need not be sorry that he is stopped by meeting the treasure on the way.

Overcome with conviction about their own vileness
Besides those who are overcome with conviction and distress, I have seen many of late who have had their bodily strength taken away with a sense of the glorious excellence of the Redeemer, and the wonders of his dying love; with a very uncommon sense of their own littleness and exceeding vileness attending it, with all expressions and appearances of the greatest abasement and abhorrence of themselves. Not only new converts, but many who, we hope. were already converted, have had their love and joy attended with a flood of tears, and a great appearance of contrition and humiliation, especially for their having lived no more to God's glory since their conversion. These have had a far greater sight of their vileness, and the evil of their hearts, than ever they had; with an exceeding earnestness of desire to live better for the

time to come, but attended with greater self-diffidence than ever; and many have been overcome with pity for the souls of others, and longing for their salvation.

I might mention many other things in this extraordinary work, answering to every one of those marks which have been insisted on. If the apostle John knew how to give signs of a work of the true Spirit, this is such a work.

Providence has cast my lot in a place where the work of God has *formerly* been carried on. I had the happiness to be settled in that place for two years with the venerable Stoddard; and was then acquainted with a number who, at that time, were wrought upon under his ministry, before that period, in a manner agreeable to the doctrine of all orthodox divines. And recently a work has been carried on there with very uncommon operations, but it is evidently the same work that was carried on there at other times, though attended with some new circumstances. And if this is not in general the work of God, we must certainly throw out all talk of conversion and Christian experience; and not only that, but we must throw out our Bibles, and give up revealed religion. Not that I suppose the degree of the Spirit's influence is to be determined by the degree of effect on people's bodies; or that the experiences which have the greatest influence on the body are always the best.

Imprudences, irregularities and delusions
As for the imprudences, irregularities, and mixture of delusion that has been observed, it is not at all to be wondered at that a reformation, after a long-continued and almost universal deadness, should be accompanied by such things at first, when the revival is new. In the first creation God did not make a complete world at once, but there was a great deal of imperfection, darkness, and mixture of chaos and confusion after God first said, 'Let there be light,' before the whole stood forth in perfect form. When God at first began his great work for the deliverance of his people, after their long-continued bondage in Egypt, there were false wonders mixed with the true for a while; which hardened the unbelieving Egyptians, and made them doubt the divinity of the whole work. When the children of Israel first went to bring up the ark of God,

after it had been neglected, and had been long absent, they did not seek the Lord in the proper way (1 Chron. 15:13). At the time when the sons of God came to present themselves before the Lord, Satan came among them too. And Solomon's ships, when they brought gold, silver, and pearls, also brought apes and peacocks. When daylight first appears after a night of darkness, we must expect to have darkness mixed with light for a while, and not have perfect day and the run risen at once. The fruits of the earth are green at first, before they are ripe, and they come to their perfection gradually; and so, Christ tells us, is the kingdom of God. 'So is the kingdom of God; as if a man should cast seed into the ground, and should sleep, and rise night and day; and the seed should spring and grow up, he knoweth not how: for the earth bringeth forth fruit of herself; first the blade, then the ear, after that the full corn in the ear' (Mark 4:26–8).

Mainly young people

The imprudences and errors that have accompanied this work are the less to be wondered at when it is considered that chiefly young people have been the subjects of it, who have less steadiness and experience, and being in the heat of youth are much more ready to run to extremes. Satan will keep people secure as long as he can; but when he can do that no longer, he often endeavours to drive them to extremes, and so to dishonour God, and wound religion in that way. And doubtless it has been one occasion of much misconduct, that in many places people see plainly that their ministers have an ill opinion of the work; and therefore, with good reason, dare not go to them as their guides in it; and so are without guides. No wonder then that when a people are like sheep without a shepherd, they wander out of the way. A people in such circumstances stand in great and continual need of guides, and their guides are in continual need of much more wisdom than they have of their own.

And if a people have ministers that favour the work, and rejoice in it, it is still not to be expected that either the people or ministers should know so well how to conduct themselves in such an extraordinary state of things – while it is new, and something they never had any experience of before, and time to see their tendency, consequences, and result. The happy influence of experience is very manifest at this day in the people among whom God has settled me to live. The work which has been carried on there this year has been much purer than what happened there six years earlier: it has seemed to be more purely spiritual, free from natural and corrupt mixtures, and anything savouring of enthusiastic wildness and extravagance. It has wrought more by deep humiliation and abasement before God and men; and they have been much freer from imprudences and irregularities. And particularly there has been a remarkable difference in this respect, that whereas many before, in their comforts and rejoicings, did too much forget their distance from God, and were ready in their conversation together of the things of God, and of their own experiences, to talk with too much lightness; but now they seem to have no disposition that way, but rejoice with a more solemn, reverential, humble joy, as God directs (Ps. 2:11). Not because the joy is not as great, and in many instances much greater. Many among us who were wrought upon in that earlier period have now had much greater communications from heaven than they had then. Their rejoicing operates in another manner; it abases them, breaks their hearts, and brings them into the dust. When they speak of their joys, it is not with laughter, but a flood of tears. Thus those who laughed before weep now, and yet by their united testimony, their joy is vastly purer and sweeter than that which before raised their animal spirits more. They are now more like Jacob, when God appeared to him at Bethel, when he saw the ladder that reached to heaven, and said, 'How dreadful is this place!' And like Moses, when God showed him his glory on the mount, when he made haste and 'bowed himself unto the earth'.

Do not oppose the work
Let this warn us all not by any means to oppose the work, or do anything in the least to clog of hinder it; but, on the contrary, do our utmost to promote it.

Now Christ is come down from heaven in a remarkable and wonderful work of his Spirit, it becomes all his professed disciples to acknowledge him, and give him honour.

The example of the Jews in Christ's time
The example of the Jews in Christ's and the apostles' times is
enough to make those who do not acknowledge this work very jealous of themselves, and to make them exceedingly cautious of what
they say or do. Christ then was in the world, and the world did not
receive him. That coming of Christ had been much spoken of in
the prophecies of Scripture which they had in their hands, and it
had been long expected; and yet because Christ came in a manner
they did not expect, and which did not agree with their carnal
reason, they would not own him.

   Indeed, they opposed him, counted him a madman, and pronounced the spirit by which he worked to be the spirit of the devil.
They stood and wondered at the great things done, and know not
what to make of them; but they still met with so many stumbling-
blocks that they finally could not acknowledge him. And when the
Spirit of God came to be poured out so wonderfully in the apostles'
days, they looked upon it as confusion and distraction. They were
astonished by what they saw and heard, but not *convinced*. And especially was the work of God then rejected by those who were most
conceited of their own understanding and knowledge, as Isaiah
29:14 said: 'Therefore, behold, I will proceed to do a marvellous
work amongst this people, even a marvellous work and a wonder;
for the wisdom of their wise men shall perish, and the understanding of their prudent men shall be hid.' And many who had had a
reputation for religion and piety had a great spite against the
work, because they saw it tended to diminish their honour, and to
reproach their formality and lukewarmness. Some, upon these
accounts, maliciously and openly opposed and reproached the
work of the Spirit of God, and called it the work of the devil,
against inward conviction, and so were guilty of the unpardonable
sin against the Holy Spirit.

A spiritual coming of Christ
There is another, a spiritual coming of Christ, to set up his kingdom in the world, that is as much spoken of in Scripture prophecy

as that first coming, and which has long been expected by the church of God. We have reason to think, from what is said of this, that it will be in many respects parallel with the other. And certainly that low state into which the visible church of God has lately been sunk is very parallel with the state of the Jewish church when Christ came; and it is therefore no wonder at all that when Christ comes his work should appear a strange work to most people; indeed, it would be a wonder if it were otherwise. Whether or not the present work is the beginning of that great and frequently predicted coming of Christ to set up his kingdom, it is evident from what has been said that it is a work of the same Spirit, and of the same nature.

And there is no reason to doubt that the conduct of people who continue long to refuse to acknowledge Christ in the work – especially those who are teachers in his church – will be similarly provoking to God, as it was in the Jews of old, while refusing to acknowledge Christ; notwithstanding what they may plead of the great stumbling-blocks that are in the way, and the cause they have to doubt the work. The teachers of the Jewish church found innumerable stumbling-blocks that were insuperable to them. Many things appeared in Christ, and in the work of the Spirit after his ascension, which were exceedingly strange to them; they seemed assured that they had just cause for their scruples. Christ and his work were to the Jews a stumbling-block. 'But blessed is he,' says Christ, 'whosoever shall not be offended in me.' As strange and as unexpected as the manner of Christ's appearance was, yet he had not been long in Judea working miracles before all those who had opportunity to observe, and yet refused to acknowledge him, brought fearful guilt upon themselves in the sight of God; and Christ condemned them, that though they could discern the face of the sky, and of the earth, yet they could not discern the signs of the times. 'Why,' he asks, 'even of yourselves, judge ye not what is right?' (Luke 12).

A silence which provokes God

It is not to be supposed that the great Jehovah has bowed the heavens and appeared here now for so long a time, in such a glorious work of his power and grace – in so extensive a manner, in the most public places of the land, and in almost all parts of it – without giving such evidences of his presence that great numbers and even many teachers in his church can remain guiltless in his sight, without ever receiving and acknowledging him, and giving him honour, and appearing to rejoice in his gracious presence; or without so much as once giving him thanks for so glorious and blessed a work of his grace, wherein his goodness does more appear than if he had bestowed on us all the temporal blessings that the world affords.

A long-continued silence in such a case is undoubtedly provoking to God; especially in ministers. It is a secret kind of opposition that really tends to hinder the work. Such silent ministers stand in the way of the work of God, as Christ said of old, 'He that is not with us is against us.' Those who stand wondering at this strange work, not knowing what to make of it, and refusing to receive it – and ready it may be sometimes to speak contemptibly of it, as was the case with the Jews of old – would do well to consider, and to tremble at St Paul's words to them: 'Beware therefore lest that come upon you,which is spoken of in the prophets, Behold, ye despisers, and wonder, and perish; for I work a work in your days, which you shall in no wise believe, though a man declare it unto you' (Acts 13:40–1). Those who cannot the believe the work to be true because of the extraordinary degree and manner of it should consider how it was with the unbelieving lord in Samaria, who said, 'Behold, if the Lord should make windows in heaven, might this thing be?' To whom Elisha said, 'Behold, thou shalt see it with thine eyes, but shalt not eat thereof.' Let all to whom this work is a cloud and darkness – as the pillar of cloud and fire was to the Egyptians – take heed that it be not their destruction, while it gives light to God's Israel.

A work of God without stumbling-blocks is never to be expected
I would entreat those who quiet themselves, that they proceed on a principle of prudence, and are waiting to see how things turn out – and what fruits those that are the subjects of this work will bring forth in their lives and conversations – to consider whether this

will justify long refraining from acknowledging Christ when he appears so wonderfully and graciously present in the land. It is probably that many of those who are thus waiting do not know what they are waiting for. If they wait to see a work of God without difficulties and stumbling-blocks, it will be like the fool's waiting at the river side to have the water all run by. A work of God without stumbling-blocks is never to be expected. 'It must need be that offences come.' There never yet was any great manifestation that God made of himself to the world, without many difficulties attending it. It is the same with God's works as it is with his word: they seem at first full of things that are strange, inconsistent, and difficult to the carnal unbelieving hearts of men. Christ and his work always was, and always will be, a stone of stumbling, and rock of offence, a gin and a snare to many. The prophet Hosea, speaking of a glorious revival of religion in God's church — when God would be as the dew unto Israel, who would grow as the lily, and put out roots like Lebanon, whose branches would spread, etc. — concludes: 'Who is wise, and he shall understand these things? prudent, and he shall know them? for the ways of the Lord are right, and the just shall walk in them: but the transgressors shall fall therein' (Hos. 14:9).

Future stumbling-blocks
It is probable that the stumbling-blocks that now attend this work will in some respects be increased, and not diminished. We will probably see more instances of apostasy and gross iniquity among people who claim to be believers. And if one kind of stumbling-blocks are removed, it is to be expected that others will come. It is with Christ's works as it was with his parables; things that are difficult to men's dark minds are ordered purposely, to test their corrupt minds and spiritual sense; and so that those of corrupt minds and of an unbelieving, perverse, cavilling spirit, 'seeing might see and not understand'. Those who are now waiting to see how this work turns out think they will be better able to determine later on; but probably many of them are mistaken. The Jews that saw Christ's miracles waited to see better evidences of his being the Messiah; they wanted a sign from heaven; but they waited in vain;

their stumbling-blocks did not diminish, but increased. They found no end to them, and so were more and more hardened in unbelief. Many have been praying for that glorious reformation spoken of in Scripture, and did not know want they have been praying for (as it was with the Jews when they prayed for the coming of Christ), and if it came they would not acknowledge or receive it.

A prudence or an imprudence?

This pretended prudence, in people waiting so long before they acknowledged this work, will probably in the end prove the greatest imprudence. Hereby they will fail to receive any share of so great a blessing, and will miss the most precious opportunity of obtaining divine light, grace, and comfort, heavenly and eternal benefits, that God ever gave in New England. While the glorious fountain is set open in so wonderful a manner, and multitudes flock to it and receive a rich supply for the needs of their souls, they stand at a distance, doubting, wondering, and receiving nothing, and are likely to continue thus till the precious season is past.

It is indeed to be wondered at that those who have doubted the work, which has been attended with such uncommon external appearances, should be easy in their doubts, without taking thorough pains to inform themselves, by going where such things have been to be seen, narrowly observing and diligently inquiring into them; not contenting themselves with observing two or three instances, nor resting till they were fully informed by their own observation. I do not doubt that if this course had been taken, it would have convinced all whose minds are not shut up against conviction. How greatly have they erred, when they have ventured to speak slightly of these things when they have only the uncertain reproofs of others! That caution of an unbelieving Jew might teach them more prudence: 'Refrain from these men, and let them alone; for if this counsel or this work be of men, it will come to nought; but if it be of God, ye cannot overthrow it; lest haply ye be found to fight against God' (Acts 5:38-9).

Whether or not what has been said in this discourse is enough to produce conviction that this is the work of God, I hope that for the future they will at least listen to this caution of Gamaliel, so as not to oppose it, or say anything which has even an indirect tendency to bring it into discredit, lest they should be found opposers of the Holy Spirit. There is no kind of sin so hurtful and dangerous to the souls of men as those committed against the Holy Spirit. We had better speak against God the Father, or the Son, than to speak against the Holy Spirit in his gracious operations on the hearts of men. Nothing will so much tend for ever to prevent our having any benefit of his operations on our own souls.

If there are any who still resolutely go on to speak contemptibly of these things, I would beg them to take heed that they are not guilty of the unpardonable sin. When the Holy Spirit is much poured out, and men's lusts, lukewarmness, and hypocrisy are reproached by its powerful operations, then is the most likely time of any for this sin to be committed. If the work goes on, it is well if among the many that show an enmity against it, some are not guilty of this sin, if none have been already. Those who maliciously oppose and reproach this work, and call it the work of the devil, want but one thing of the unpardonable sin, and that is, doing it against inward conviction. And though some are so prudent as not openly to oppose and reproach this work, it is still to be feared – at this day, when the Lord is going forth so gloriously against his enemies – that many who are silent and inactive, especially ministers, will bring that curse of the angel of the Lord upon themselves: 'Curse ye Meroz, said the angel of the Lord, curse ye bitterly the inhabitants thereof; because they came not to the help of the Lord, to the help of the Lord against the mighty' (Judg. 5:23).

Happiness or misery?
Since the great God has come down from heaven, and manifested himself in so wonderful a manner in this land, it is vain for any of us to expect any other than to be greatly affected by it in our spiritual state and circumstances, respecting the favour of God, one way or another. Those who do not become more happy by it will become far more guilty and miserable. It is always so; such a season as proves an acceptable years, and a time of great favour to

those who accept it and benefit from it, proves a day of vengeance to others (Is. 59:2). When God sends forth his *word*, it will not return to him void; much less his *Spirit*. When Christ was upon earth in Judea, many people slighted and rejected him; but it proved in the end to be no matter of indifference to them. God made all that people to feel that Christ had been among them; those who did not feel it to their comfort felt it to their great sorrow. When God only sent the prophet Ezekiel to the children of Israel, he declared that whether they would hear or whether they would forbear, they would still know that there had been a prophet among them. How much more may we suppose that when God has appeared so wonderfully in this land, he will make everyone know that the great Jehovah had been in New England.

Avoid all errors and misconduct

In the last place, I now come to apply myself to those who are the friends of this work, who have been partakers of it, and are zealous to promote it. Let me earnestly exhort such people to give diligent heed to themselves to avoid all errors and misconduct, and whatever may darken and obscure the work; and to give no occasion to those who stand ready to reproach it. The apostle was careful to cut off occasion from those that desired occasion. The same apostle exhorts Titus to maintain a strict care and watch over himself, that both his preaching and behaviour might be such as could not be condemned; that he who was of the contrary part might be ashamed, having no evil thing to say of them (Titus 2:7–8). We need to be wise as serpents and harmless as doves. It is of no small consequence that we should at this day behave ourselves innocently and prudently. We must expect that the great enemy of this work will especially try his utmost with us; and he will especially triumph if he can prevail in anything to blind and mislead us. He knows it will do more to further his purpose and interest than if he prevailed against a hundred others. We need to watch and pray, for we are only little children; this roaring lion is too strong for us, and this old serpent too subtle for us.

Watch out for spiritual pride

Humility and self-diffidence, and an entire dependence on our Lord Jesus Christ, will be our best defence. Let us therefore maintain the strictest watch against spiritual pride, or being lifted up with extraordinary experiences and comforts, and the high favours of heaven, that any of us may have received. We need after such favours to keep a specially strict and jealous eye upon our own hearts, lest there should arise self-exalting reflections upon what we have received, and high thoughts or ourselves as being some of the most eminent of saints and particular favourites of heaven, and that the secret of the Lord is specially with us.

Let us not presume to think that we above all are fit to be advanced as the great instructors and censors of this evil generation; and, in a high conceit of our own wisdom and discerning, assume the airs of prophets, or extraordinary ambassadors of heaven. When great revelations of God are given to our souls, we should not shine bright in our own eyes. Moses, when he had been conversing with God in the mountain, though his face shone so as to dazzle the eyes of Aaron and the people, still did not shine in his own eyes; 'he wist not that his face shone'. Let no one think themselves out of danger of this spiritual pride, even in their best frames. God saw that the apostle Paul (though probably the most eminent saint that ever lived) was not out of danger of it, no, not when he had just been conversing with God in the third heaven: see 2 Corinthians 12:7. Pride is the worst viper in the heart; it is the first sin that ever entered into the universe, lies lowest of all in the foundation of the whole building of sin, and is the most secret, deceitful, and unsearchable in its ways of working, of any lust whatever. It is ready to mix with everything; and nothing is so hateful to God, contrary to the spirit of the gospel, or of so dangerous consequence; and there is no one sin that does so much let in the devil into the hearts of the saints, and expose them to his delusions. I have seen it in many instances, and that in eminent saints. The devil has come in at this door presently after some eminent experience and extraordinary communion with God, and has woefully deluded and led them astray, till God has mercifully opened their eyes and delivered them; and they themselves have afterwards been made aware that it was pride that betrayed them.

Do not give too much attention to strong impulses
Some of the true friends of the work of God's Spirit have erred in giving too much heed to impulses and strong impressions on their minds, as though they were messages direct from heaven to them of something that was to happen, or something that it was the mind and will of God that they should do, which was not signified or revealed anywhere in the Bible without those impulses. These impressions, if they are truly from the Spirit of God, are of a quite different nature from his gracious influences on the hearts of the saints: they are of the nature of the extraordinary gifts of the Spirit, and are properly inspiration, such as the prophets and apostles and others had of old; which the apostle distinguishes from the *grace* of the Spirit (1 Cor. 13).

One reason why some people have been ready to lay weight on such impulses is an opinion they have had, that the glory of the approaching happy days of the church would partly consist in restoring those extraordinary gifts of the Spirit. This opinion, I believe, arises partly through lack of duly considering and comparing the nature and value of those two kinds of influences of the Spirit, namely those that are ordinary and gracious, and those that are extraordinary and miraculous. The former are by far the most excellent and glorious; as the apostle shows at length (1 Cor. 12:31, etc.). Speaking of the extraordinary gifts of the Spirit, he says, 'But covet earnestly the best gifts; and yet I show you a more excellent way'; i.e. a more excellent way of the influence of the Spirit.

And then he goes on, in the next chapter, to show what that more excellent way is – the grace of that Spirit, which summarily consists in charity, or divine love. And throughout that chapter he shows the great preference of that above inspiration. God communicates his own nature to the soul in saving grace in the heart, more than in all miraculous *gifts*. The blessed image of God consists in *that* and not in *these*. The excellence, happiness, and glory of the soul immediately consists in the former. That is a root which bears infinitely more excellent fruit. Salvation and the eternal enjoyment of God is promised to divine grace, but not to inspiration. A man may have those extraordinary gifts, and yet be abominable to God, and go to hell. The spiritual and eternal life of the soul consists in the grace of the Spirit, which God bestows only on his favourites and dear children. He has sometimes thrown out the other as it were to dogs and swine, as he did to Balaam, Saul, and Judas; and some who, in the earliest times of the Christian church, committed the unpardonable sin (Heb. 6). Many wicked men at the day of judgment will plead, 'Have we not prophesied in thy name, and in thy name cast out devils, and in thy name done many wonderful works.' The greatest privilege of the prophets and apostles was not their being inspired and working miracles, but their eminent holiness. The grace that was in their hearts was a thousand times more their dignity and honour than their miraculous gifts. The things in which we find David comforting himself are not his being a king, or a prophet, but the holy influences of the Spirit of God in his heart, communicating to him his divine light, love, and joy. The apostle Paul abounded in visions, revelations, and miraculous gifts, above all the apostles; but yet he esteems all things but loss for the excellence of the spiritual knowledge of Christ.

It was not the gifts but the grace of the apostles that was the proper evidence of their names being written in heaven; in which Christ directs them to rejoice, much more than in the devils being subject to them. To have grace in the heart is a higher privilege than the blessed Virgin herself had, in having the body of the second person of the Trinity conceived in her womb, by the power of the Highest overshadowing her: 'And it came to pass as he spake these things, a certain woman of the company lift up her voice, and said unto him; Blessed is the womb that bare thee, and the paps that thou hast sucked! But he said, Yea, rather blessed are they that hear the word of God and keep it' (Luke 11:27–28; see also Matt.12:47ff.).

The influence of the Holy Spirit, or divine charity in the heart, is the greatest privilege and glory of the highest archangel in heaven; indeed, this is the very thing by which the creature has fellowship with God himself, with the Father and the Son, in their beauty and happiness. By this the saints are made partakers of the divine nature, and have Christ's joy fulfilled in themselves.

The ordinary sanctifying influences of the Spirit of God are the *purpose* of all extraordinary gifts, as the apostle shows in Ephesians 4:11–13. They are good for nothing, any further than as they are subordinate to this end; they will be so far benefiting anyone without it, that they will only aggravate their misery. This is, as the apostle observes, the most excellent way of God's communicating his Spirit to his church; it is the greatest glory of the church in all ages. This glory is what makes the church on earth most like the church in heaven, when prophecy and tongues and other miraculous gifts cease.

And God communicates his Spirit only in that more excellent way of which the apostle speaks, namely *charity*, or divine love, 'which never faileth'. Therefore the glory of the approaching happy state of the church does not at all require these extra-ordinary gifts. As that state of the church will be the nearest of any to its perfect state in heaven, so I believe it will be like it in this, that all extraordinary gifts will have ceased and vanished away; and all those stars, and the moon, with the reflected light they gave in the night, or in a dark season, will be swallowed up in the sun of divine love. The apostle speaks of these gifts of inspiration as childish things in comparison with the influence of the Spirit in divine love – things given to the church only to support it in its minority, till the church has a complete standing rule established, and all the ordinary means of grace are settled; but as things that would cease as the church advanced to the state of manhood. 'When I was a child, I spake as a child, I understood as a child, I thought as a child; but when I became a man, I put away childish things' (1 Cor. 13:11 – compare the three preceding verses).

Is immaturity linked to miraculous gifts?
When the apostle, in this chapter, speaks of prophecies, tongues, and revelations ceasing, and vanishing away in the church – when the Christian church advances from a state of minority to a state of manhood – he seems to be referring to its coming to an adult state

in this world, as well as in heaven; for he speaks of a state of man-hood in which those three things, Faith, Hope, and Charity, remain after miracles and revelations had ceased; as in the last verse, and 'now abideth [remaineth] Faith, Hope, and Charity, these three'. The apostle's manner of speaking here shows an evident reference to what he had just been saying before; and here is a manifest *antithesis* between *remaining* and that *failing, ceasing,* and *vanishing away* spoken of in verse 8. The apostle had been showing how all those gifts of inspiration, which were the leading-strings of the Christian church in its infancy, would vanish away when the church came to a state of manhood. Then he returns to observe what things remain after those had failed and cased; and he observes that those three things shall remain in the church, Faith, Hope, and Charity; and therefore the adult state of the church he speaks of is the more perfect one at which it will arrive on earth, especially in the latter ages of the world. And this was the more properly observed to the church at Corinth, upon two accounts: because the apostle had previously observed to that church that they were in a state of infancy (3:1–2), and because that church seems above all others to have abounded with miraculous gifts.

When the expected glorious state of the church comes, the increase of light will be so great that it will in some respects answer what is said in verse 12 of *seeing face to face*. (See Isaiah 24:23 and 25:7.)

Therefore I do not expect a restoration of these miraculous gifts in the approaching glorious times of the church, nor do I desire it. It appears to me that it would add nothing to the glory of those times, but rather diminish it. For my part, I would rather enjoy the sweet influences of the Spirit, showing Christ's spiritual divine beauty, infinite grace, and dying love, drawing out the holy exercise of faith, divine lore, sweet complacence, and humble joy in God, one quarter of an hour, than to have prophetic visions and revelations the whole year. It appears to me much more probable that God should give immediate revelations to his saints in the dark times of prophecy than now in the approach of the most glorious and perfect state of his church on earth. It does not appear to me that there is any need of those extraordinary gifts to introduce this happy state, and set up the kingdom of God through the world; I have seen so much of the power of God in a more excellent way, as to convince me that God can easily do it without.

I would therefore entreat the people of God to be very cautious how they give heed to such things. I have seen them fail in very many instances, and know by experience that impressions made with great power, and on the minds of true and eminent saints – even in the midst of extraordinary exercises of grace, and sweet communion with God, and attended with texts of Scripture strongly impressed on the mind – are no sure signs of their being revelations from heaven. I have known such impressions fail, in some instances, attended with all these circumstances. Those who leave the sure word of prophecy – which God has given to us as a light shining in a dark place – to follow such impressions and impulses, leave the guidance of the polar star to follow a jack-o'-lantern. No wonder therefore that sometimes they are led into woeful extravagancies.

Do not despise human learning

Moreover, seeing inspiration is not to be expected, *let us not despise human learning*. Those who assert that human learning is of little or no use in the work of the ministry do not well consider what they say; if they did, they would not say it. By human learning I mean, and suppose others to mean, the use of common knowledge by human and outward means. And therefore, to say that human learning is of no use is as much as to say that the education of a child, or the common knowledge which a grown man has more than a little child, is of no use. At this rate, a child of four years old is as fit for a teacher in the church of God, with the same degree of grace – and capable of doing as much to advance the kingdom of Christ by his instruction – as a very knowing man of thirty years of age. If adult persons have greater ability and advantage to do service, because they have more knowledge than a little child, then doubtless if they have more human knowledge still, with the same degree of grace, they would have still greater ability and advantage to do service. An increase of knowledge, without doubt, increases a man's advantage either to do good or harm, according as he is disposed. It is too obvious to be denied that God made great use of human learning in the apostle Paul, as he also did in Moses and Solomon.

And if knowledge, obtained by human means, is not to be despised, then it will follow that the means of obtaining it are not to be neglected, namely *study*; and that this is of great use in order to prepare for public instruction of others. And though having the heart full of the powerful influences of the Spirit of God may at some time enable people to speak profitably, indeed most excellently, without study; yet this will not warrant us needlessly to cast ourselves down from the pinnacle of the temple, depending upon it that the angel of the Lord will bear us up, and keep us from dashing our foot against a stone, when there is another way to go down, though it may not be as quick. And I would pray that *method* in public discourses, which tends greatly to help both the understanding and memory, may not be wholly neglected.

Beware of judging other Christians

Another thing I would beg the dear children of God to consider more fully is how far, and upon what grounds, the rules of the Holy Scriptures will truly justify their censuring other professing Christians as hypocrites and ignorant of real religion. We all know that there is a judging and censuring of some sort or other that the Scripture very often and very strictly forbids. desire that those rules of Scripture may be looked into, and thoroughly weighed; and that it may be considered whether our taking it upon us to discern the state of others – and to pass sentence upon them as wicked men, though they are professing Christians, and of good behaviour – is not really forbidden by Christ in the New Testament. If it is, then doubtless the disciples of Christ ought to avoid this practice, however qualified they may think themselves for it; or however needful, or useful, they may think it. It is plain that the sort of judgement which God claims as his prerogative, whatever that is, is forbidden.

We know that a certain judging of the hearts of the children of men is often spoken of as the great prerogative of God, and which belongs only to him; as in 1 Kings 8:39 – 'Forgive, and do, and give unto every man according to his ways, whose heart thou knowest; for thou, even thou only, knowest the hearts of all the children of men.' And if we examine, we shall find that the judging of hearts which is spoken of as God's prerogative relates not only to the aims and suppositions of men's hearts in particular actions, but chiefly to the state of their hearts as the professors of religion, and with regard to that profession. This will appear very manifest by looking over the following scriptures: 1 Chronicles 28:9; Psalm 7:9–11; Psalm 26; Proverbs 16:2; 17:3; 21:2; Job 2:23–5; Revelation 2:22–3. The sort of judging which is God's own business is forbidden: 'Who art thou that judgest another man's servant? to his own master he standeth or falleth' (Rom. 14:4). 'There is one lawgiver that is able to save or destroy; who art thou that judgest another?' (Jas. 4:12). 'But with me it is a very small thing, that I should be judged of you, or of man's judgement; yea I judge not mine own self; but he that judgeth me is the Lord' (2 Cor. 4:13–14).

Again, whatever kind of judging is the proper work and business of the day of judgement is what we are forbidden: 'Therefore judge nothing before the time, until the Lord come; who both will bring to light the hidden things of darkness, and will make manifest the counsels of the heart; and then shall every man have praise of God' (1 Cor. 4:5). But to distinguish hypocrites from true saints, when they have the form of godliness and the behaviour of godly men – or to separate the sheep from the goats – is the proper business of the day of judgement. Indeed, it is represented as the main business and purpose of that day. Therefore people greatly err when they take it upon them positively to determine who are sincere and who are not – to draw the dividing line between true saints and hypocrites, and to separate between sheep and goats, setting the one on the right hand and the other on the left – and to distinguish and gather out the tares from amongst the wheat.

Many of the servants of the owner of the field are very ready to think themselves sufficient for this, and are forward to offer their service to this end; but their Lord Jesus says, 'Nay, lest while ye gather up the tares, ye root up also the wheat with them. Let both grow together until the harvest.' And in the time of harvest will take care to see a thorough separation made (Matt. 13:28–30). This is in keeping with the apostle's prohibition mentioned above: 'Judge nothing before the time' (1 Cor. 4:5).

   In this parable, the servants who have the care of the fruit of the field doubtless mean the same as the servants who have the car of the fruit of the vineyard (Luke 20), and who are elsewhere represented as servants of the Lord of the harvest, appointed as labourers in his harvest. These we know are ministers of the gospel. *Now* is that parable in Matthew 13 fulfilled: 'While men sleep,' (during a long, sleepy, dead time in the church) 'the enemy has sowed tares.' Now is the time 'when the blade is sprung up,' and religion is reviving; and now some of the servants who have the care of the field say, 'Let us go and gather up the tares.'

The older I get the more suspicious I become . . .
I know that men who suppose they have some experience of the power of religion are very apt to think themselves capable of discerning and determining the state of others by a little conversation with them; and experience has taught me that this is an error. I once did not imagine that the heart of man has been so unsearchable as it is. I am less charitable, and less uncharitable than once I was. I find more things in wicked men that may counterfeit, and make a fair show of piety; and more ways that the remaining corruption of the godly may make them appear like carnal men, formalists, and dead hypocrites, than once I knew of. The longer I live, the less I wonder that God challenges it as his prerogative to try the hearts of the children of men, and directs that this business should be let alone till harvest. I desire to adore the wisdom of God, and his goodness to me and my fellow-creatures, that he has not committed this great business into the hands of such a poor, weak, and dim-sighted creature – one of so much blindness, pride, partiality, prejudice, and deceitfulness of heart – but has committed it into the hands of one infinitely fitter for it, and has made it his prerogative.

   The talk of some persons, and the account they give it their experiences, is exceedingly satisfying, and such as forbids and banishes the thought of their being any other than the precious

children of God. It obliges, and as it were forces, full charity; but
yet we must allow the Scriptures to stand good that speak of everything in the saint, belonging to the spiritual and divine life, as hidden (Col. 3:3–4). Their food is the hidden manna; they have meat
to eat that others know not of; a stranger does not intermeddle
with their joys. The heart in which they possess their divine distinguishing ornaments is the hidden man, and in the sight of God
only (1 Pet. 3:4). Their new name, which Christ has given them, no
man knows but he that receives it (Rev. 2:17). The praise of the
true Israelites, whose circumcision is that of the heart, is not of
men but of God (Rom. 2:29); that is, they can be certainly known
and discerned to be Israelites, so as to have the honour that
belongs to such, only by God; as appears from the use of the same
expression by the same apostle in 1 Corinthians 4:5. Here he
speaks of its being God's prerogative to judge who are upright
Christians, and what he will do at the day of judgment, adding,
'and then shall every man have praise of God'.

Judas

The instance of *Judas* is remarkable. Though he had been so much
amongst the rest of the disciples, all persons of true experience,
but his associates never seem to have entertained a thought of his
being any other than a true disciple, till he revealed himself by his
scandalous practice.

Ahitophel

And the instance of *Ahitophel* is also very remarkable. David did
not suspect him, though he was so wise and holy a man, so great a
divine, and had such a great acquaintance with Scripture. He knew
more than all his teachers, more than the ancients; he had grown
old in experience, and was in the greatest ripeness of his judgement. He was a great prophet, and was intimately acquainted with
Ahitophel, being his familiar friend, and most intimate companion
in religious and spiritual concerns. Yet David not only never discovered him to be a hypocrite, but relied on him as a true saint. He
relished his religious discourse, it was sweet to him, and he
counted him an eminent saint; so that he made him above any

other man his guide and counsellor in soul matters; but yet he was not only no saint, but a notoriously wicked man, a murderous, vile wretch. 'Wickedness is in the midst thereof; deceit and guile depart not from her streets: for it was not an open enemy that reproached me, then I could have borne it; neither was it he that hated me, that did magnify himself against me, then I would have hid myself from him: but it was thou, a man mine equal, my guide and mine acquaintance: we took sweet counsel together, and walked unto the house of God in company' (Ps. 55:11–14).

To suppose that men have ability and right to determine the state of the souls of visible Christians, and so to make an open separation between saints and hypocrites, that true saints may be of one visible company, and hypocrites of another, separated by a partition that men make, carries in it an inconsistency, for it supposes that God has given men power to make another visible church, within his visible church; for by visible Christians or visible saints is meant people who have a right to be received as such in the eye of public charity. None can have a right to exclude any one of this visible church except in the way of that regular ecclesiastical proceeding which God has established in his visible church.

I beg those who have a true zeal for promoting this work of God to consider these things carefully. I am persuaded that whichever of them have much to do with souls, if they do not listen to me now, they will be of the same mind when they have had more experience.

Beware of attacking your opponents
And another thing that I would entreat the zealous friends of this glorious work of God to avoid, is managing the controversy with opposers with too much heat, and appearance of an angry zeal; and particularly insisting very much in public prayer and preaching, on the persecution of opposers. If their persecution were ten times as great as it is, I think it would not be best to say so much about it. If it becomes Christians to be like lambs, not apt to complain and cry when they are hurt, it becomes them to be dumb and not to open their mouth, after the example of our dear Redeemer; and not to be like swine, that are apt to scream aloud when they are touched. We

should not be ready to think and speak straightaway of fire from heaven, when the Samaritans oppose us and will not receive us into their villages. God's zealous ministers would do well to think of the direction the apostle Paul gave to a zealous minister: 'And the servant of the Lord must not strive, but be gentle unto all men, apt to teach, patient, in meekness instructing those that oppose themselves; if God peradventure will give them repentance, to the acknowledging of the truth; and that they may recover themselves out of the snare of the devil, who are taken captive by him at his will' (2 Tim. 2:24–6).

I would humbly recommend to those that love the Lord Jesus Christ, and would advance his kingdom, to follow that excellent rule of prudence which Christ has left us: 'No man putteth a piece of new cloth into an old garment; for that which is put in to fill it up, taketh from the garment, and the rent is made worse. Neither do men put new wine into old bottles; else the bottles break and the wine runneth out, and the bottles perish. But they put new wine into new bottles, and both are preserved' (Matt. 9:16–17). I am afraid the wine is now running out in some parts of this land, for lack of attendance to this rule. For though I believe we have confined ourselves too much to a certain stated method and form in the management of our religious affairs; which has had a tendency to cause all our religion to degenerate into mere formality; yet whatever has the appearance of a great innovation – that tends much to shock and surprise people's minds, and to set them talking and disputing – tends greatly to hinder the progress of the power of religion. It raises the opposition of some, diverts the minds of others, and perplexes many with doubts and scruples. It causes people to swerve from their great business, and turn aside to vain jangling. Therefore that which is very much beside the common practice had better be avoided, unless it is of considerable importance in its own nature. In this we shall follow the example of one who had the greatest success in propagating the power of religion: 'Unto the Jews I became as a Jew, that I might gain the Jews; to them that are under the law, as under the law, that I might gain them that are under the law; to them that are without law, as without law, (being not without law to God, but under to Christ,) that I might gain them that are without law. To the weak I became as weak, that I might gain the weak. I am made all things to all men, that I might by all means save some. And this I do for the gospel's sake, that I might be partaker thereof with you' (1 Cor. 9:20–3).

Jonathan Edwards: A Treatise Concerning Religious Affections

TRUE RELIGION, IN GREAT PART, CONSISTS IN THE AFFECTIONS.

'Be ye fervent in spirit'

Who will deny that true religion consists, in a great measure, in vigorous and lively actings of the *inclination* and *will* of the soul, or the fervent exercises of the *heart*? The religion which God requires, and will accept, does not consist in weak, dull, and lifeless wishes, scarcely raising us above a state of indifference. God, in his word, greatly insists that we should be in good earnest, *fervent in spirit,* and our hearts vigorously engaged in religion: 'Be ye fervent in spirit, serving the Lord' (Rom. 12:11; see also Deut. 10:12; 6:4–5; 30:6).

'Baptised with the Holy Ghost and with fire'

If we are not in good earnest in religion, and our wills and inclinations are not strongly exercised, we are nothing. The things of religion are so great that the exercises of our hearts cannot be suitable to their nature and importance unless they are lively and powerful. Vigour in the actings of our inclinations is requisite in nothing so much as in religion; and in nothing is lukewarmness so odious. True religion is evermore a powerful thing; and its power appears, first, in its exercises in the heart, its principal and original seat. Hence true religion is called the *power of godliness*, in distinction from external appearances, which are *the form* of it: 'Having a form of godliness, but denying the power of it' (2 Tim. 3:5). The Spirit of God, in those who have sound and solid religion, is a

Spirit of powerful holy affection; and therefore God is said to have given 'the Spirit of power, and of love, and of a sound mind' (2 Tim. 1:7). And such people, when they receive the Spirit of God in his sanctifying and saving influences, are said to be 'baptised with the Holy Ghost, and with fire', by reason of the power and fervour of those exercises which the Spirit of God excite sin them, and by which *their hearts*, when grace is in exercise, may be said to *burn within them* (Luke 24:32).

Affections are the spring of actions

The Author of our nature has not only given us affections, but has made them very much the spring of actions. As the *affections* not only necessarily belong to the *human nature* but are a very *great part* of it, so (inasmuch as by regeneration people are renewed in the whole man) *holy affections* not only necessarily belong to *true religion*, but are a very great part of such religion. And as true religion is practical, and God has so constituted the human nature that the affections are very much the spring of people's actions, this also shows that true religion must consist very much in the affections.

Religion takes hold of us as we are affected

Nothing is more manifest *in fact* than that the things of religion take hold of men's souls no further than they *affect* them. Multitudes hear the peremptory commands of God, his gracious counsels and warnings, and the sweet invitations of the gospel. Yet they remain as before, with no perceptible alteration either in heart or practice, because they are not *affected* with what they hear. I am bold to assert that there never was any considerable change wrought in the mind or conversation of any person, by anything of a religious nature that ever he read, heard, or saw, who did not have his affections moved. Never was a natural man engaged earnestly to seek his salvation; never were any such brought to cry after wisdom, and lift up their voice for understanding, and to wrestle with God in prayer for mercy; and never was one humbled, and brought to the feet of God, from anything that ever he heard or imagined of his own unworthiness and deservings of God's displeasure; nor was ever one induced to fly for refuge to Christ, while his heart remained unaffected. Nor was there ever a saint awakened out of a cold, lifeless frame, or recovered from a declining state in religion, and brought back from a lamentable departure from God, without having his heart affected. And, in a word, there never was anything considerable brought to pass in the heart or life of anyone living, by the things of religion, that had not his heart deeply affected by those things.

Christ was tender-hearted

He whom God sent into the world to be the light of the world and the head of the whole church, and the perfect example of true religion and virtue for the imitation of all, the Shepherd whom the whole flock should follow wherever he goes – the Lord Jesus Christ – was of a remarkably tender and affectionate heart; and his virtue was expressed very much in the exercise of holy affections. He was the greatest instance of ardent, vigorous, and strong *love*, to both God and man, that ever was. It was these affections which got the victory in that mighty struggle and conflict of his affections, in his agonies, when *he prayed more earnestly, and offered strong crying and tears,* and wrestled in tears and in blood. Such was the power of the exercises of his holy love that they were stronger than death, and in that great struggle overcame those strong exercises of the natural affections of fear and grief, when his soul was exceeding sorrowful, even unto death.

He also appeared to be full of affection in the course of his life. We read of his great *zeal*, fulfilling the expression in Psalm 60: 'The zeal of thine house hath eaten me up' (John 2:17). We read of his *grief* for the sins of men: 'He looked round about on them with anger, being grieved for the hardness of their hearts' (Mark 3:5). And we read of his breaking out in tears and exclamations, thinking about the sin and misery of ungodly men, and at the sight of the city of Jerusalem, which was full of such inhabitants: 'And when he was come near, he beheld the city, and wept over it, saying, If thou hadst known, even thou, at least in this thy day, the things which belong unto thy peace! but now they are hid from thine eyes' (Luke 19:41–2). 'O Jerusalem, Jerusalem, which killest the prophets and stonest them that are sent unto thee: how often would I have gathered thy children together, as a hen doth gather her brood under her wings, and ye would not!' (Luke 13:34). We reads of Christ's earnest *desire*: 'With desire have I desired to eat this passover with you before I suffer' (Luke 22:15). We often read of the affection of *pity* or *compassion* in Christ (Matt. 15:32 and 18:34; Luke 7:13), and of his being *moved with compassion* (Matt. 9:36 and 14:14; Mark 6:34). And how tender did his heart appear to be on the occasion of Mary's and Martha's mourning for their brother, and coming to him with their complaints and tears! Their tears soon drew tears from his eyes; he was affected with their grief, and *wept* with them; though he knew their sorrow would soon be turned into joy by their brother being raised from the dead: see John 11. And how ineffably affectionate was that last and dying discourse which Jesus had with his eleven disciples the evening before he was crucified – when he told them he was going away, and foretold the great difficulties and sufferings they would meet with in the world, when he had gone; and comforted and counselled them, as his dear little children; and bequeathed to them his Holy Spirit, and therein his peace, his comfort and joy, as it were in his last will and testament (John 13–16); and concluded the whole with that affectionate intercessory prayer for them, and his whole church, in chapter 17. Of all the discourses ever penned or uttered by the mouth of any man, this seems to be the most affectionate and affecting.

Hardness of heart and tenderness of heart

I am far from supposing that all affections manifest a tender heart; hatred, anger, vain-glory, and other selfish and self-exalting affections may greatly prevail in the hardest heart. But yet it is evident that *hardness of heart* and *tenderness of heart* are expressions that relate to the affections of the heart, and denote its being susceptible to, or shut up against, certain affections, of which I shall have occasion to speak more afterwards.

Without holy affection, there is no true religion

On the whole, I think it clearly and abundantly evident that true religion lives very much inthe affections. Not that I think that religion in the hearts of the truly godly is ever in exact proportion to the degree of affection and present emotion of the mind: for, undoubtedly, there is much affection in the true saints which is not spiritual; their religious affections are often mixed; all is not from grace, but much from nature. And though the affections do not have their seat in the body, yet the consitution of the body may very much contribute to the present emotion of the mind. The degree of religion is to be estimated by the fixedness and strength of habit exercised in affection, whereby holy affection is habitual, rather than by the degree of the present exercise; and the strength of that habit is not always in proportion to outward effects and manifestations, or indeed inward ones, in the hurry, vehemence, and sudden changes of the course of the thoughts. But yet it is evident that religion consists so much in the affections that without holy affection there is no true religion. No light in the understanding is good if it does not produce holy affection in the heart; no habit or principle in the heart is good if it has no such exercise; and no external fruit is good if it does not proceed from such exercises.

Three conclusions

1. The error of discarding religious affections

From this we may learn how great is the error of those who are for discarding all religious affections as having nothing solid or substantial in them. There seems to be too much of a disposition this way prevailing at this time. Because many who, in the recent extraordinary time, appeared to have great religious affections, did not manifest a right temper of mind, and run into many errors in the heat of their zeal; and because the high affections of many seem to have come to nothing so soon, and some who seemed to be mightily raised and swallowed with joy and zeal for a while seem to have returned like the dog to his vomit – therefore religious affections in general have become discredited with great numbers, as though true religion did not consist in them at all. Thus we easily and naturally run from one extreme to another.

A little while ago we were in the other extreme: there was a prevalent disposition to look upon all high religious affections as eminent exercises of true grace, without much inquiry into the nature and source of those affections, and the manner in which they arose. If people only appeared to be indeed very much moved and raised, so as to be full of religious talk, and express themselves with great warmth and earnestness, and to be *filled*, or to be *very full*, as the phrases were, it was too much the manner, without further examination, to conclude such persons were full of the Spirit of God, and had eminent experience of his gracious influences. This was the extreme which was prevailing three or four years ago. But of late, instead of esteeming and admiring all religious affections, without distinction, it is much more prevalent to reject and discard all without distinction. In this we see the subtlety of Satan. While he saw that affections were much in vogue, knowing the greater part were not versed in such things, and had not had much experience of great religious affections, enabling them to judge well, and to distinguish between true and false, then he knew he could best play his game by sowing tares among the wheat, and mingling false affections with the works of God's Spirit. He knew this to be a likely way to delude and eternally ruin many souls, and entangle them in a dreadful wilderness, and by and by to bring all religion into disrepute.

But now, as the ill consequences of these false affections appear, and it has become very apparent that some of those emotions which made a glaring show, and were greatly admired by many, were in reality nothing, the devil sees it to be for his interest to work another way, and to endeavour to his utmost to propagate and establish a persuasion that all affections and emotions of the mind in religion are not to be regarded at all, but are rather to be avoided, and carefully guarded against, as things of a pernicious tendency. He knows this is the way to bring all religion to a mere lifeless formality, and effectually to shut out the power of godliness and everything spiritual.

For although to true religion there must indeed be something else besides affection, yet true religion consists so much in the affections that there can be no true religion without them. He who has no religious affections is in a state of spiritual death, and is wholly destitute of the powerful, quickening, saving influences of the Spirit of God upon his heart. As there is not true religion where there is nothing else but affection, so there is no true religion where there is no religious affection. As on the one hand there must be light in the understanding, as well as an affected, fervent heart; or where there is heat without light, there can be nothing divine or heavenly in that heart; so, on the other hand, where there is a kind of light without heat, a head stored with notions and speculations with a cold and unaffected heart, there can be nothing divine in that light, that knowledge is no true spiritual knowledge of divine things. If the great things of religion are rightly understood, they will affect the heart. The reason why men are not affected by such infinitely great, important, glorious, and wonderful things as they often hear and read of in the word of God, is undoubtedly because they are blind. If they were not so, it would be impossible, and utterly inconsistent with human nature, that their hearts should be otherwise than strongly impressed and greatly moved by such things.

This manner of slighting all religious affections is the way exceedingly to harden the hearts of men, to encourage them in their stupidity and senselessness, to keep them in a state of spiritual death as long as they live, and bring them at last to death eternal. The prevailing prejudice against religious affections at this day is apparently of awful effect to harden the hearts of sinners, to damp the graces of the saints, to preclude the effect of ordinances, and hold us down in a state of dullness and apathy; and this undoubtedly causes many people greatly to offend God, in entertaining mean and low thoughts of the extraordinary work he has recently done in this land. For people to despise and cry down all religious affections is the way to shut all religion out of their own hearts, and to make thorough work in ruining their souls.

Those who condemn high affection in others are certainly not likely to have high affections themselves. And let it be considered that those who have but little religious affection certainly have little religion. And those who condemn others for the religious affections, and have none themselves, have no religion. There are false affections, and there are true. A man's having much affection does not prove that he has any true religion, but is he has *no* affection it proves that he has no true religion. The right way is not to reject all affections, nor to approve all, but to distinguish between them, approving some and rejecting others; separating between the wheat and the chaff, the gold and the dross, the precious and the vile.

2. *Desire things that move the affections*

If true religion lies much in the affections, we may infer that we are to desire such means as have much tendency to move the affections. Such books, and such a way of preaching the word and the administration of ordinances, and such a way of worshipping God in prayer and praises as has a tendency deeply to affect the hearts of those who attend these means, is much to be desired.

Such kind of means would formerly have been highly approved, and applauded by the generality of people as the most excellent and profitable, and having the greatest tendency to promote the ends of the means of grace. But the prevailing taste seems of late to be strangely altered: that feeling manner of praying and preaching which would formerly have been admired and extolled because it has such a tendency to move the affections, now immediately excites disgust in many people, and moves no other affections than those of displeasure and contempt.

Perhaps, formerly, the generality (at least of the common people) were in the extreme of looking too much to an affectionate address in public performances; but now a very great part of the people seem to have gone far to the opposite extreme. Indeed there *may* be such means as have a great tendency to stir up the passions of weak and ignorant people, and yet have none to benefit their souls; for though they may have a tendency to excite affections, they have little or none to excite *gracious* affections. But, undoubtedly, if the things of religion in the means used are treated according to their nature and exhibited truly, tending to convey just apprehensions and a right judgement of them, then the more they tend to move the affections the better.

3. Be ashamed that we are not more affected

If true religion lies much in the affections, we may learn what great cause we have to be ashamed and confounded before God, that we are no more affected with the great things of religion. It appears from what has been said that this arises from our having so little true religion.

God has given affections to mankind for the same purpose as that for which he has given all the faculties and principles of the human soul, namely that they might be subservient to man's chief end, and the great business for which God has created him, that is, the business of religion. And yet how common it is among mankind that their affections are much more exercised and engaged in other matters than in religion! In matters which concern men's worldly interest, their outward delights, their honour and reputation, and their natural relations, they have their desires eager, their appetites vehement, their love warm and affectionate, their zeal ardent; in these things their hearts and tender and sensitive, easily moved, deeply impressed, much concerned, very perceptibly affected, and greatly engaged; much depressed with grief at worldly losses, and highly raised with joy at worldly successes and prosperity. But how insensitive and unmoved are most men about the great things of another world! How dull are their affections! How heavy and hard their hearts in these matters! Here their love is cold, their desires languid, their zeal low, and their gratitude small. How they can sit and hear of the infinite height and depth and length and breadth of the love of God in Christ Jesus – of his giving his infinitely dear So to be offered up a sacrifice for the sins of men – and of the unparalleled love of the innocent, holy Lamb of God manifested in his dying agonies, his bloody sweat, his loud and bitter cries and bleeding heart – and all this for enemies, to redeem them from deserved, eternal burnings, and to bring to unspeakable and everlasting joy and glory; and yet be cold, heavy, insensitive, and regardless! Where are the exercises of our affections proper, if not here? What is it that more requires them? And what can be a fit occasion of their lively and vigorous exercise, if not such as this? Can anything greater and more important be set in our view? Anything more wonderful and surprising, or that concerns our interest more closely? Can we suppose that the wise Creator implanted such principles in our nature as the affections, to lie still on such an occasion as this? Can any Christian, who believes the truth of these things, entertain such thoughts?

If we ought ever to exercise our affections at all, and if the Creator has not unwisely constituted the human nature in making these principles a part of it, then they ought to be exercised about those objects which are most worthy of them. But is there anything in heaven or earth so worthy to be the objects of our admiration and love, our earnest and longing desires, hope, rejoicing, and fervent zeal, as those things which are held out to us in the gospel of Jesus Christ? There not only are things declared most worthy to affect us, but they are exhibited in the most affecting manner. The glory and beauty of the blessed Jehovah, which is most worthy in itself to be the object of our admiration and love, is there exhibited in the most affecting manner that can be conceived of; as it appears shining in all its lustre, in the face of an incarnate, infinitely loving, meek, compassionate, dying Redeemer. All the virtues of the Lamb of God, his humility, patience, meekness, submission, obedience, love, and compassion, are exhibited to our view in a manner the most tending to move our affections of any that can be imagined; for they all had their greatest trial, their highest exercise, and brightest manifestation, when he was in the most affecting circumstances; even when he was under his last sufferings, those unutterable and unparalleled sufferings which he endured from his tender love and pity to us. There, also, the hateful *nature* of our *sins* is manifested in the most affecting manner possible; as we see the dreadful effects of them, in what our Redeemer, who undertook to answer for us, suffered for them. And there we have the most affecting manifestations of God's *hatred* of sin, and his wrath and justice in punishing it; as we see his justice in the strictness and inflexibleness of it, and his wrath in its terribleness, in so dreadfully punishing our sins, in one who was infinitely dear to him, and loving to us. Thus has God disposed things in the affair of our redemption, and in his glorious dispensations revealed to us in the gospel, as though everything were purposely contrived in such a manner as to have the greatest possible tendency to reach our hearts in the most tender part, and move our affections most perceptibly and strongly. How great cause have we therefore to be humbled to the dust, that we are no more affected!

John Wesley
(1703–91)

English clergyman, travelling preacher and founder of Methodism by his organising of the new believers who had responded to his preaching.

Wesley arrives in Georgia: 1736

Friday 6. About eight in the morning, we first set foot on American ground. It was a small uninhabited island, over against Tybee. Mr Oglethorpe led us to a rising ground, where we all kneeled down to give thanks. He then took boat for Savannah. When the rest of the people had come on shore, we called our little flock together to prayers.

Saturday 7. Mr Oglethorpe returned from Savannah with Mr Spangenberg, one of the pastors of the Germans. I soon found what spirit he was of; and asked his advice with regard to my own conduct. He said, 'My brother, I must first ask you one or two questions. Have you the witness within yourself? Does the Spirit of God bear witness with your spirit, that you are a child of God?' I was surprised, and knew not what to answer. He observed it, and asked, 'Do you know Jesus Christ?' I paused, and said, 'I know he is the saviour of the world.' 'True,' replied he; 'but do you know he has saved you?' He only added, 'Do you know yourself?' I said, 'I do.' But I fear they were vain words.

The Journal of John Wesley, 6th–7th February 1736.

The voyage to England: 1738

Tuesday 24. We spoke with two ships, outward-bound, from

whom we had the welcome news of our being only one hundred and sixty leagues short of Land's End. My mind was now full of thought; part of which I wrote down as follows:

I went to America, to convert the Indians; but oh, who shall convert me? who, what is he that will deliver me from this evil heart of mischief? I have a far summer religion. I can talk well; nay, and believe myself, while no danger is near; but let death look me in the face, and my spirit is troubled. Nor can I say, 'To die is gain!'

> I have a sin of fear, that when I've spun
> My last thread, I shall perish on the shore!

I think, verily, if the gospel be true, I am safe: for I not only have given, and do give, all my good to feed the poor; I not only give my body to be burned, drowned, or whatever God shall appoint for me; but I follow after charity (though not as I ought, yet as I can), if haply I may attain it. I now believe the gospel is true. 'I show my faith by my works,' by staking my all upon it. I would do the same again and again a thousand time, if the choice were still to make.

Whoever sees me, sees I would be a Christian. Therefore 'are my ways not like other men's ways'. There I have been, I am, I am content to be 'a by-word, a proverb of reproach'. But in a storm I think, 'What, if the gospel be not true? Then you are all men most foolish. For what cause have you given up your goods, your ease, your friends, your reputation, your country, your life? For what cause are you wandering over the face of the earth? A dream, a cunningly devised fable!'

Oh, who will deliver me from this fear of death? What shall I do? Where shall I fly from it? Should I fight against it by thinking, or by not thinking of it? A wise man advised me some time ago, 'Be still and go on.' Perhaps this is best, to look upon it as my cross; when it comes, to let it humble me, and quicken all my good resolutions, especially that of praying without ceasing; and at other times, to take no thought about it, but quietly to go on 'in the work of the Lord.'

The Journal of John Wesley, 24th January 1738.

Peter Bohler's advice

I found my brother at Oxford, recovering from his pleurisy; and with him Peter Bohler; by whom, in the hand of the great God, I was, on Sunday 5, clearly convinced of unbelief, of the lack of that faith whereby alone we are saved.

Immediately it struck into my mind: 'Leave off preaching. How can you preach to others, who have not faith yourself?' I asked Bohler whether he thought I should leave it off or not. He answered, 'By no means.' I asked, 'But what can I preach?' He said: 'Preach faith till you have it; and then, because you have it, you will preach faith.'

The Journal of John Wesley, 4th March 1738.

'I felt my heart strangely warmed'

In the evening I went very unwillingly to a society in Aldersgate Street, where someone was reading Luther's preface to the Epistle to the Romans. About a quarter before nine, while he was describing the change which God works in the heart through faith in Christ, I felt my heart strangely warmed. I felt I did trust in Christ, Christ alone, for salvation; and an assurance was given me that he had taken away my sins, even mine, and saved me from the law of sin and death.

I began to pray with all my might for those who had in a more especial manner despitefully used me and persecuted me. I then testified openly to all there that what I now first felt in my heart. But it was not long before the enemy suggested, 'This cannot be faith; for where is your joy?' Then was I taught that peace and victory over sin are essential to faith in the Captain of our salvation; but that, as to the transports of joy that usually attend the beginning of it, especially in those who have mourned deeply, God sometimes gives, sometimes withholds them, according to the counsels of his own will.

After my return home, I was much buffeted with temptations; but cried out, and they fled away. They returned again and again. I as often lifted up my eyes, and he 'sent me help from his holy place'. And I found the difference between this and my former state chiefly consisted in this. I was striving, yes, fighting with all my might under the law, as well as under grace. But then I was sometimes, if not often, conquered; now, I was always conqueror.

Thursday 25. The moment I awoke, 'Jesus, Master' was in my heart and in my mouth; and I found all my strength lay in keeping my eye fixed on him, and my soul waiting on him continually.

The Journal of John Wesley, 24th–25th May 1738.

In London alone I found 652 members of our Society who were exceeding clear in their experience, and whose testimony I could see no reason to doubt. And every one of these, without a single exception, has declared that his deliverance from sin was instantaneous; that the change was wrought in a moment. Had half of these, or one third, or one in twenty, declared it was gradually wrought in them, I should have believed this, with regard to them, and thought that some were gradually sanctified and some instantaneously. But as I have not found, in so long a space of time, a single person speaking thus, I cannot but believe that sanctification is commonly, if not always, an instantaneous work.

Tyerman, *Life of Wesley,* vol. 1, p. 463.

The witness of the Spirit is immediate in the believer

The Spirit beareth witness with our spirits that we are the sons of God (Romans 8:18). This witness is an inward impression on the soul, whereby the Spirit of God directly witnesses to my spirit, that I am a child of God; that Jesus Christ hath loved me: that all my sins are blotted out, and I, even I, am reconciled to God.

Wesley's sermon *The Witness of the Spirit* in *Collected Works,* vol. 1, p. 202.

The Holy Spirit's anointing for evangelism: 'This New Year Pentecost'

Mr Hall, Kinchin, Ingham, Whitefield, Hutchins and my brother Charles, were present at our love-feast in Fetter Lane, with about sixty of our brethren. About three in the morning, as we were continuing in prayer, the power of God came mightily upon us, insomuch that many cried out for exceeding joy, and many fell to the ground. As soon as we were recovered a little from that awe and amazement at the presence of his Majesty, we broke out with one voice, 'We praise thee, O God; we acknowledge thee to be the Lord.'

The Journal of John Wesley, 1st January 1739.

Methodist paroxysms start in London

We were surprised in the evening, when I was expounding in the Minories. A well-dressed, middle-aged woman suddenly cried out as in the agonies of death.

The Journal of John Wesley, 21st January 1739.

Preaching in Bristol

We called upon God to confirm his word. Immediately one that stood by (to our surprise) cried aloud, with the utmost vehemence, even as in the agonies of death. But we continued in prayer, till a new song was put in her mouth. Soon after, two people were seized with strong pain, and constrained to roar for the disquietness of their heart. But it was not long before they likewise burst forth into praise to God their Saviour. The last who called on God as out of the belly of hell was I.E., a stranger to Bristol. And in a short space he also was overwhelmed with joy and love.

The Journal of John Wesley, 17th April 1739.

Bristol first witnessed large numbers of people shrieking etc.

Shriekings, Roarings, Groanings, Gnashings, Yellings, Cursings, Blasphemies and Despairings . . .

George Lavington, *The Enthusiasm of Methodists and Papists Compared* (1749), vol. 2, p. 152.

They dropped on every side as thunderstruck

[During Wesley's sermon at Newgate, Bristol] One, and another, and another sunk to the earth; they dropped on every side as thunderstruck.

The Journal of John Wesley, 26th April 1739.

Talking with Whitefield about outward signs

I had an opportunity to talk with Whitefield about those outward signs which had so often accompanied the inward work of God. I found his objections were chiefly grounded on gross misrepresentations of matter of fact. But the next day he had an opportunity of informing himself better: for no sooner had he begun (in the application of his sermon) to invite all sinners to believe in Christ, than four people sank down, close to him, almost in the same moment.

The Journal of John Wesley, 7th July 1739.

'I think Satan is let loose'

I was sent for to Kingswood again, to one of those who had been so ill before. A violent rain began just as I set out, so that I was thoroughly wet in a few minutes. Just at that time the woman (then three miles off) cried out, 'Yonder comes Wesley, galloping as fast as he can.'

'She is mine; her soul is mine'

When I was come, I was quite cold and dead, and fitter for sleep than prayer. She burst out into a horrid laughter, and said, 'No power, no power; no faith, no faith. She is mine; her soul is mine. I have her, and will not let her go.'

We begged of God to increase our faith. Meanwhile her pangs increased more and more; so that one would have imagined, by the violence of the throes, her body must have been shattered to pieces. One who was clearly convinced this was not natural disorder, said, 'I think Satan is let loose. I fear he will not stop here.' And added, 'I command you, in the name of the Lord Jesus, to tell if you have commission to torment any other soul.' It was immediately answered, 'I have. L.C. and S.J.' (two who lived at some distance, and were then in perfect health).

We betook ourselves to prayer again; and ceased not till she began, about six o'clock, with a clear voice and composed, cheerful look: 'Praise God, from whom all blessings flow.'

Sunday 28: Returning in the evening, I called at Mrs J.'s in Kingswood. S.J. and L.C. were there. It was scarcely a quarter of an hour before L.C. fell into a strange agony; and presently after, S.J. The violent convulsions all over their bodies were too horrid to be borne, till one of them, in a tone not to be expressed, said: 'Where is your faith now? Come, go to prayers. I will pray with you. "Our Father, which art in heaven."' We took the advice, from whomsoever it came, and poured out our souls before God, till L.C.'s agonies so increased, that it seemed she was in the pangs of death. But in a moment God spoke: she knew his voice; and both her body and soul were healed.

'I burn! I burn! O what shall I do?'

We continued to pray till near one, when S.J.'s voice was also changed, and she began strongly to call upon God. This she did for the greatest part of the night. In the morning we renewed our prayers, while she was crying continually, 'I burn! I burn! O what shall I do? I have a fire within me. I cannot bear it. Lord Jesus! Help!' – Amen, Lord Jesus! when your time comes.

The Journal of John Wesley, 27th–28th October 1739.

A spirit of laughter

I was a little surprised by some, who were buffeted of Satan in an unusual manner, by such a spirit of laughter as they could in no way resist.

The Journal of John Wesley, 9th May 1740.

Hysteria or a spirit of laughter?

They laughed whether they would or no, almost without ceasing. Thus they continued, a spectacle to all, for two days; and were then, upon a prayer made for them, delivered in a moment.

The Journal of John Wesley, 23rd May 1740.

Shaking

Great indeed was the shaking among them; lamentation and great mourning were heard.

The Journal of John Wesley, 11th June 1742.

Exorcism by prayer and fasting

I was with a gentlewoman whose distemper has puzzled the most eminent physicians for many years; it being such as they could neither give any rational account of, nor find any remedy for. The plain case is, she is tormented by an evil spirit, following her day and night. Yea, try all your drugs over and over; but at length it will plainly appear that this kind goeth not out but by prayer and fasting.

The Journal of John Wesley, 10th July 1742.

Groaned and trembled

Men, women and children wept and groaned and trembled exceedingly; many cried with a loud and bitter cry.

The Journal of John Wesley, 17th November 1743.

Wesley's view of the Montanists

After reading an old book, *The General Delusion of Christians with Regard to Prophecy*, I was fully convinced of what I had once suspected:

1. That the Montanists, in the second and third centuries, were real, scriptural Christians.

2. That the grand reason why the miraculous gifts were so soon withdrawn, was not only that faith and holiness were well nigh lost, but that dry, formal, orthodox men began even then to ridicule whatever gifts they had not themselves, and to decry them all as either madness or imposture.

The Journal of John Wesley, 15th August 1750.

A remarkable premonition fulfilled

I rode to Tullamore; where one of the Society, Edward Willis, gave me a very surprising account of himself. He said:

'When I was about twenty years old, I went to Waterford for business. After a few weeks I resolved to leave it; and packed up my things, in order to set out the next morning. This was Sunday; but my landlord pressed me much not to go till the next day. In the afternoon we walked out together, and went into the river. After a while, leaving him near the shore, I struck out into the deep. I soon heard a cry, and, turning, saw him rising and sinking in the channel of the river. I swam back with all speed, and, seeing him sink again, dived down after him. When I was near the bottom, he clasped his arm round my neck, and held me so fast that I could not rise.

'Seeing death before me, all my sins came into my mind, and I faintly called for mercy. In a while my sense went away, and I thought I as in a place full of light and glory, with abundance of people. While I was thus, he who held me died, and I floated up to the top of the water. I then immediately came to myself, and swam to the shore, where several stood who had seen us sink, and said they never knew such a deliverance before; for I had been under the water full twenty minutes. It make me more serious for two or three months. Then I returned to all my sins.

'But in the midst of all, I had a voice following me everywhere, "When an able minister of the gospel comes, it will be well with you!" Some years after I entered into the army: our troop lay at Phillipstown, when Mr W. came. I was much affected by his preaching; but not so as to leave my sins. The voice followed me still, and when Mr J. W. came, before I saw him I had an unspeakable conviction that he was the man I looked for: and soon after I found peace with God, and it was well with me indeed.'

The Journal of John Wesley, 28th April 1756.

John Berridge, minister in the Everton parish

The windows being filled within and without, and even the outside of the pulpit to the very top; so that Mr. Berridge seemed almost stifled by their breath. The text was, 'Having a form of godliness, but denying the power thereof.' When the power of religion began to be spoken of, the presence of God really filled the place. And while poor sinners felt the sentence of death in their souls, what sounds of distress did I hear!

Level-headed John Berridge preaches in agricultural East Anglia

Great numbers, feeling the arrows of conviction, fell on the ground, some of whom seemed dead, and others in the agony of death, the violence of their bodily convulsions exceeding all description.

Selina, Countess of Huntingdon, *Life and Times* (1839), vol. 1, p. 398, note.

Others fell down as dead

The greatest number of them who cried or fell were men; but some women, and several children, felt the power of the same almighty Spirit, and seemed just sinking into hell.

Great numbers wept without any noise; others fell down as dead; some sinking in silence, some with extreme noise and violent agitation.

[Berridge held another meeting for seekers who squeezed into his vicarage.] And now did I see such a sight as I do not expect again on this side of eternity. The faces of all the believers present did really shine; and such a beauty, such a look of extreme happiness, and at the same time of Divine love and simplicity did I never see in human faces until now.

The Journal of John Wesley, 20th May 1759.

Extraordinary trances at Everton

I talked at length with Ann Thorn and two others, who had been several times in trances. What they all agreed on was:

1. That when they went away, as they termed it, it was always at the time they were fullest of the love of God.

2. That it came upon them in a moment, without any previous notice, and took away all their senses and strength.

3. That there were some exceptions, but in general, from that moment, they were in another world, knowing nothing of what was done or said by all that were round about them.

About five in the afternoon I heard them singing hymns. Soon after, Mr B. came up, and told me Alice Miller (fifteen years old) had fallen into a trance. I went down immediately, and found her sitting on a stool, and leaning against the wall, with her eyes open and fixed upwards. I made motion as if going to strike, but they continued immovable. Her face showed an unspeakable mixture of reverence and love, while silent tears stole down her but not enough to cause any sound.

I do not know whether I ever saw a human face look so beautiful; sometimes it was covered with a smile, as from joy, mixing with love and reverence; but the tears fell still though not so fast. Her pulse was quite regular. In about half an hour I observed her countenance change into the form of fear, pity, and distress; then she burst into a flood of tears, and cried out, 'Dear Lord; they will be damned! They will all be damned!' But in about five minutes her smiles returned, and only love and joy appeared in her face.

About half an hour after six, I observed distress take place again; and soon after she wept bitterly and cried out, 'Dear Lord, they will go to hell! The world will go to hell!' Soon after, she said, 'Cry aloud! Spare not!' And in a few moments her look was composed again, and spoke a mixture of reverence, joy, and love. Then she said aloud, 'Give God the glory.'

About seven her senses returned. I asked, 'Where have you been?'

'I have been with my saviour.'

'In heaven, or on earth?'

'I cannot tell; but I was in glory.'

'Why then did you cry?'

'Not for myself, but for the world; for I saw they were on the brink of hell.'

'Whom did you desire to give the glory to God?'

'Ministers that cry aloud to the world: else they will be proud; and then God will leave them, and they will lose their own souls.'

The Journal of John Wesley, 6th July 1759.

Wesley knelt there, shaken with sobs

[Writing about himself, Wesley records in his Journal:] I shook from head to foot, while tears of joy ran down my face. . . . I no sooner kneeled by him than the consolations of God came upon me, so that I trembled and wept much . . . I no sooner sat down by her than the Spirit of God poured the same blessedness into my soul.

. . . J.D. was kneeling when the fit came. We laid him on the ground, where he soon became as stiff as last night, and prayed in like manner. Afterwards his body grew flexible by degrees, but was convulsed from head to foot. . . . God had broken down seventeen people last week by the singing of hymns only. . . . It seemed as if the Lord came upon him mightily, taking him by the neck and shaking all his bones in pieces.

The Journal of John Wesley, 29th July 1759.

Examples of Wesley following 'unaccountable impulses'

[I received] directions from God in an affair of the greatest importance.

[On visiting a Quaker family] I was led, I know not how, to speak to them largely, then to pray.

The Journal of John Wesley, 24th March 1785; 26th December 1762.

Revival in Bristol: like a rushing mighty wind

God broke in on our boys in a surprising manner, like a rushing mighty wind, which made them cry aloud for mercy. Last night, I hope, will never be forgotten, when about twenty were in the utmost distress. While I am writing,k the cries of the boys, from their several apartments, are sounding in my ears. Their age is from eight to fourteen. There are but few who withstand the work.

The Journal of John Wesley, 27th April 1768.

An indignant Quaker

A Quaker, who stood by, was not a little displeased at the dissimulation of these creatures and was biting his lips and knitting his brows, when he dropped down as thunderstruck. The agony he was in was even terrible to behold. We besought God not to lay folly to his charge. And he soon lifted up his head and cried aloud: 'Now I know thou art a prophet of the Lord!'

The Journal of John Wesley, 1st May 1769.

One of Wesley's opponents

[John Haydon witnessed the above event, recorded in Wesley's Journal for 1st May 1769, and then spoke against Wesley and the danger of his meetings. Wesley records the following incident in a letter to his brother, Samuel dated 10th May 1769.]

A bystander, one John Haydon, was quite enraged at this, and, being unable to deny something supernatural in it, laboured beyond all measure to convince all his acquaintance, that it was a delusion of the devil.

I was met in the street the next day by one who informed me that John Haydon was fallen raving mad. It seems he had sat down to dinner, but wanted first to make an end to a sermon he was reading. At the last page he suddenly changed colour, fell off his chair, and began screaming terribly, beating himself against the ground.

I found him on the floor, the room being full of people, whom his wife would have kept away; but he cried out, 'No; let them all come; let all the world see the judgement of God.'

Two or three were holding him as well as they could. He immediately fixed his eyes on me, and said, 'Aye, this is he I said deceived the people; but God hath overtaken me. I said it was a delusion of the devil; but this is no delusion.'

Then he roared aloud, 'O thou devil! Thou cursed devil! Yes, thou legion of devils! Thou canst not stay in me. Christ will cast thee out. I know his work is begun. Tear me to pieces if thou wilt. But thou canst not hurt me.'

He then beat himself again, and groaned again, with violent sweats, and heaving of the breast. We prayed with him, and God put a new song in his mouth. The words were, which he pronounced with a clear, strong voice, 'This is the Lord's doing, and it is marvellous in our eyes. This is the day which the Lord hath made: We will rejoice and be glad in it. Blessed be the Lord God of Israel, from this time forth for evermore.'

The Works of John Wesley (Peabody (Mass.): Hendrickson, 1872), vol. 1, pp. 234–6.

Four young men remained on their knees for five hours

On Sunday afternoon, December 1, as William Hunter was preaching, the power of God fell on the congregation in a wonderful manner. Many being cut to the heart, cried aloud for mercy.

On [the following] Saturday night we met at six, and three of us sang and prayed. But before the third was done, his voice could not be heard for the cries of the people. Seven of these soon arose, praising and blessing God.

We had nothing to do, but to stand and see the wonderful work of God. And ho how dreadful, yet pleasing, was the sight. All this time many were crying for mercy. Among these were four young men who remained on their knees five hours together.

One was asked, what he thought of this. He answered, I wish it be all real. He then turned to go home; but, after taking a few steps, began to cry aloud for mercy. He cried till his strength was quite gone, and then lay as one dead till about four o'clock in the morning.

At our meeting on Tuesday, eleven more were filled with the peace of God. Yet one young man seemed quite unconcerned. But suddenly the power of God fell upon him; he cried for two hours with all his might. On Saturday evening God was present through the whole service, but especially towards the conclusion. Then one and another dropped down, till six lay on the ground together roaring.

Four young men came out of curiosity. That evening six were wounded. One of them, hearing the cry, rushed through the crowd to see what was the matter. He was no sooner got to the place, than he dropped down himself, and cried as loud as any. The other three, pressing on, one after another, were struck in just the same manner. And indeed all of them were in such agonies, that many feared they were struck with death. Edward Farles was struck to the ground, so distressed that he was convulsed all over.

The Journal of John Wesley, 4th June 1772.

A plea for spiritual consolations to be allowed

[From one of Wesley's sermons:] . . . A delicate device of Satan to destroy the whole religion of the heart; the telling them not to regard frames or feelings, but to live by naked faith; that is, in plain terms, not to regard either love, joy, peace, or any other fruit of the Spirit; not to regard whether they feel these or the reverse, whether their souls be in a heavenly or hellish frame.

The Journal of John Wesley, 1st May 1775.

The existence of witchcraft

I cannot give up to all the Deists in Great Britain the existence of witchcraft, till I give up the credit of all history, sacred and profane. And at the present time I have not only as strong but stronger proofs of this, from eye and ear witnesses, than I have of murder; so that I cannot rationally doubt of one any more than the other.

The Journal of John Wesley, 23rd May 1776.

Wesley's sermon, assessing the Awakening, at the opening of the City Road Chapel, London

The Awakening's extent
This revival of religion has spread to such a degree as neither we nor our fathers had known. How extensive has it been! There is scarce a considerable town in the kingdom where some have not been made witnesses of it. It has spread to every age and sex, to most orders and degrees of men; and even to abundance of those who, in time past, were accounted monsters of wickedness.

The Awakening's speed of expansion
Consider the swiftness as well as extent of it. In what age has such a number of sinners been recovered from the error of their ways? When has true religion, I will not say since the Reformation, but since the time of Constantine the Great, made so large a progress in any nation, within so small a space? I believe hardly can either ancient or modern history afford a parallel instance.

The Awakening's depth
We may likewise observe the depth of the work so extensively and swiftly wrought. Multitudes have been thoroughly convinced of sin; and, shortly after, so filled with joy and love, that whether they were in the body or out of the body, they could hardly tell; and in the power of this love they have trampled under foot whatever the world accounts either terrible or desirable, having evidenced, in their severest trails, an invariable and tender goodwill to mankind, and all the fruits of holiness. Now so deep a repentance, so strong a faith, so fervent a love, and so unblemished holiness, wrought in so many persons in so short a time, the world has not seen for many ages.

The Journal of John Wesley, 1st Janùary 1778.

Chapel-en-le-Frith: bringing the real work into contempt

Frequently three or four, yes, ten or twelve, pray aloud all together. Some of them, perhaps many, scream all together as

loud as they possibly can. Some of them use improper, yes, indecent expressions in prayer. Several drop down as dead, and are
as stiff as a corpse; but in a while they start up and cry, Glory,
glory, perhaps twenty times together. Just so do the French
prophets, and very lately the Jumpers in Wales, bringing the real
work into contempt. Yet whenever we reprove them, it should be
in the most mild and gentle manner possible.

The Journal of John Wesley, 3rd April 1786.

Bristol 1788: the strangest incident of the kind I ever remember

About the middle of the discourse, when there was on every side
attention still as night, a vehement noise arose, none could tell
whence, and shot like lightning through the whole congregation.
The terror and confusion was inexpressible. You might have
imagined it was a city taken by storm. The people rushed upon
each other with the utmost violence, the benches were broken in
pieces, and nine tenths of the congregation appeared to be struck
with the same panic. In about six minutes the storm ceases.

It is the strangest incident of the kind I ever remember, and I
believe none can account for it without supposing some supernatural influence. Satan fought, lest his kingdom should be
delivered up.

The Journal of John Wesley, 3rd March 1788.

John Wesley: *Thoughts on Christian Perfection*

At the Conference in 1759, perceiving some danger that a diversity of thinking should imperceptibly take a hold on us, we again
considered this doctrine in detail. Soon after this I published
Thoughts on Christian Perfection, prefaced with the following adver-
tisement:

The following tract is by no means designed to gratify the curiosity
of any man. It is not intended to prove the doctrine at large, in
opposition to those who explode and ridicule it; no, nor to answer

the numerous objections against it, which may be raised even by serious men. All I intend here is simply to declare what are my sentiments on the main point; what Christian Perfection does, according to my apprehension, include, and what it does not; and to add a few practical observations and directions relative to the subject.

As these thoughts were at first thrown together by way of question and answer, I let them continue in the same form. They are just the same that I have entertained for above twenty years.

QUESTION   What is Christian Perfection?
ANSWER   The loving God with all our heart, mind, soul, and strength. This implies, that no wrong frame of mind, nothing contrary to love, remains in the soul; and that all the thoughts, words and actions, are governed by pure love.
Q   Do you affirm that this perfection excludes all infirmities, ignorance and mistakes?
A   I continually affirm quite the opposite, and have always done so.
Q   But how can every thought, word and work, be governed by pure love, and the man be subject at the same time to ignorance and mistake?
A   I see no contradiction here: 'A man may be filled with pure love, and still be liable to mistake.' Indeed I do not expect to be freed from actual mistakes till this mortal puts on immortality. I believe this to be a natural consequence of the soul's dwelling in flesh and blood. For we cannot now think at all, but by the mediation of those bodily organs which have suffered equally with the rest of our frame. And hence we cannot avoid sometimes thinking wrong, till this corruptible shall have put on incorruption.
Q   If people live without sin, does not this exclude the necessity of a Mediator?
A   Firstly, not only sin, properly so called (that is, a voluntary transgression of a known law), but sin, incorrectly so called (that is, an involuntary transgression of a divine law, known or unknown), needs the atoning blood.
Secondly, I believe there is no such perfection in this life as

excludes these involuntary transgressions which I apprehend to be naturally consequent on the ignorance and mistakes inseparable from mortality.

Thirdly, therefore, 'sinless perfection' is a phrase I never use, lest I should seem to contradict myself.

Fourthly, I believe a person filled with love of God is still liable to these involuntary transgressions.

Fifthly, such transgressions you may call sins, if you please: I do not, for these reasons above-mentioned.

Q   How shall we avoid setting perfection too high or too low?
A   By keeping to the Bible, and setting it just as high as the scripture does. It is nothing higher and nothing lower than this – the pure love of God and man; the loving of God with all our heart and soul, and our neighbour as ourselves. It is love governing the heart and life, running through our whole mentality, words, and actions.

Q   Is it proof that a person is not perfect if he is surprised or thrown into confusion by a noise, a fall, or some sudden danger?
A   It is not; for one may jump, tremble, change colour, or be otherwise disordered in body, while the soul is calmly stayed on God, and remains in perfect peace.

Q   Is death to sin, and renewal in love, gradual or instantaneous?
A   A man may be dying for some time; yet he does not, properly speaking, die till the instant the soul is separated from the body; and in that instant he lives the life of eternity. In the same way he may be dying to sin for some time; yet he is not dead to sin, till sin is separated from his soul; and in that instant he lives the full life of love.

A Plain Man's Guide to Christian Holiness, ed. H. C. Backhouse (London: Hodder and Stoughton, 1988), pp. 55–61.

Brief Thoughts on Christian Perfection

1   By perfection I mean the humble, gentle, patient love of God and our neighbour, ruling our minds, words and actions.

I do not include an impossibility of falling from it, either in part or in whole. Therefore, I retract several expressions in our hymns, which partly express, partly imply, such an impossibility.

And I do not contend for the terms 'sinless', though I do not object against it.

2   As to the manner, I believe this perfection is always wrought in the soul by a simple act of faith, consequently, in an instant. But I believe a gradual work, both preceding and following that instant.

3   As to the time, I believe this instant generally is the instant of death, the moment before the soul leaves the body. But I believe it may be ten, twenty, or forty years before.

I believe it is usually many years after justification, but that it may be within five years or five months after it. I know no conclusive argument to the contrary.

A Plain Man's Guide to Christian Holiness, ed. H. C. Backhouse (London: Hodder and Stoughton, 1988), p. 122.

Advice to those caught up in spiritual renewal

Beware of that daughter of pride, enthusiasm. Oh, keep at the utmost distance from it! You are in danger of enthusiasm every hour, if you depart ever from scripture; yea, or from the plain, literal meaning of any text, taken in connection with the context; and so you are, if you despise, or lightly esteem, reason, knowledge, or human learning; every one of which is an excellent gift of God, and may serve the noblest purposes.

A Plain Man's Guide to Christian Holiness, ed. H. C. Backhouse (London: Hodder and Stoughton, 1988), p. 88.

'Have you received this or that blessing?'

Another ground of these, and a thousand mistakes is the not considering deeply that love is the highest gift of God – humble, gentle, patient love; that all visions, revelations, manifestations whatever, are little things compared to love; and that all the gifts above mentioned are either the same with it or infinitely inferior to it.

It were well you should be thoroughly sensible of this – the heaven of heavens is love. There is nothing higher in religion – there is, in effect, nothing else; if you look for anything but more love, you are looking wide of the mark, you are getting out of the royal way. And when you are asking others, 'Have you received this or that blessing?' if you mean anything but more love, you mean wrong; you are leading them out of the way, and putting them upon a false scent. Settle it in your heart, that you are to aim at nothing more, but more of that loved described in the thirteenth of Corinthians. You can go no higher than this till you are carried into Abraham's bosom.

A Plain Man's Guide to Christian Holiness, ed. H. C. Backhouse (London: Hodder and Stoughton, 1988), p. 94.

Distinguishing between imagination and visions from God

In 1762, God's work greatly increased in London. Many, who had until then cared nothing for these things, were deeply convinced about their lost condition; many found redemption in the blood of Christ; not a few backsliders were healed; and a considerable number of people believed that God had saved them from all sin. Because it was easy to predict that Satan would try to sow tares among the wheat, I took great pains to warn them of the danger, particularly about pride and enthusiasm. And while I stayed in town, I had reason to hope they continued both humble and sober-minded.

But almost as soon as I was gone enthusiasm broke in. Two or three began to substitute their own imaginations for visions from God, and from there to suppose they should never die; and these, working hard to bring others into the same opinion, brought about much noise and confusion. Soon after, the same people, with a few others, fell into more extreme ideas; claiming that they could not be tempted; that they could feel no more pain; and that they had the gift of prophecy, and of distinguishing between spirits. On my return to London in the autumn, some of them stood reproved; but others had risen above instruction.

A Plain Man's Guide to Christian Holiness, ed. H. C. Backhouse (London: Hodder and Stoughton, 1988), p. 71.

Satan sows tares, especially on any remarkable outpouring of his Spirit

At about this time (1762), a friend who lived some distance from London wrote me the following letter: ·

'Be not over alarmed that Satan sows tares among the wheat of Christ. It ever has been so, especially on any remarkable outpouring of his Spirit; and ever will be so, till Satan is chained up for a thousand years. Till then he will always ape, and endeavour to counteract, the work of the Spirit of Christ. One melancholy effect of this has been that a world, who is always asleep in the arms of the evil one, has ridiculed every work of the Holy Spirit.

'But what can real Christians do? Why, if they would act worthily of themselves, they should,

'1   Pray that every deluded soul may be delivered;

'2   endeavour to reclaim them in the spirit of meekness; and,

'3   lastly, take the utmost care, both by prayer and watchfulness, that the delusion of others may not lessen their zeal in seeking after that universal holiness of soul, body and spirit, 'without which no man will see the Lord.'

Indeed this complete new creature is mere madness to a mad world. But it is, notwithstanding, the will and wisdom of God. May we all seek after it!

But some who maintain this doctrine in its full extent are too often guilty of limiting the Almighty. He dispenses his gifts just as he pleases; therefore, it is neither wise nor modest to affirm that a person must be a believer for any length of time before he is capable of receiving a high degree of the Spirit of holiness.

God's usual method is one thing, but his sovereign pleasure in another. He has wise reasons both for hastening and retarding his work. Sometimes he comes suddenly, and unexpected; sometimes not till we have long looked for him.

Indeed it has been my opinion for many years, that one great cause why men make so little improvement in the divine life is their own coldness, negligence and unbelief. And yet I here speak of believers.

Many the Spirit of Christ give us a right judgment in all things, and 'fill us with all the fullness of God' (see Eph. 3:10); that so we may be 'mature and complete, not lacking anything' ['perfect and entire, wanting nothing'] (Jas 1:4 [AV]).

A Plain Man's Guide to Christian Holiness, ed. H. C. Backhouse (London: Hodder and Stoughton, 1988), pp. 72–3.

You will be sanctified in a moment

A gradual work of grace constantly precedes the instantaneous work both of justification and sanctification, but the work itself is undoubtedly instantaneous . . . after a gradually increasing conviction of inbred sin you will be sanctified in a moment.'

The Letters of Rev. John Wesley, 21st June, 1784

James Robe
(1688–1753))

Minister in the Scottish parish of Kilsyth during the 1742 revival.

Signs of revival appear on 16th May 1742

While pressing all the unregenerate to seek to have Christ formed within them, an extraordinary power of the Divine Spirit accompanied the word preached. There was great mourning in the congregation, as for an only son. Many cried out, and these not only women, but some strong and stout-hearted young men.

Cries . . . groans . . . weeping

After the congregation was dismissed, an attempt was made to get the distressed into my barn, but their number being so great this was impossible, and I was obliged to convene them in the kirk. I sung a psalm and prayed with them, but when I essayed to speak to them I could not be heard, so great were their bitter cries, groans and the voice of their weeping. After this I requested that they might come into my closet one by one. I sent for the Rev. Mr

John Oughterson, minister of Cumbernauld, who immediately came to assist me in dealing with the distressed. In the meantime, I appointed psalms to be sung with those in the kirk, and that the precentor and two or three of the elders should pray with them.

Narrative of the Revival of Religion at Kilsyth, pp. 31–32; quoted in A. Skevington Wood, *The Inextinguishable Blaze* (Paternoster, 1960), pp. 123–4.

John Cennick
(1718–55)

John Cennick became Wesley's first lay preacher.

A wonderful revival began all the more gladdening because here also [in Wiltshire], as in Yorkshire, gross spiritual darkness had hitherto prevailed; ignorance and superstition, almost heathenish in its character, abounded; the gospel was but rarely preached, so that its proclamation came to the people as something new and refreshing. Speedily it proved its divine power; it exercised everywhere its old attractive influence. Curiosity gave place to thought; indifference was changed to conviction of sin. The dry bones were stirred, they came together 'an exceeding great army'; the Spirit of God entered into them, and behold! they lived.

E. R. Hasse, *The Moravians* (London, 1911), p. 79.

Thomas Walsh

One of Wesley's preachers.

Walsh's diary entry: 8th March 1750

This morning the Lord gave me a language I knew not of, raising my soul to Him in a wondrous manner.

Quoted by Michael Harper, *As At the Beginning* (London: Hodder & Stoughton), p. 21.

Charles Wesley
(1707–88)

English clergyman, writer of many famous hymns; brother of John Wesley.

Break my heart

> Break my heart
> Bleeding love – I long to feel it!
>   Let the smart Break my heart;
> Break my heart and heal it.

J. R. Tyson, *Charles Wesley on Sanctification* (Grand Rapids, 1986), p. 131.

Pentecost: a taste of heaven

> O might we each receive the grace
> By Thee to call the Saviour mine!
> Come, Holy Ghost, to all our race,
> Bring in the righteousness divine,
> Inspire the sense of sin forgiven,
> And give our earth a taste of heaven.

I will heal their backsliding. Hosea 14:4

> How am I healed, if still again
> I must relapse with grief and pain
>   Into my old disease?
> If Christ, with all His power and love,
> Can never perfectly remove
>   My desperate wickedness?

> But, Lord, I trust, Thy gracious skill
> Shall throughly my backslidings heal,
>   My sinfulness of soul,
> Destroy the bent to sin in me,
> Cure my original malady,
>   And make, and keep me whole.

George Whitefield
(1714–70)

English clergyman who attracted huge crowds to his open-air preaching in both Britain and America.

Whitefield's conversion

God was pleased to remove the heavy load, to enable me to lay hold of his dear Son by a living faith, and by giving me the spirit of adoption, to seal me, even to the day of everlasting redemption. O! With what joy – joy unspeakable – even joy that was full of and big with glory, was my soul filled, when the weight of sin went off, and an abiding sense of the pardoning love of God broke in upon my disconsolate soul!

Surely it was a day to be had in everlasting remembrance! My joys were like a spring tide, and overflowed the banks.

Arnold A. Dallimore, *George Whitefield* (Edinburgh: Banner of Truth, 1980), p. 21.

Whitefield and the Quakers

Dined with many Quakers at Frenchay, who entertained me and my friends with much Christian love. I think their ideas about walking and being led by the Spirit are right and good.

The Journals of George Whitefield, 23rd March 1739.

White gutters made by the tears of the Kingswood colliers

[Whitefield's hearers were so affected by what they heard that] the white gutters made by their tears, which plentifully fell down their black cheeks as they came out of their coal pits.

J. Gillies, *Memoirs of the Life of George Whitefield*, pp. 37–8.

The Holy Spirit's gifts and graces

Preached, after earnest and frequent invitation, at Hackney, in a field belonging to one Mr Rudge, to about ten thousand people. I insisted much upon the reasonableness of the doctrine of the new birth, and the necessity of our receiving the Holy Spirit in his sanctifying gifts and graces, as well now as formerly. God was pleased to impress it most deeply upon the hearers. Great numbers were in tears, and I could not help exposing the impiety of those letter-learned teachers who say we are not now to receive the Holy Spirit, and who count the doctrine of the new birth as 'enthusiasm'. Out of your own mouths will I condemn you. Did you not, at the time of ordination, tell the bishop that you were inwardly moved by the Holy Spirit to take upon you the administration of the church? Surely at that time you acted the crime of Ananias and Sapphira over again. You lied, not to man, but to God.

The Journals of George Whitefield, 28th May 1739.

'I have experienced some blessed teachings of his Holy Spirit'

[On board the *Elizabeth,* bound from England to Philadelphia.] The power of writing has been in a great measure taken from me, but God has been with me in reading, expounding, and other exercises of devotion. I have experienced some blessed teachings of his Holy Spirit, in convicting me of the pride, sensuality and blindness of my own heart, and of the advantages Satan has gained over me by working on them. I have also been more enlightened to see into the mystery of godliness, God manifest in the flesh, and behold more and more of God's goodness, in letting me have this time of retirement to search my spirit. I would not have lost this voyage for a thousand worlds; it has been sweet and profitable to my soul. Lord I want to know myself and you. Oh let not the hurry of business, which awaits me on shore, prevent my hearing the still small voice of your Holy Spirit.

The Journals of George Whitefield, 9th October 1739.

Daniel Rowlands
(1713–90)

A revival preacher in Wales

Letters written to Whitefield about Daniel Rowlands

While one is praying, another is laughing; some howl and beat their hands together; others are weeping and groaning; and others are grovelling on the ground in a swoon, making various kinds of antic postures; then they laugh out all at once, and continue laughing for about a quarter of an hour.

The power that continues with Brother Rowlands is uncommon. Such crying out and heart-breaking groans, silent weeping and holy joy and shouts of rejoicing, I never saw. 'Tis very common when he preaches for scores to fall down by the power of the Word, pierced or wounded or overcome by the love of God, and sights of beauty and excellency of Jesus.

. . . It is not only by means of outward manifestations, such as shouting, jumping, laughing, that I conclude that God is in the Church and visiting his people. They are zealous, not for secondary matters of faith, but for the essential issues of salvation.

Eifon Evans, *Daniel Rowlands and the Great Evangelical Awakening in Wales* (Edinburgh: Banner of Truth, 1985), pp. 158, 217, 321.

New York: 'God's Spirit came upon the preacher and the people'

Preached this morning from a scaffold erected for that purpose, to a somewhat less congregation than last night, but with much greater power; for towards the conclusion of my talk God's Spirit came upon the preacher and the people, so that they were melted down exceedingly.

The Journals of George Whitefield, 30th April 1740.

Philadelphia: 'A wonderful power was in the room'

Though God has shown me great things already in this place, yet today I have seen greater. I preached twice, and to larger congregations than ever. In the evening I went to settle a Society of young women who, I hope, will prove wise virgins. As soon as I entered the room and heard them singing, my soul was delighted. When the hymn was over I desired to pray before I began to converse; but my soul was so carried out that I had not time to talk at all. A wonderful power was in the room, and with one accord they began to cry out and weep most bitterly for half an hour. They seemed to be under the strongest convictions, and did indeed seek Jesus sorrowing. Their cries might be heard a great way off. When I had done, I thought it right to leave them at their devotions.

'Seemed affected as those who were in fits'

They continued in prayer for over an hour, confessing their most secret faults; and at length the agonies of some were so strong that five of them seemed affected as those who were in fits. The present captain of our sloop going near the waterside was called in to a group almost in the same circumstances, and at midnight I was desired to come to one who was in strong agonies of body and mind but felt something of joy and peace, after I had prayed with her several times. Her case reminded me of the young man whom the devil tore when he was coming to Jesus. Such-like bodily agonies, I believe, are from the devil; and now the work of God is going on he will, no doubt, endeavour by these to bring an evil report upon it. O Lord, for your mercy's sake rebuke him; and though he may be permitted to bite your people's heel, fulfil your promise and let the seed of the woman bruise his head! Amen, Amen!

The Journals of George Whitefield, 10th May 1740.

Nottingham (USA): 'Such demonstration of the Spirit as few saw before'

Preached at Nottingham, both morning and evening, with such demonstration of the Spirit and such a wonderful movement among the hearers as few ever saw before. It surprised me to see such a multitude gathered together at so short a notice, and in such a desert place. I believe there were about twelve thousand. I had not spoken long before I perceived numbers melting. As I proceeded, the influence increased till at last (both in the morning and the afternoon) thousands cried out, so that they almost drowned my voice. Never did I see a more glorious sight. Oh what tears were shed and poured out after the Lord Jesus. Some fainted; and when they had got a little strength they would hear and faint again. Others cried out in a manner as if they were in the sharpest agonies of death. Oh what thoughts and words did God put into my heart!

The Journals of George Whitefield, 14th May 1740.

Whitefield and the 1740 Awakening

Whitefield was the greatest single factor in the Awakening of 1740. He zealously carried the work up and down the colonies from New England to Georgia. Among the revivalists, his influence alone touched every section of the country and every denomination. Everywhere he supplemented and augmented the work with his wonderful eloquence. He literally preached to thousands as he passed from place to place. He was the one preacher to whom people everywhere listened — the great undying agency in the Awakening, the great moulding force among the denominations.

Wesley M. Gewehr, *The Great Awakening in Virginia, 1740–1790* (Durham (NC), 1930), pp. 8–9.

Like a mighty rushing wind

But when we came to public prayer, the Holy Spirit seemed to come into the congregation like a mighty rushing wind, carrying all before it. I had not long begun before several young men and maidens, old men and children, were all dissolved in tears, and mourning after Jesus. I believe there were scarcely half a dozen in the whole congregation who were not deeply affected.

The Journals of George Whitefield, 6th June 1741.

Northampton (USA): Plentiful effusion of the Spirit upon believers

Mr [Jonathan] Edwards is a solid, excellent Christian, but, at present, weak in body. I think I have not seen his like in all New England. When I came to his pulpit, I found my heart drawn out to talk of scarcely anything besides the consolations and privileges of saints, and the plentiful effusion of the Spirit upon believers. When I came to remind them of their former experiences, and how zealous and lively they were at that time, both minister and people wept much.

The Journals of George Whitefield, 17th October 1741.

Baskinridge (USA): 'He is come! He is come!'

Mr Gilbert Tennent preached first; and I then began to pray and give an exhortation. In about six minutes, one cried out, 'He is come! He is come!' and could scarcely sustain the manifestation of Jesus to his soul. The eager crying of others, for a similar favour, obliged me to stop; and I prayed over them as I saw their agonies and distress increase. At length we sang a hymn, and then retired to the house where the man that received Christ continued praising and speaking of him till near midnight. My own soul was so full that I retired, and wept before the Lord, under a deep sense of my own vileness and the sovereignty and greatness of God's everlasting love. Most of the people spent the remainder of the night in prayer and praises. It was a night much to be remembered.

The Journals of George Whitefield, 5th November 1741.

Made anew by the Holy Spirit

As it may be said of a piece of gold, that was once in the ore, after it has been cleansed, purified and polished, that it is a new piece of gold; as it may be said of a bright glass that has been covered over with filth, when it is wiped, and so become transparent and clear, that it is new glass, so our souls thought still the same as to essence, yet are so purged, purified and cleansed from their natural dross by the blessed influence of the Holy Spirit, that they may be properly said to be made anew.

George Whitefield, *Sermons on Important Subjects* (London, 1828), p. 545.

Whitefield complains to Wesley about convulsions

Honoured Sir, I cannot think it right in you to give so much encouragement to these convulsions which people have been thrown into under your ministry. Were I to do so, how many would cry out every night?

Quoted in Lunn, *John Wesley,* p. 138.

What happened when Whitefield preached, the day after he complained to Wesley about convulsions

Four people sunk down close to him, almost in the same moment. One of them lay without sense or motion. A second trembled exceedingly. The third had strong convulsions all over his body, but made no noise, unless by groans. The fourth, equally convulsed, called upon God, with strong cries and tears.

From the time I trust we shall all suffer God to carry on his own work in the way that pleases him.

The Journal of John Wesley, 7th July 1739.

Whitefield's preaching in America produces swooning

Some were struck pale as death, others were wringing their hands, others lying on the ground, others sinking into the arms of their friends.

J. P. Gledstone, *Life and travels of Whitefield* (London, 1871), p. 215.

Some uttered the worst blasphemies against our Saviour

One night more than twenty roared and shrieked together while I was preaching. Some of them confessed they were demoniacs. Sally Jones could not read and yet would answer if persons talked to her in Latin or Greek. They could tell who was coming into the house, who would be seized next, what was doing in other places.

I have seen people so foam and violently agitated that six men could not hold one, but he would spring out of their arms or off the ground, and tear himself, as in hellish agonies. Others I have seen sweat uncommonly, and their necks and tongues swell and twist out of all shape. Some prophesied and some uttered the worst blasphemies against our Saviour.

John Cennick (one of Whitefield's preacher-associates), as quoted by Arnold A. Dallimore, *George Whitefield* (Edinburgh: Banner of Truth, 1980), vol. 1, p. 327.

Hell within would begin to roar

I think the case was often this; the word of God would come with convincing light and power into the hearts and consciences of sinners, whereby they were so far awakened that the peace of the strong man armed would be disturbed; hell within would begin to roar; the devil, who before, being unmolested, lay quiet in their hearts, would now be stirred up.

Ralph Humphries (an associate of Whitefield and Wesley), quoted by Arnold A. Dallimore, *George Whitefield* (Edinburgh: Banner of Truth, 1980), vol. 1, p. 326.

A critical view of 'enthusiasm'

The shrieks they catch from one to another, till a great part of the congregation is affected. They move others, and bring forward a general scream. Visions now become common, and trances also. Subjects report that they are conversed with Christ and holy angels; had opened to them the book of Life, and were permitted to read the names of people there, and the like. Laughing, loud hearty laughing, was one of the ways in which our new converts, almost everywhere, were wont to join together in expressing their joy and the conversion of others.

At the same time, some would be praying, some exhorting, some singing, some clapping their hands, some laughing, some crying, some shrieking and roaring out. It is in the evening, or more late in the night, that there is the screaming and shrieking to the greatest degree.

The Great Awakening: Documents on the Revival of Religion, 1740–45, ed. Richard Bushman (New York: Atheneum, 1970), pp. 118–9.

Others cried out as if they were in the sharpest agonies of death

Some fainted; and when they had got a little strength they would hear and faint again. Others cried out in a manner as if they were in the sharpest agonies of death. Oh what thoughts and words did God put into my heart!

The Journals of George Whitefield, 14th November 1740.

Others lying on the ground

The bitter cries and groans were enough to pierce the hardest heart. Some of the people were as pale as death; others were wringing their hands; others lying on the ground; others sinking into the arms of friends; and most lifting up their eyes to heaven and crying to God for mercy. One would imagine none could have withstood the power, or avoided crying out, 'Surely God is in this place.'

The Journals of George Whitefield, 15th November 1740.

'I preached to the whole congregation of upwards of twenty thousand persons'

On the Sabbath, scarce ever was such a sight seen in Scotland. Two tents were set up, and the holy sacrament was administered in the fields. When I began to serve a table, the people crowded so upon me, that I was obliged to desist, and go to preach in one of the tents, while the ministers served the rest of the tables. There was preaching all day, by one or another; and in the evening, when the sacrament was over, at the request of the ministers, I preached to the whole congregation of upwards of twenty thousand persons.

I preached about an hour and a half. It was a time much to be remembered. On Monday morning I preached again to near as many. I never before saw such a universal stir. The motion fled, as swift as lightning, from one end of the auditory to the other. Thousands were bathed in tears – some wringing their hands, others almost swooning, and others crying out and mourning over a pierced Saviour. In the afternoon, the concern was again very great. Much prayer had been previously put up to the Lord. All night, in different companies, persons were praying to God, and praising him. The children of God came from all quarters. It was like the Passover in Josiah's time.

Tyerman, *Whitefield*, vol. 2, pp. 6–7; quoted in A. Skevington Wood, *The Inextinguishable Blaze* (London: Paternoster, 1960), pp. 121–2.

Henry Venn observes Whitefield's preaching in a churchyard, 1757

Under Mr Whitefield's sermon, many of the immense crowd that filled every part of the burial ground, were overcome with fainting. Some sobbed deeply; others wept silently. When he came to impress the injection of the text several of the congregation burst into the most piercing bitter cries. Mr Whitefield, at this juncture, made a pause and then burst into a flood of tears.

During this short interval Mr Madan and myself stood up, and requested people to restrain themselves as much as possible, from making any noise. Twice afterwards we had to repeat the same counsel. When the sermon was ended people seemed chained to the ground. We found ample employment in endeavouring to comfort those broken down under a sense of guilt.

Quoted in Arnold A. Dallimore, *George Whitefield* (Edinburgh: Banner of Truth, 1980), vol 2, pp. 392–3.

A holy warmth

For what is a Christian without a holy warmth?

George Whitefield, *Works* (London and Edinburgh, 1771), vol. 2, p. 341.

Draw down God's Holy Spirit into your hearts

The words which you have read ('devoutly and daily' from the Bible), may be inwardly engrafted in your hearts, and bring forth in you the fruits of good life. Do this and you will with a holy violence, draw down God's Holy Spirit into your hearts; you will experience his gracious influence, and feel him enlightening, quickening and inflaming your souls.

George Whitefield, *Sermons on Important Subjects* (London, 1828), p. 429.

Imagination mistaken for revelation?

I am a man of like passions with others, and consequently may have sometimes mistaken nature for grace, imagination for revelation.

J. P. Gledstone, *Whitefield* (1900), p. 162.

God's Spirit, or my own spirit?

Alas! Alas! in how many things I have judged and acted wrong. I have been too bitter in my zeal. Wild-fire has been mixed with it, and I find that I frequently wrote and spoke too much in my own spirit, when I thought I was writing and speaking entirely by the assistance of God.

J. P. Gledstone, *Whitefield* (1900), vol. 2, p. xxiii.

The revival in Cambuslang
(1742)

Such a commotion surely was never heard of, especially at eleven at night. It far outdid all that I ever saw in America. For about an hour and a half there was such weeping, so many falling into deep distress, and expressing it in various ways. Their cries and agonies were exceedingly affecting.

Mr McCullough preached after I had ended, till past one in the morning, and then could scarce persuade them to depart. All night in the fields might be heard the voice of prayer and praise. Some young ladies were found by a gentlewoman praising God at break of day. She went and joined with them.

Arnold A. Dallimore, *George Whitefield* (Edinburgh: Banner of Truth, 1980), vol. 2, p. 125.

David Brainerd
(1718–47)

US evangelist to American Indians

In a mournful melancholy state, on July 12, 1739, I was attempting to pray; but found no heart to engage in that or any other duty; my former concern, exercise, and religious affections were now gone. I thought that the Spirit of God had quite left me; but still was not distressed; yet disconsolate, as if there was nothing in heaven or earth could make me happy. Having been thus endeavouring to pray – though, as I thought, very stupid and senseless – for near half an hour; then, as I was walking in a thick grove, unspeakable glory seemed to open to the apprehension of my soul. I do not mean any external brightness, nor any imagination of a body of light, but it was a new inward apprehension or view that I had of God, such as I never had before, nor anything which had the least resemblance to it. I had no particular apprehension of any one person in the Trinity, either the Father, the Son, or the Holy Spirit; but it appeared to be Divine glory.

My soul rejoiced with joy unspeakable, to see such a God, such a glorious Divine Being; and I was inwardly pleased and satisfied that he should be God over all for ever and ever. My soul was so captivated and delighted with the excellency of God that I was even swallowed up in him; at least to that degree that I had no thought about my own salvation, and scarce reflected that there was such a creature as myself. I continued in this state of inward joy, peace, and astonishing, till near dark without any abatement;

and then began to think and examine what I had seen; and felt sweetly composed in my mind all the evening following. I felt myself in a new world, and everything about me appeared with a different aspect from what it was wont to do.

Jonathan Edwards and S. E. Dwight, *Life of Brainerd* (New Haven, 1822), pp. 45–7.

Thursday, October 25 (1744)

Was very sensible of my absolute dependence on God in all respects; saw that I could do nothing, even in those affairs that I have sufficient natural faculties for, unless God should smile upon my attempt. 'Not that we are sufficient of ourselves, to think any thing as of ourselves,' I saw was a sacred truth.

Friday, October 26

In the morning my soul was melted with a sense of divine goodness and mercy to such a vile unworthy worm. I delighted to lean upon God, and place my whole trust in him. My soul was exceedingly grieved for sin, and prized and longed after holiness; it wounded my heart deeply, yet sweetly, to think how I had abused a kind God. I longed to be perfectly holy, that I might not grieve a gracious God; who will continue to love, notwithstanding his love is abused! I longed for holiness more for this end, that I did for my own happiness' sake: and yet this was my greatest happiness, never more to dishonour, but always to glorify, the blessed God.

Saturday, September 14 (At Shaumoking)

In the evening my soul was enlarged and sweetly engaged in prayer; especially that God would set up his kingdom in this place, where the devil now reigns in the most eminent manner. And I was enabled to ask this for God, for his glory, and because I longed for the enlargement of his kingdom, to the honour of his dear name. I could appeal to God with the greatest freedom, that he knew it was his dear cause, and not my own, that engaged my heart: and my soul cried:

'Lord, set up thy kingdom, for thine own glory. Glorify thyself; and I shall rejoice. Get honour to thy blessed name; and this is all I desire. Do with me just what thou wilt. Blessed be thy name for ever, that thou art God, and that thou wilt glorify thyself. O that the whole world might glorify thee! O let these poor people be brought to know thee, and love thee, for the glory of thy dear ever-blessed name!'

I could not but hope, that God would bring in these miserable, wicked Indians; though there appeared little human probability of it; for they were dancing and revelling, as if possessed by the devil. But yet I hoped, though against hope, that God would be glorified, and that his name would be glorified by these poor Indians. I continued long in prayer and praise to God; and had great freedom, enlargement, and sweetness, remembering dear friends in New England, as well as the people of my charge. Was entirely free from the dejection of spirit with which I am frequently exercised. Blessed be God!

David Brainerd's Journal

[The *Journal* was first printed with the following title:
'Mirabilia Dei inter Indicos;'
Or the Rise and Progress of a remarkable Work of Grace
Among a number of Indians, in the Province of New Jersey and Pennsylvania;
Justly represented in a Journal
kept by order of the Honourable Society (in Scotland)
for Propagating Christian Knowledge.
by David Brainerd.

August 7, 1745
Preached to the Indians for Isaiah 53:3—10. There was a remarkable influence attending the word, and great concern in the assembly. Most were much affected and in great distress for their souls; and some few could neither go nor stand, but lay flat on the ground, as if pierced at heart, crying incessantly for mercy. Several were newly awakened, and it was remarkable, that as fast as they came from remote places round about, the Spirit of God seemed to seize them with concern for their souls.

August 8, 1745

In the afternoon I preached to the Indians; their number was about sixty-five people, men, women and children. I spoke from Luke 14:16–23 and was favoured with uncommon freedom in my discourse. There was much visible concern among them while I was speaking, but afterwards when I spoke with them individually, the power of God seemed to descend on the assembly 'like rushing mighty wind,' and with an astonishing energy bore down all before it.

I stood amazed at the influence that seized the audience almost universally, and could compare it to nothing more aptly than the irresistible force of a mighty torrent or swelling deluge, that with its insupportable weight and pressure bears down and sweeps before it whatever is in its way. Almost everyone, of all ages, were bowed down with concern together, and hardly anyone was able to withstand the shock of this surprising work. Old men and women who had been drunken wretches for many years, and some little children not more than six or seven years of age, appeared in distress for their souls, as well as middle-aged people.

A leader among the Indians who had been previously most self-righteous told me, 'he had been a Christian more than ten years' but was now brought under a solemn concern for his soul, and wept bitterly. Another man, advanced in years, who had been a murderer, a powwow (conjurer), and a notorious drunkard now cried with many tears for God's mercy.

There was one remarkable instance of awakening this day, that I cannot but take particular notice of here. A young Indian woman, who I believe never knew before she had a soul, nor ever thought of any such thing, hearing that there was something strange among the Indians, came it seems to see what was the matter. On her way to the Indians she called at my lodgings, and when I told her I intended to shortly preach to the Indians she laughed. Nevertheless she joined them. By the time I had finished preaching she was so convinced about her sin and misery, and so distressed about her soul's salvation, that she seemed like one pierced through with a dart, and cried out incessantly.

She could neither go nor stand, nor sit on her seat without being

held up. After the service was over she lay flat on the ground praying earnestly, and would take no notice of, nor give any answer to,
anyone who spoke to her. I tried to listen to what she said, and perceived that the burden of her prayer was, Guttummaukalummeh
wechaumeh melch Ndah, that is, 'Have mercy on me, and help me
to give you my heart.' She continued to pray like this for hour
upon hour. This was indeed a surprising day of God's power and
seemed enough to convince an atheist of the truth and importance, and power of God's word.

John Woolman
(1720–72)

American Quaker, author of a distinctive, widely read Journal.

A vivid spiritual experience: before dawn 1757

It was yet dark and no appearance of day nor moonshine, and as I
opened my eyes I saw a light in my chamber at the apparent distance of five feet, about nine inches diameter, of a clear, easy
brightness and near the centre the most radiant. As I lay still without any surprise looking upon it, words were spoken to my inward
ear which filled my whole inward man. They were not the effect of
thought nor any conclusion in relation to the appearance, but as
the language of the Holy One spoken in my mind. The words
were, 'Certain Evidence of Divine Truth', and were repeated
exactly in the same manner, whereupon the light disappeared.

St Serafim of Sarov
(1759–1833)

*Russian monk who spent ten years in a hermitage, three years of which were
spent as a pillar hermit, standing or kneeling on rock.*

N. A. Motovilov visited Serafim in his hermitage in 1831 and discovered what 'in the fullness of the Holy Spirit' meant.

Motovilov observed a mysterious light which seemed to both come from and envelop Serafim. Motovilov said to Serafim, 'Your face looks brighter than the sun and my eyes hurt to look at you.'

Serafim replied, 'You, too, have become as radiant as I am. You are also in the fullness of the Spirit of God now, or you would not be able to see me as I am.'

V. N. Il'in, *Prepodobnyi Serafim Sarovskii* (Paris, 1930), p. 113.

Charles Grandison Finney
(1792–1875)

US evangelist and author of Lectures on Revivals in Religion.

Finney's intense encounter with God's presence

All my feelings seemed to rise and flow out; and the utterance of my heart was, 'I want to pour my whole soul out to God.' The rising of my soul was so great that I rushed into the back room of the front office, to pray. There was no fire and no light in the room; nevertheless it appeared too me as if it were perfectly light. As I went in and shut the door after me, it seemed as if I met the Lord Jesus face to face. It did not occur to me then, nor did it for some time afterwards, that it was wholly a mental state. On the contrary, it seemed to me that I saw him as I would see any other man. He said nothing, but looked at me in such a manner as to break me right down at his feet. I have always since regarded this as a most remarkable state of mind; for it seemed to me a reality that he stood before me, and I fell down at his feet and poured out my soul to him. I wept aloud like a child, and made such confessions as I could with my choked utterance. It seemed to me that I bathed his feet with my tears; and yet I had no distinct impression that I touched him, that I recollect. I must have continued in this state for a good while; but my mind was too absorbed with the interview to recollect anything that I said. But I know, as soon as my mind became calm enough to break off from the interview, I returned to the front office, and found that the fire that I had made of large wood was nearly burned out. But as I turned as was about to take a seat by the fire, I received a mighty baptism of the Holy Spirit.

Without any expectation of it, without ever having the thought in my mind that there was any such thing for me, without any recollection that I had ever heard the thing mentioned by anyone in the world, the Holy Spirit descended on me in a manner that seemed to go through me, body and soul. I could feel the impression, like a wave of electricity, going through and through me. Indeed, it seemed to come in waves and waves of liquid love; for I could not express it in any other way. It seemed like the very breath of God. I can recollect distinctly that it seemed to fan me, like immense wings.

No words can express the wonderful love that was shed abroad in my heart. I wept aloud with joy and love; and I do not know but I should say I literally bellowed out the unutterable gushings of my heart. These waves came over me, and over me, and over me, one after the other, until I recollect I cried out, 'I shall die if these waves continue to pass over me.' I said, 'Lord, I cannot bear any more:' yet I had no fear of death.

How long I continued in this state, with this baptism continuing to roll over me and go through me, I do not know. But I know it was late in the evening when a member of my choir – for I was the leader of the choir – came into the office to see me. He was a member of the church. He found me in this state of loud weeping, and said to me, 'Mr Finney, what ails you?' I could make him no answer for some time. He then said, 'Are you in pain?' I gathered myself as best I could, and replied, 'No, but so happy that I cannot live.'

E. D. Starbuck, *The Psychology of Religion* (1899).

What a revival of religion is

It presupposes that the church is sunk down in a backslidden state, and a revival consists in the return of the church from her backslidings, and in the conversion of sinners.

1. A revival always includes conviction of sin on the part of the church.

2. Backslidden Christians will be brought to repentance. A revival is nothing else than a new beginning of obedience to God.

3. Christians will have their faith renewed. They will be filled with tender and burning love for souls.

4. A revival breaks the power of the world and of sin over Christians.

5. When the churches are thus awakened and reformed, the reformation and salvation of sinners will follow.

Lectures on Revivals of Religion (Manchester: Simpkin, Marshall, 1840), pp. 6–7.

Revival and the sovereignty of God

Mistaken notions concerning the sovereignty of God have greatly hindered revivals.

Lectures on Revivals of Religion (Manchester: Simpkin, Marshall, 1840), p. 10.

Prayer and revival

A revival may be expected when Christians have a spirit of prayer for a revival: that is, when they pray as if their hearts were set upon a revival. Sometimes, Christians are not engaged in prayer for a revival, not even when they are warm in prayer.

Prayer is the state of the heart. The spirit of prayer is a state of continual desire and anxiety of mind for the salvation of sinners. It is something that weighs them down. A Christian who has this spirit of prayer feels anxious for souls.

When this feeling exists in a church, unless the spirit is grieved away by sin, there will infallibly be a revival. This anxiety and distress increases till the revival commences. A clergyman in W——n told me of a revival among his people, which commenced with a zealous and devoted woman in the church. She became anxious about sinners, and went to praying for them; and she prayed, and her distress increased; and she finally came to her minister, and talked with him, and asked him to appoint an anxious meeting (a meeting of a minister with awakened sinners). After initially refusing to hold such a meeting the minister eventually agreed and announced in church that if there were any who wished to converse with him about the salvation of their souls, he would meet them on such an evening. He did not know of one, but when he went to the place, to his astonishment, he found a large number of anxious inquirers. Now don't you think that that woman knew there was going to be a revival? Call it what you please, a new revelation, or an old revelation, or anything else – I say it was the Spirit of God that taught that praying woman there was going to be a revival.

Lectures on Revivals of Religion (Manchester: Simpkin, Marshall, 1840), pp. 19–20.

The danger of paying too much attention to the evils of revival

We see why it is that those who have been making the ado about new measures have not been successful in promoting revivals.

They have been taken up with the evils, real or imaginary, which have attended this great and blessed work of God. That there have been evils no one will pretend to deny. But I do believe that no revival ever existed since the world began, of so great power and extent as the one that has prevailed for the last ten years [i.e., 1825–35] which has not been attended with a great or greater evils. Still a large portion of the church have been frightening themselves and others, by giving constant attention to the evils of revival. While men are taken up with the evils instead of the excellencies of the blessed work of God, how can it be expected that they will be useful in promoting it?

Lectures on Revivals of Religion (Manchester: Simpkin, Marshall, 1840), pp. 237–8.

Hindrances to revival

A revival is a work of God, and so is a crop of wheat; and God is as much dependent on the use of means in one case as in the other.

And therefore a revival is as liable to be injured as a wheat field.

1. A revival will stop whenever the church believe it is going to cease. The church are the instruments with which God carries on this work. Nothing is more fatal to a revival than for its friends to predict that it is going to stop.

2. A revival will cease when Christians consent that it should cease.

3. A revival will cease when Christians become mechanical in their attempts to promote it.

4. A revival will cease whenever Christians get the idea that the work will go on without their aid. The church are co-workers with God in promoting a revival.

5. The work will cease when the church prefer to attend to their own concerns rather than God's business.

6. When Christians get proud of their great revival, it will cease.

7. The revival will stop when the church gets exhausted by labour.

Multitudes of Christians commit a great mistake here, in time of revival. They are so thoughtless, and have so little judgment, that they will break up all their habits of living, neglect to eat and sleep at the proper hours, and let the excitement run away with them, so that they overdo their bodies, and are so imprudent that they soon become exhausted, and it is impossible for them to continue in the work. Revivals often cease, and declensions follow, from negligence and imprudence, in this respect, on the part of those engaged in carrying them on.

8. A revival will cease when the church begin to speculate about abstract doctrines, which have nothing to do with practice.

9. When Christians begin to proselytise from other Christian denominations.

10. When Christians refuse to render to the Lord according to the benefits received. God gives people up if they show a niggardly spirit.

11. When the church, in any way, grieve the Holy Spirit.

a. When they do not feel their dependence on the Spirit.

b. The Spirit may be grieved by a spirit of boasting of the revival.

c. The Spirit may be grieved by saying or publishing things that are calculated to undervalue the work of God.

12. A revival may be expected to cease when Christians lose the Spirit brotherly love.

13. A revival will decline and cease, unless Christians are frequently reconverted. By this I mean, that Christians, in order to keep in the spirit of a revival, commonly need to be frequently convicted, and humbled, and broken down before God, and reconverted. This is something which many do not understand. But the fact is, that in a revival the Christian's heart is liable to get crusted over, and lose its exquisite relish for divine things; his unction and prevalence in prayer abates, and then he must be converted over again. It is impossible to keep him in such a state as not to do injury to the work, unless he pass through such a process every few days.

I have never laboured in revivals in company with any one who would keep in the work and be fit to manage a revival continually, who did not pass through this process of breaking down as often as once in two or three weeks. Revivals decline, commonly, because it is found impossible to make the church feel their guilt and dependence, so as to break down before God. It is important that ministers should understand this, and learn now to break down the church, and break down themselves when they need it, or else Christians will soon become mechanical in their work, and lose their fervour and their power of prevailing with God.

This is the process through which Peter passed, when he had denied the Saviour, and by which breaking down the Lord prepared him for the great work on the day of Pentecost. I was surprised a few years ago to find that the phrase 'breaking down' was a stumbling-block to certain ministers and professors of religion. They laid themselves open to the rebuked administered to Nicodemus, 'Art thou a master in Israel, and knowest not these things?' I am confident that until some of them know what it is to be 'broken down,' they never will do much more for the cause of revivals.

14. A revival cannot continue when Christians will not practice selfdenial.

15. A revival will be stopped by controversies about new measures.

16. Revivals can be put down by the continued opposition of the old school, combined with a bad spirit in the new school.

17. Any diversion of the public mind will hinder a revival. Any thing that succeeds in diverting public attention, will put a stop to revival.

18. Resistance to the temperance reformation will put a stop to revivals in a church.

19. Revivals are hindered when ministers and churches take wrong ground in regard to any question involving human rights, such as the subject of slavery.

20. Another thing that hinders revivals is neglecting the claims of missions.

21. When a church rejects the calls of God upon them for educating young men for the ministry, they will hinder and destroy a revival. Look at the Presbyterian church, look at the 200,000 souls converted within ten years, and means enough to fill the world with ministers, and yet the ministry is not increasing so fast as the population of our own country.

22. Slandering revivals will often put them down.

The great revival in the days of President Edwards suffered greatly by the conduct of the church in this respect. It is to be expected that the enemies of God will revile, misrepresent, and slander revivals. But when the church herself engages in this work, and many of her most influential members are aiding and abetting in calumniating and misrepresenting a glorious work of God, it is reasonable that the Spirit should be grieved away. It cannot be denied, that this has been done to a grievous and God-dishonouring extent.

It has been estimated that in one year, since this revival commenced, 100,000 souls were converted to God in the United States. This is undoubtedly the greatest number that were ever converted in one year, since the world began. It could not be expected that, in an excitement of this extent among human beings, there should be nothing to deplore. To expect perfection in such a work as this, of such extent, and carried on by human instrumentality, is utterly unreasonable and absurd. Evils doubtless did exist, and have existed. They were to be expected of course, and guarded against as far as possible. And I do not believe the world's history can furnish one instance, in which a revival, approaching to this in extent and influence, has been attended with so few evils, and so little that is honestly to be deplored.

But how has this blessed work of God been treated? At the General Assembly, that grave body of men who represent the Presbyterian Church, in the middle of this great revival, instead of appointing a day of thanksgiving, instead of praising God for the greatness of his work, we hear from them the voice of rebuke. They sent a 'Pastoral Letter' finding fault and carping about evils. When I read what was done at that General Assembly, when I read their speeches, when I saw the pastoral letter, my soul was sick, an unutterable feeling of distress came over my mind, and I felt that God would 'visit' the Presbyterian church for conduct like this; and ever since, the glory has been departing, and departing, and revivals have been becoming less and less frequent – less and less powerful.

23. Ecclesiastical difficulties are calculated to grieve away the Spirit, and destroy revivals. President Edwards was forced to attend ecclesiastical councils, taking up is time.

24. Another thing by which revivals may be hindered, is censoriousness on either side, and especially in those who have been engaged in carrying forward a revival. The greatest hindrance to an universal Revival of the work of God, is the divided state of the church of Christ.

Lectures on Revivals of Religion (Manchester: Simpkin, Marshall, 1840), pp. 243–55.

Lack of brotherly love

Where there is a lack of brotherly love and Christian confidence among professors of religion, then a revival is needed. Then there is a loud call for God to revive his work.

Lectures on Revivals of Religion.

Backslidden

It presupposes that the church is sunk down in a backslidden state, and a revival consists in the return of the church from her backslidings, and in the conversion of sinners. A revival is nothing else than a new beginning of obedience to God.

Lectures on Revivals of Religion.

The need for personal revival

I said to myself: 'What is this? I must have grieved the Holy Spirit entirely away. I have lost all my conviction. I have not a particle of concern about my soul; and it must be that the Spirit has left me.'

'Why!' thought I, 'I never was so far from being concerned about my own salvation in my life.' I tried to recall my convictions, to get back again the load of sin under which I had been labouring. I tried in vain to make myself anxious. I was so quiet and peaceful that I tried to feel concerned about that, lest it should be the result of my having grieved the Spirit away.

Memoirs (1875), pp. 17–18.

Falling down signals the outbreak of revival

I had not spoken to them . . . more than an hour when all at once an awful solemnity seemed to settle down upon them. The congregation began to fall from their seats in every direction and cry for mercy. If I had had a sword in each hand I could not have cut them off their seats as fast as they fell. Indeed, nearly the whole congregation were either on their knees or prostrate in less than two minutes from this first shock that fell upon them.

Autobiography (Bethany, 1977), pp. 82–3.

Finney speaks out against induced excitement

Charles Finney, who was all in favour of genuine manifestations as the natural accompaniment of true revival, considered it his duty to speak out against the spurious. On one occasion Finney visited a camp meeting in New York State where, after several sermons and much exhortation, prayer and singing, there was still little or no visible excitement. Several of the leaders consulted together and then one of the most energetic came down from the platform and stood in front of a row of women. He began to clap his hands with great vigour while bellowing at the top of his voice, 'Power! Power!! Power!!!' The fervour spread, as one after another began to clap, shout, shriek and fall to the ground. The platform party then proclaimed that the power of God was revealed from heaven, and left the meeting much gratified.

Finney's critique is justly severe: 'In the getting up of this excitement there was not a word of truth communicated; there was no prayer or exhortation – nothing but a most vociferous shouting. . . . So for as such efforts to promote revivals are made, they are undoubtedly highly disastrous, and should be entirely discouraged.'

Reflections on Revival, pp. 50–1.

19TH CENTURY

Charles Hodge
(1797–1878)

Charles Hodge was professor of biblical literature and theology at Princeton for over fifty years and wrote well-known commentaries on Romans, Ephesians and 1 and 2 Corinthians.

Comment on Romans 12:6–8

In these verses we have the application of the preceding comparison to the special object in view. 'If Christians are all members of the same body, having different offices and gifts, instead of being puffed up one above another, and instead of envying and opposing each other they should each discharge their respective duties diligently and humbly for the good of the whole, and not for their own advantage.' It is a common opinion that the apostle, in specifying the various gifts to which he refers, meant to arrange them under the two heads of *prophesying* and *administering*; or that he specifies the duties of two classes of officers, the prophets and deacons. To the former would then belong prophesying, teaching, exhortation; to the latter, ministering, giving, ruling, showing mercy. This view of the passage requires that the terms prophet and deacon should be taken in their widest sense. Both are used frequently with great latitude, the former being applied to anyone who speaks as the mouth of God, or who explains his will; and the latter to any ministering officer in the church (1 Cor. 3:5; Eph. 3:7; Col. 1:7, 23, etc.). Although this interpretation is consistent with the usage of the words, and in some measure simplifies the passage, yet it is by no means necessary. There is no appearance of such a systematic arrangement; on the contrary, Paul seems to refer without any order to the various duties which the officers and even private members of the church were called upon to perform.

'Having therefore gifts differing according to the grace given unto us'
That is, Just as there are in the one body various offices and gifts, let every one act in a manner consistent with the nature and design of the particular gift which he has received.

'Whether prophecy,' let us prophecy *'according to the proportion of faith'*
The first gift specified is that of prophecy, with regard to the precise nature of which there is no little diversity of opinion. The original and proper meaning of the Hebrew word rendered *prophet* in the Old Testament is *interpreter,* the one who explains or delivers the will of another. And to this idea the Greek term also answers. It matters little whether the will or purpose of God which the prophets were called upon to deliver had reference to present duty or to future events. They derived their Hebrew name not from predicting what was to come to pass, which was but a small part of their duty, but from being the interpreters of God, men who spoke in his name. We accordingly find the term *prophet* applied to all classes of religious teachers under the old dispensation. Of Abraham it is said, 'He is a prophet, and he shall pray for thee and thou shalt live' (Gen. 20:7). The name is often applied to Moses as the great interpreter of the will of God to the Hebrews (Deut. 18:18); and the writers of the historical books are also constantly so called. The passage in Exodus 7:1 is peculiarly interesting, as it clearly exhibits the proper meaning of this word. 'And the Lord said unto Moses, See, I have made thee a god to Pharaoh; and Aaron thy brother shall be thy prophet,' i.e., he shall be your interpreter. In Exodus 4:16 it is said, 'He shall be a mouth to thee'; and of Jeremiah, God says, 'Thou shalt be as my mouth' (Jer.

15:19; compare Deut. 18:18). Anyone, therefore, who acted as the mouth of God, no matter what was the nature of the communication, was a prophet. And this is also the meaning of the word in the New testament; it is applied to anyone employed to deliver a divine message (Matt. 10:41; 13:57; Luke 4:24; 7:26–9; John 4:19; Acts 15:32; 1 Cor. 12:28; 14:29–32). From these and numerous similar passages, it appears that the prophets in the Christian church were men who spoke under the immediate influence of the Spirit of God, and delivered some divine communication relating to doctrinal truths, to present duty, to future events, etc., as the case might be. The point of distinction between them and the apostles, considered as religious teachers, appears to have been that the inspiration of the apostles was abiding, they were the infallible and authoritative messengers of Christ; whereas the inspiration of the prophets was occasional and transient. The latter differed from the teachers inasmuch as these were not necessarily inspired, but taught to others what they themselves had learned from the Scriptures, of from inspired men.

In line with this view of the office of the prophets, we find the sacred writers speaking of the gift of prophecy as consisting in the communication of divine truth by the Spirit of God, intended for instruction, exhortation, or consolation: see 1 Corinthians 13:2; 14:3, 24.

'According to the proportion of faith'
The gift of which Paul here speaks is not, therefore, the faculty of predicting future events, but that immediate, occasional inspiration, leading the recipient to deliver, as the mouth of God, the particular communication which he had received, whether designed for instruction, exhortation, or comfort. The apostle required that those who enjoyed this gift should exercise it 'according to the proportion of faith'. This clause admits of different interpretations. The word rendered 'proportion' may mean either 'proportion', or 'measure, rule, standard'. The choice between the two meaning of the word must depend on the sense given to the word 'faith', and on the context. 'Faith' may here mean inward confidence or belief; or it may mean the gift received, i.e., 'that which

is confided'; or finally, that which is believed, truths divinely revealed. If the first of these three senses be adopted, the passage means, 'Let him prophesy according to his internal convictions; that is, he must not exceed in his communication what he honestly believes to have been divinely communicated, or to allow himself to be carried away by enthusiasm, to deliver, as from God, what is really nothing but his own thoughts'. If the second sense be preferred, the clause then means, 'Let him prophesy according to the proportion of the gifts which he has received; i.e., let everyone speak according to the degree and nature of the divine influence, or the particular revelation imparted to him'. If, however, 'faith' here means, as it does in so many other places, the object of faith, or the truths to be believed (see Gal. 1:23; 3:25; 6:10; Eph. 4:5; 1 Thess. 3:5; etc.), then 'according to the proportion' signifies 'agreeably to the rule or standard', and the apostle's direction to the prophets is that in all their communications they are to conform to the rule of faith, and not contradict those doctrines which had been delivered by men whose inspiration had been established by indubitable evidence. In favour of this view of the passage is the frequent use of the word 'faith' in this sense. The ordinary subjective sense of the word does not suit the passage. The amount or strength of faith does not determine either the extent to which the gift of prophecy is enjoyed, or the manner in which it is exercised. There were prophets who had no saving faith at all; just as many performed miracles who were not the true disciples of Christ (see Matt. 7:22–3).

The second sense given to 'faith', 'that which is confided to anyone, i.e., a gift,' is without any authority. The objective sense of the word, although denied by many of the strict philological interpreters, is nevertheless well established by such expressions as 'obedience to the faith', 'doer of faith', 'faith once delivered to the saints', and is perfectly familiar in ecclesiastical usage.

Similar directions are given in other passages respecting those who consider themselves prophets or inspired persons: see 1 Corinthians 14:37. No one had a right to consider himself inspired, or to require other so to regard him, when he did not conform himself to the instructions of men whose inspiration was beyond doubt. Thus, too, the apostle John commands Christians, 'Believe not every spirit, but try the spirits whether they are of God; because many false prophets are gone out into the world' (1 John 4:1). And the standard by which these prophets were to be tried, he gives in verse 6: 'We are of God: he that knoweth God, heareth us; he that is not of God, heareth not us. Hereby we know the spirit of truth and the spirit of error.' It was obviously necessary that Christians, in the age of immediate inspiration, should have some means of discriminating between those who were really under the influence of the Spirit of God, and those who were either enthusiasts or deceivers. And the test to which the apostles directed them was rational, and easily applied. There were inspired men to whose divine mission and authority God had borne abundant testimony by 'signs and wonders, and divers miracles, and gifts of the Holy Spirit'. As God cannot contradict himself, it follows that anything inconsistent with the teachings of these men, though proceeding from one claiming to be a prophet, must be false, and the pretension of its author to inspiration unfounded. Accordingly, the apostle directed that while one prophet spoke, the others were to judge, i.e., decide whether he spoke according to the analogy of faith; and whether his inspiration was real, imaginary, or feigned.

This interpretation also exactly suits the context. Paul, after giving the general direction contained in the preceding verses, as to the light in which the gifts of the Spirit were to be viewed, and the manner in which they were to be used, in this and the following verses, gives special directions with respect to particular gifts. Those who thought themselves prophets should be careful to speak nothing but truth, to conform to the standard; those who ministered should devote themselves to their appropriate duties, etc.

Ministry
The terms 'minister' and 'ministry' ('deacon' and 'deaconship') are used in the New Testament both in a general and a restricted sense. In the former, they are employed in reference to all classes of ecclesiastical officers, even the apostles; see 1 Cor. 3:5; 2 Cor.

6:4; Eph. 3:7; 6:21; Col. 1:7, 23; 1 Tim. 4:6; Acts 1:17, 25; 20:24; Rom. 11:13; 1 Cor. 12:5; 2 Cor. 4:1, etc. In the latter, they are used in reference to a particular class of officers, to whom were committed the management of the external affairs of the church, the care of the poor, attention to the sick, etc.; see Acts 6:1–3; Phil. 1:1; 1 Tim. 3:8–13, etc. It is doubtful in which of these senses the latter of the above-mentioned words is here used by the apostle, most probably in the restricted sense. The apostle exhorts different classes of officers to attend to their own particular vocation, and to exercise their superior endowments. The deacons, therefore, were to attend to the poor and the sick, and not attempt to exercise the office of teachers. Luther, and many others, give the words their wide sense: 'If a man has an office, let him attend to it.' But this would render unnecessary the specifications which follow. The apostle, in this context, refers to definite ecclesiastical offices in connection with ordinary Christian duties. That is, he exhorts both church officers and private Christians.

'He that teacheth, on teaching'
Teachers are elsewhere expressly distinguished from prophets: see 1 Corinthians 12:28–9. And in this passage they are not to be confused, nor is teaching to be regarded, in this place, as one part of prophesying. As remarked above on verse 6, the teachers were distinguished from prophets, inasmuch as the former were not necessarily inspired, and were a regular and permanent class of officers. Those who had the gift of prophecy were to exercise it aright; those who were called to the office of deacons were to devote themselves to their appropriate duties; and those who had the gift of teaching were to teach.

'He that exhorteth, on exhortation'
Teaching is addressed to the understanding; exhortation is addressed to the conscience and feelings. There was probably no distinct class of officers called exhorters, as distinguished from teachers; but as the apostle is speaking of gifts as well as officers, his direction is that he who had the gift of teaching should teach, and that he who had a gift for exhortation should be content to exhort.

'He that giveth,' let him do it 'with simplicity; he that ruleth, with diligence; he that showeth mercy, with cheerfulness'

These directions refer to the manner in which the duties of church officers and of private Christians ought to be performed. In this connection, the former no doubt are principally, though not exclusively, intended. Paul is thinking of the duties of imparting or distributing to the needs of the saints. This duty, whoever performs it, is to be done with 'simplicity', i.e., with purity of motive, free from all improper designs. This same word is rendered 'singleness of heart' in Ephesians 6:5 and Colossians 3:22, and occurs in the same sense in the phrase 'simplicity and godly sincerity' in 2 Corinthians 1:12. Considered in reference to private Christians, this clause may be rendered, 'he that giveth, with liberality' (see 2 Cor. 8:2; 9:11, 13).

'He that ruleth, with diligence'

Here again the right discharge of ecclesiastical duties is principally intended (see 1 Thess. 5:12). There is a considerable diversity of opinion about the meaning of the word rendered 'he that ruleth'. The Greek word properly means 'one who is placed over', who presides, or rules. It is, however, used in a more restricted sense, for a patron, one who befriends others, and especially strangers. Hence in 16:2, Phoebe is called a 'patroness', one who befriended strangers. As what precedes and what follows, giving and showing mercy, relate to acts of kindness, the one to the poor, the other to the sick, so this word, it is urged, should be understood to mean showing kindness to strangers. There is certainly force in this consideration. But as there is very slight foundation for giving this meaning of the word in the New testament, and as it is elsewhere used in its ordinary sense (see 1 Thess. 5:12, and compare 1 Tim. 5:17), it is commonly understood to refer to rulers. Some take it to refer to rulers in general, others specifically to the pastor or bishop of the congregation. The objection against this restricted reference to the presiding officer of a church is the introduction of the term in the enumeration of ordinary Christian duties. He that gives, he that acts as pastor, he that shows mercy, is rather an incongruous association. It is more common, therefore, to understand it to refer to anyone who exercises authority in the church.

Those who were called to exercise the office of ruler were required to do it with 'diligence', i.e., with attention and zeal. This is opposed to inertness and carelessness. The government of the church, in correcting abuses, preventing disorders, and in the administration of discipline, calls for constant vigilance and fidelity.

'He that showeth mercy, with cheerfulness'

As the previous direction referred to the care of the poor, this relates to the care of the sick and afflicted. These were the two great departments of the deacon's duties. The former was to be discharged with alacrity and kindness. On this, the value of any service rendered to the children of sorrow mainly depends.

A Commentary on Romans (1864; reprinted Edinburgh: Banner of Truth, 1972), pp. 387–93.

Comment on Romans 15:19

Through mighty signs and wonders, by the power of the Spirit of God
That is, by miracles, and by the influences of the Holy Spirit. The Greek says 'by the power of (i.e., which comes from) signs and wonders, and, the power which flows from the Holy Spirit.' It was thus Christ rendered the labours of Paul successful. He produced conviction, or the obedience of faith in the minds of the Gentiles, partly by miracles, partly and mainly by the inward working of the Holy Spirit. That Christ exercises divine power both in the external world and in the hearts of men, clearly proves that he is a divine person.

'Signs and wonders' are the constantly recurring words to designate those external events which are produced, not by the operation of second causes, but by the immediate efficiency of God. They are called 'signs' because evidences of the exercise of God's power, and proofs of the truth of his declarations, and 'wonders' because of the effect which they produce on the minds of men. This passage is, therefore, analogous to that in 1 Corinthians 2:4 – Paul relied for success not on his own skills or eloquence, but on the powerful demonstration of the Spirit. This demonstration of the Spirit consisted partly in the miracles which he enabled the first preachers of the gospel to perform, and partly in the influence with which he attended the truth to the hearts and consciences of those that believed: see Gal. 3:2–5; Heb. 2:4.

A Commentary on Romans (1864; reprinted Edinburgh: Banner of Truth, 1972), pp. 440–1.

Comment on Ephesians 4:11–12

'He who gave' – he, the ascended Saviour, to whom all power and all resources have been given – he gave 'some to be apostles, some to be evangelists, and some to be pastors and teachers.' These were among the gifts which Christ gave to his church, which, though implying diversity of grace and office, were necessary to its unity as an organised whole These officers are mentioned in the order of their importance:

1. The *apostles* – the immediate messengers of Christ; his witnesses concerning his doctrines, his miracles, and his resurrection; infallible as teachers and absolute as rulers because of the gift of inspiration and because of their commission. No man, therefore, could be an apostle unless:

a. He was appointed by Christ.

b. He had seen Christ after his resurrection and had received the knowledge of the gospel by direct revelation.

c. He was made infallible by the gift of inspiration.

These things constituted the office and were essential to its authority. Those who claimed the office without having these gifts and qualifications are called 'false apostles'.

2. *Prophets*. A prophet is someone who speaks on behalf of someone else, a spokesman, as Aaron was the prophet of Moses. Those whom God spoke through to people were prophets, whether their communications were doctrinal, moral, or prophetic, in the restricted sense of the term. Everyone who spoke by inspiration was a prophet. The New Testament prophets differed from the apostles in that their inspiration was occasional, and therefore their authority as teachers was subordinate. As the gift of infallibility

was essential for the apostolic office, so the gift of infallibility was essential for the prophetic office. It is inconceivable that God should invest any set of men with the authority claimed and exercised by the apostles and prophets of the New Testament, requiring everyone to believe their teaching and submit to their authority on pain of perdition, without his giving the inner gifts qualifying them for their work.

Evangelists. There are two views about the nature of the office of the evangelists. Some regard them as appointees of the apostles – men commissioned by them for a definite purpose and clothed with special powers for the time being, similar to the Roman Catholic apostolic vicars or to the temporary superintendents appointed after the Reformation in the Scottish church, clothed for a limited time and for a definite purpose with power to be presbyters – i.e., to a certain extent with the power of a presbytery, the power to ordain, install and depose. Evangelists, in this sense, were temporary officers. This view of the nature of the office prevailed at the time of the Reformation.

According to this view, evangelists were itinerant preachers, as Theodoret and other early writers describe them. They were really missionaries sent to preach the gospel where it had not previously been known. This is the commonly received view, and in its favour are the following points: First, the word by itself means nothing more than preacher of the gospel. Second, Philip was an evangelist, but was in no sense an appointee of the apostles. And when Timothy was exhorted to do the work of an evangelist, the exhortation was simply to be a faithful preacher of the gospel. Acts 21:8, Ephesians 4:11, and 2 Timothy 4:5 are the only passages in which the word occurs, and in none of them does the context, or any other consideration, demand any other meaning than the one commonly followed. Third, the words 'evangelists' and 'pastors' are both used about making the gospel known; but when,as here, the evangelist is distinguished from the teacher, the only distinction is between the person who makes the gospel known where it had not been heard and an instructor of those who were already Christians.

The use of 'preach the gospel' in such passages as Acts 8:4 and

14:7, 1 Corinthians 1:17, and 2 Corinthians 10:16 serves to confirm the commonly received opinion that an evangelist is one who makes the gospel known. That Timothy and Titus were in some sense apostolic appointees – i.e., men clothed with special powers for a special purpose and for a limited time – may be admitted, but this does not determine the nature of the office of an evangelist. They exercised these powers not as evangelists but as delegates or commissioners.

Pastors and teachers. According to one interpretation, we have two distinct officers here – that of pastor and that of teacher. The latter, says Calvin, 'had nothing to do with disciplines, nor with the administration of the sacraments, nor with admonitions or exhortations, but simply with the interpretation of Scripture' (*Institutes*, 4.3–4). All this is inferred from the meaning of the word 'teachers'. There is no evidence from Scripture that there was then a set of men authorised to teach but not authorised to exhort. The thing is impossible. One function includes the other. The man who teaches duty and the grounds of it does at the same time admonish and exhort. It was, however, on the ground of this unnatural interpretation that the Westminster Directory made 'teachers' a distinct and permanent class of officers in the church. The Puritans in New England endeavoured to reduce the theory to practice and appointed 'doctors' as distinct from preachers. But the attempt proved to be a failure. The two functions could not be kept separate. The whole theory rested on a false interpretation of Scripture.

The absence of the article before 'teachers' proves that the apostles intended to designate the same persons both 'pastors' and 'teachers'. The former term designates them as pastors, 'overseers', the latter as instructors. Every pastor or bishop was required to be apt to teach. This interpretation is given by Augustine and Jerome. Modern commentators almost without exception agree with this interpretation. It is true the article is at times omitted between two substantives referring to different classes, where the two constitute one order – as in Mark 15:1; the elders and scribes formed one body. But in such a list as that contained in this verse, the rules of the language require 'of the teachers' if the apostle had intended to distinguish the teachers from the pastors. 'Pastors and teachers', therefore, must be taken as a twofold name for the same officers, who were both the guides and instructors of the people.

Having mentioned the officers Christ gave his church, the apostle states why this gift was conferred. It was 'to prepare God's people for works of service, so that the body of Christ may be built up'.

Both the meaning of the words and the relationship of the different clauses in this verse are uncertain. The word 'prepare' has a variety of interpretations. The root of the word means 'to unite' or 'to bind together'. Hence it signifies 'united, complete, perfect', and from this comes the verb 'to mend' (Matthew 4:21); to reduce to order, to render complete of perfect (Luke 6:40; 2 Corinthians 13:11); to prepare or make fit for us (Hebrews 10:5; 13:21). The substantive may express the action of the verb in the various modifications of its meaning. Hence it has been translated here:

a. For the completion of the saints – i.e., of their number.
b. For their renewing or restoration.
c. For their reduction to order and union as one body.
d. For their preparation (for service).
e. For their perfecting.

This last one is to be preferred, because it agrees with the frequent use of the verb by this apostle and because it gives the sense which suits the context best.

The word 'service' may express that service which one person gives to another, as in Luke 10:40, 'to do the work', or especially the service given to Christians, as in 1 Corinthians 16:15, 'devoted themselves to the service of the saints', or to the official service of the ministry. Hence the phrase 'for works of service' may mean 'the work of mutual service or kind offices' or to the work of the ministry in the official sense. The lastter is the normal interpretation and is preferred not only because the word is more frequently used in that sense but also because of the context, as the apostle is speaking here about the different kinds of ministers of the Word.

The principal difficulty connected with this verse concerns the relation of its different clauses.

1. Some people propose to invert the first and second, so that

the sense would be, 'Christ appointed the apostles, etc., for the work of the ministry, the purpose of which is that God's people become mature, and the building of the body of Christ'. Although this sense is good and pertinent, the transposition is arbitrary.

2. Others regard the clauses as coordinate. 'These officers were given so God's people could become mature, for the work of service, for the building up of the body of Christ.' But objections against this are the change in the prepositions and the incongruity of the thoughts, for the expressions are not parallel.

3. The two latter clauses may be made subordinate to the first: 'Christ has appointed the ministry with the view of preparing God's people for the work of serving one another [compare 1 Cor. 16:15] and for the building up of his body.' This, however, assumes that 'service' has a sense which does not suit the context.

4. Others make the second and third clauses explanations of the first clause: 'Christ appointed these officers for the preparation of God's people, some for the work of service and some for the building up of his body.' But this is inconsistent with the structure of the passage. It would require the introduction of 'some for this, and some for that'.

5. Others again give the sense in this way: 'To prepare God's people, Christ appointed these officers for the work of the ministry, for the building up of his body.' The 'work of the ministry' is that work which the ministry performs – namely, the building up of the body of Christ. This last view is perhaps the best.

'He could not,' says Calvin, 'exalt the ministry of the Word more highly than by attributing this effect to it. For what higher work can there be than to build up the church that it may reach its perfection? Therefore, they are insane who, neglecting this means, hope to be perfect in Christ, as is the case with fanatics, who pretend to secret revelations of the Spirit; and the proud, who content themselves with the private reading of the Scripture, and imagine they do not need the ministry of the church.' If Christ has appointed the ministry for the edification of his body, it is in vain to expect that end to be accomplished in any other way.

Commentary on the Epistle to the Ephesians (Wheaton (IL): Crossway Books, 1994), pp. 135–9.

Comment on 5:18–20

'Do not get drunk on wine'
This is an example of folly, a lack of sense, especially inconsistent with the intelligence of the true believer. The person who has correct discernment will not seek refreshment of excitement from wine but from the Holy Spirit. Therefore, the apostle adds, 'instead, be filled with the Spirit'. In drunkenness, he says, there is 'debauchery' – 'revelry', 'riot', whatever tends to destruction. the word is derived from a word which means 'what cannot be saved', one given up to a destructive course of life. Compare Titus 1:6; 1 Peter 4:4.

People are said to be filled with wine when they are completely under its influence; so they are said to be 'filled with the Spirit' when he controls all their thoughts, feelings, words, and actions. The expression is a common one in Scripture. Of our Lord himself it was said that he was 'full of the Holy Spirit' (Luke 4:1), and of Stephen that he was 'full of faith and of the Holy Spirit' (Acts 6:5), and also of Barnabas (Act 11:24), etc. To the Christians, therefore, the source of strength and joy is not wine, but the blessed Spirit of God. As drunkenness produces rioting and debauchery, so the Holy Spirit produces a joy which expresses itself in 'psalms, hymns and spiritual songs'.

'Speak to one another'
'Speak to one another' – as in Ephesians 4:32 and elsewhere – not 'to ourselves'. Compare Colossians 3:16, where we read, 'teach and admonish one another'. 'Speak to one another' signifies the interchange of thoughts and feelings expressed in the psalms and hymns used. This is supposed to refer to responsive singing in the private assemblies and public worship of Christians. Whether the passage refers to the responsive method of singing or not, which is somewhat doubtful from the parallel passage in Colossians (where Paul speaks of their teaching one another), it at least proves that singing was from the beginning a part of Christian worship, and that not only psalms but hymns were also used.

The early use of the words for 'psalms, hymns and spiritual

songs' appears to have been as loose as that of the corresponding English terms. A psalm was a hymn, and a hymn a song. Still there was a distinction between them, as there is still. A 'psalm' was, as its etymology shows, a song designed to be sung with the accompaniment of instrumental music. It was one of the sacred poems contained in the book of Psalms, as in Acts 13:33, 'in the second Psalm', and Acts 1:20, 'in the book of Psalms'. It could also be any sacred poem formed on the model of the Old Testament Psalms, as in 1 Corinthians 14:26, where 'psalm' appears to mean such a song given by divine inspiration, and not one of the psalms of David. A 'hymn' was a song of praise to God, a divine song. Psalms and hymns then, as now, were religious songs; 'songs' were religious or secular, and therefore those intended here are described as 'spiritual'. The word may mean either 'inspired' – i.e., derived from the Spirit – or expressing spiritual thoughts and feelings. The latter is the more probable, as it is not only inspired people who are said to be 'filled with the Spirit', but all those who in their ordinary thoughts and feelings are governed by the Holy Spirit.

'Sing and make music in your heart to the Lord'
If this clause is considered as co-ordinate with the preceding one, then it refers to a different kind of singing. The former, expressed by 'speak to one another', is singing audibly; the latter, indicated by 'make music in your heart', is the music of the heart, the rhythm of the affections not clothed in words. In favour of this view, which is adopted by several of the best modern commentators, such as Harless, Rückert, Olshausen, and Meyer, it is urged that the apostle says 'in your heart', and not simply 'in heart' – 'from the heart'; also, the pronoun 'your' would be unnecessary had he meant only that the singing was to be cordial.

Besides, the singing referred to here is that of those 'filled with the Spirit', and therefore the caution that it should not be mere lip service is out of place. Notwithstanding these reasons, the great majority of commentators make this clause subordinate to the preceding one and descriptive of the kind of singing required: 'You are to commence with psalms and hymns, singing in your heart.' Compare Romans 1:9, where the apostle says, 'whom I serve with my whole heart' and 1 Corinthians 14:15. There is no sufficient reason for departing from the ordinary view of the passage.

'Sing and make music'

These are two forms of expressing the same thing. The latter term is the more comprehensive. To sing is to make music with the voice; to make music is to make music in any way – literally, to play on a stringed instrument, then to sing in concert with such an instrument, then to sing or chant. See 1 Cor. 14:15; Jas. 5:13; Rom. 15:9.

'To the Lord'

That is, to Christ. In the parallel passage, Colossians 3:16,. it is 'to God'. In either form the idea is the same. In worshipping Christ we worship God. God in Christ, however, is the definite, special object of Christian worship, to whom the heart when filled with the Spirit instinctively turns. This special worship of Christ is neither inconsistent with the worship of the Father, nor is it ever dissociated from it. The one runs into the other. Therefore the apostle connects the two: 'Be filled with the Spirit, singing hymns to Christ, and giving thanks to God, even the Father'. The Spirit dictates the one as naturally as the other.

'Always . . . for everything'

We are to give thanks always. It is not a duty to be performed once for all, nor merely when new mercies are received, but always, because we are under obligation for blessings temporal and spiritual already received, which calls for perpetual acknowledgment. We are to give thanks 'for everything' – for afflictions as well as for our joys, say the ancient commentators. This is not in the text, though Paul, as we learn from other passages, gloried in his afflictions. Here the words are limited by the context – 'for everything, in the name of our Lord Jesus'.

'In the name'

The apostles preached in the name of the Lord Jesus Christ; they worked miracles in his name. Believers are commanded to pray in his name, to give thanks in his name, and to do all things in his name. What we do in the name of Christ, we do by his authority and relying on him for success. Christ gives us access to the Father; we come to God through him; he gives us the right to come; and it is on him we depend for acceptance when we come.

'The Father'

That is, God, the Father of our Lord Jesus Christ. This is the covenant title for God under the new dispensation, and it presents the only ground on which he can be approached as our Father.

Commentary on the Epistle to the Ephesians (Wheaton (IL): Crossway Books, 1994), pp. 178–81.

Commentary on 1 Corinthians 12:1–13

The ancient prophets had clearly predicted that the Messianic period would be accompanied by a remarkable effusion of the Holy Spirit. 'And afterward,' God says in Joel 2:28, 'I will pour out my Spirit on all people. Your sons and daughters will prophesy, your old men will dream dreams, your young men will see visions.' Our Lord, before his crucifixion, promised to send the Comforter, who is the Holy Spirit, to instruct and guide his church (see John 14, etc.). And after his resurrection he said to his disciples, 'These signs will accompany those who believe: In my name they will drive out demons; they will speak in new tongues; they will pick up snakes with their hands; and when they drink deadly poison, it will not hurt them at all; they will place their hands on sick people, and they will get well' (Mark 16:17–18). And immediately before his ascension he said to the disciples, 'You will be baptised with the Holy Spirit' (Acts 1:6). Accordingly, on the day of Pentecost, these promises and prophecies were literally fulfilled.

What was special about the new dispensation was that, first of all, these gifts were not confined to any one group of people but extended to all – male and female, young and old. Secondly, these supernatural endowments were wonderfully diverse.

Under such extraordinary circumstances it was unavoidable that many disorders should arise. Some people would claim to be organs of the Spirit, when they were deluded or impostors; some would be dissatisfied with the gifts which they had received, and envy those whom they regarded as more highly favored; others would be puffed up, and make an ostentatious display of their extraordinary powers; and in the public meetings it might be expected that the greatest confusion would arise from so many people wanting to exercise their gifts at the same time. The apostle devotes this chapter and the next two to correcting these evils, all of which had manifested themselves in the Corinthian church.

It is impossible to read these chapters without being deeply impressed by the divine wisdom with which they are pervaded. After contrasting the condition of the Corinthians, as members of that body which was filled with the life-giving Spirit of God, with their former condition as the senseless worshippers of lifeless idols, Paul *first* of all lays down the criterion by which they might decide whether those who claimed to be organs of the Spirit were really under this influence. How do they speak of Christ? Do they blaspheme, or do they worship him? If they openly and sincerely recognise Jesus as the supreme Lord, then they are under the influence of the Holy Spirit (verses 1–3).

Secondly, these gifts, whether viewed as graces of the Spirit, or as forms of ministering to Christ, or the effects of God's power (that is, whether viewed in relation to the Spirit, to the Son, or to the Father), are only different manifestations of the Holy Spirit living in his people, and are all intended for the edification of the church (verses 4–7).

Thirdly, he arranges them under three headings:

1. The word of wisdom and the word of knowledge.

2. Faith, the gift of healing, the power of working miracles, prophesying, and the discerning of spirits.

3. The gift of tongues and the interpretation of tongues (verses 8–10).

Fourthly, these gifts are not only all the fruits of the Spirit, but they are distributed according to his sovereign will (verse 11).

Fifthly, there is therefore in this matter a striking analogy between the church and the human body:

1. As the body is one organic whole, because it is animated by

one spirit, so the church is one because of the indwelling of the Holy Spirit as the principle of its life.

2. As the unity of life in the body is manifested in a diversity of organs and members, so the indwelling of the Spirit in the church is manifested by a diversity of gifts and functions.

3. As the very idea of the body as an organisation supposes this diversity in unity, the same is true in regard to the church.

4. As in the human body the members are mutually dependent, and no one exists for itself alone but for the body as a whole, so also in the church there is the same dependence of its members on each other, and their various gifts are not designed for the exclusive benefit of those who exercise them, but for the edification of the whole church.

5. As in the body the position and function of each member is determined not by itself but by God, so also these spiritual gifts are distributed according to the good pleasure of their author.

6. In the body the least attractive parts are those which are indispensable to its existence, and so in the church it is not the most attractive gifts which are the most useful.

Sixthly, the apostle draws from this analogy the following inferences:

1. Everyone should be content with the gift which he has received from the Lord, just as the hand and foot are content with their position and function in the body.

2. There should be no exaltation of one member of the church over others, on the ground of the supposed superiority of his gifts.

3. There should, and must, be mutual sympathy between the members of the church, as there is between the members of the body. One cannot suffer without all the other suffering with it. No one lives, or acts, or feels for himself alone, but each in the rest (verses 12–27).

In conclusion, the apostle shows that what he had said with regard to these spiritual gifts applies in all its force to the various functions in the church, which are the organs through which the gifts of the Spirit are exercised (verses 28–31).

'Now about spiritual gifts, brothers, I do not want you to be ignorant'
Instead of beginning with 'in the second place', in continuing the list begun in 11:17, Paul passes to the second ground of censure by the simple 'now'. The misuse of the spiritual gifts, especially the gift of tongues, was the next topic of rebuke.

The Greek says simply, 'About spirituals' – the word could mean 'gifts' or 'men', depending on whether it is neuter or masculine. The former is the more natural and common explanation, because the gifts rather than the people are the subject of discussion; and because in verse 31 and in 14:1 the neuter form is used.

'I do not want you to be ignorant.' That is, I wish you to understand the origin and purpose of these extraordinary manifestations of divine power, and to be able to discriminate between the true and false claimants to them.

'You know that when you were pagans, somehow or other you were influenced and led astray to mute idols'
Here, as in Ephesians 2:11, the apostle contrasts the former state of his readers with their present state. Formerly, they were pagans, now they were Christians. Formerly, they worshipped and consulted mute idols, now they worshipped the living and true God. Formerly, they were swayed by a blind, unintelligent impulse, which carried them away, they knew not why or where; now they were under the influence of the Spirit of God. Their former state is referred to here as affording a reason why they needed instruction on this subject. It was one on which their previous experience gave them no information.

'You know that when you were pagans.' This is the comprehensive statement of their previous state. It includes the two specific things which follow. First, they were addicted to the worship of mute (that is, voiceless) idols (compare Habakkuk 2:19: 'Woe to him who says to the wood, "Come to life!" Or to lifeless stone, "Wake up!" Can it give guidance?' To worship mute idols, gods who could neither hear nor save, expresses in the strongest terms at once their folly and their misery.

Secondly, they were 'influenced and led astray' to this worship; that is, they were controlled by an influence which they could not understand or resist. For the meaning of the word used here, compare Galatians 2:13 and 2 Peter 3:17. It is often used of those who are led away to judgment, to prison, or to execution (as in Mark 13:53 and John 18:13). Paul wants to contrast this being led astray, as though by force, with being led by the Spirit. One was an irrational influence controlling the understanding and will; the other is an influence from God, congruous with our nature, and leading to good.

'Therefore I tell you that no one who is speaking by the Spirit of God says, "Jesus be cursed," and no one can say, "Jesus is Lord," except by the Holy Spirit'
'Therefore,' that is, because I do not want you to be ignorant on this subject. This first thing which he teaches is the criterion or test of true divine influence. This criterion he states first negatively and then positively. The negative statement is that 'no one who is speaking by the Spirit of God says, "Jesus be cursed"'. To speak by (or in) the Spirit is to speak under the influence of the Spirit, as the ancient prophets did. See Matthew 22:43; Mark 12:36. 'No one speaking (using his voice) calls (pronounces) Jesus to be accursed.' Or, according to another reading, utters the words 'Jesus is accursed.'

'Jesus': the historical person known among people by that name. Paul therefore uses that word and not 'Christ', which designates his function.

'Cursed': that is, anathema. The word strictly means something consecrated to God. As among the Jews any living thing consecrated in this way could not be redeemed, but must be put to death (Lev. 27:28–9), so the word was used to designate any person of thing devoted to destruction; and then with the added idea of the divine displeasure, something devoted to destruction as accursed. This last is always its meaning in the New Testament (Rom. 9:3; Gal. 1:8–9; 1 Cor. 16:22). Hence to say that Jesus is anathema is to say that he was a malefactor, someone justly condemned to death. This is what the Jews said when they invoked his blood on their heads.

'No one can say, "Jesus is Lord," except by the Holy Spirit.' The word for 'Lord' is *kyrios,* the word commonly used in the Greek

version of the Old Testament for Jehovah. To say that Jesus is the
Lord, therefore, in the apostle's sense, is to acknowledge him to be
truly God. And as the word 'Jesus' here, as before, designates the
historical person known by that name, who was born of the Virgin
Mary, saying that Jesus is Lord is to acknowledge that that person
is God revealed in the flesh. In other words, the confession
includes the acknowledgment that he is truly God and truly man.
What the apostle says is that no one can make this acknowledgment except by the Holy Spirit. This of course does not mean that
no none can utter these words unless he is under special divine
influence; it means that no one can truly believe and openly confess that Jesus is God revealed in the flesh unless he is enlightened
by the Spirit of God.

This is precisely what our Lord himself said when Peter confessed
him to be the Son of God. 'Blessed are you, Simon son of Jonah,
for this was not revealed to you by man, but by my Father in
heaven' (Matt. 16:17). The same thing is also said by the apostle
John. 'This is how you can recognise the Spirit of God: Every spirit
that acknowledges that Jesus Christ has come in the flesh is from
God, but every spirit that does not acknowledge Jesus is not from
God' (1 John 4:2–3). 'If anyone acknowledges that Jesus is the Son
of God, God lives in him and he in God' (1 John 4:15).

To blaspheme Christ, to say evil of him, was the way in which
people renounced Christianity before the Roman tribunals; and
saying, 'I believe that Jesus Christ is the Son of God' (Acts 8:37)
was the way people professed allegiance to Christ. People acknowledged themselves to be Christians by acknowledging the divinity
of Christ. These passages, therefore, teach us first, who we are to
regard as Christians, namely those who acknowledge and worship
Jesus of Nazareth as the true God; secondly, that the rest of the
divine commission of those who assume the office of teachers of the
Gospel, is not external descent, or apostolic succession, but soundness in the faith. If even an apostle or angel teach any other gospel,
we are to regard him as accursed (Galatians 1:8). And Paul tells the
Corinthians that they were to use the same criterion to discriminate between those who were really the organs of the Holy Spirit,
and those who claimed that office falsely. As it is unscriptural to

recognise as Christians those who deny the divinity of our Lord, so it is unscriptural for any person to doubt his own regeneration if he is conscious that he sincerely worships the Lord Jesus.

'There are different kinds of gifts, but the same Spirit. There are different kinds of service, but the same Lord. There are different kinds of working, but the same God works all of them in all men'
The second thing which the apostle teaches concerning these gifts is their diversity in connection with the unity of their source and purpose. However, we are not to understand him here as dividing these gifts into three classes, under the headings of 'gifts', 'service' and 'works'. He is presenting three different aspects of each and all of them. Viewed in relation to the Spirit, they are gifts; in the relation to the Lord, they are acts of service; in relation to God, they are works, that is, effects worked by his power. And it is the same Spirit, the same Lord, and the same God who are concerned in them all. That is, the same Spirit is the giver; it is he who is the immediate author of all these various endowments. It is the same Lord in whose service and by whose authority these various gifts are exercised. They are all different forms in which he is served, or ministered to. And it is the same God the Father, who having exalted the Lord Jesus to the supreme headship of the church, and having sent the Holy Spirit, works all these effects in the minds of men. There is no inconsistency between this statement and verse 11, where the Spirit is said to work all these gifts; because God works by his Spirit. So in one place we are said to be born of God, and in another to be born of the Spirit. Thus, the doctrine of the Trinity underlies the whole scheme of redemption in its execution and application as well as in its conception.

Those who understand this passage as describing three distinct classes of gifts, one derived from the Spirit, another from the Son, and a third from the Father, suppose that to the first class belong wisdom, knowledge, and faith; to the second, church offices; and to the third, the gift of miracles. But this view of the passage is inconsistent with the constant and equal reference of these gifts to the Holy Spirit – they all come under the heading of 'spiritual gifts'. It is also inconsistent with what follows in verses 8–10, where a different classification is given. That is, the nine gifts mentioned there are not classified in reference to their relation to the Father, Son, and Spirit; and therefore it is unnatural to assume such a classification here. They are all and equally gifts of the Spirit, modes of serving the Son, and effects due to the working of the Father.

'Now to each one the manifestation of the Spirit is given for the common good' Although these gifts are diverse in their manifestations, they have the same source.

'To each one': that is, to every believer, or every recipient of the Holy Spirit.

'The manifestation of the Spirit is given': that is, the Spirit who lives in all believers, as the body of Christ, manifests himself in one way in one person, and in another way in another person. The illustration which the apostle introduces later is derived from the human body. As the principle of life manifests itself in one organ as the faculty of vision, and in another as the faculty of hearing, so the Holy Spirit manifests himself variously in the different members of the church – in one as the gift of teaching, in another as the gift of healing. This is one of those pregnant truths, compressed in a single sentence, which are developed in manifold forms in different parts of the Word of God. This whole chapter is the exposition and the application of this truth.

'For the common good': that is, for edification. This is the common object of all these gifts. They are not intended exclusively or mainly for the recipients' benefit, much less for their gratification; but for the good of the church. Just as the power of vision is not for the benefit of the eye, but for the whole person. When God's gifts, natural or supernatural, are perverted as means of self-exaltation or aggrandisement, therefore, it is a sin against their giver, as well as against those for whose benefit they were intended.

With regard to the gifts mentioned in the following verses, note first that the listing is not intended to include all the forms in which the Spirit manifested his presence in the people of God. Gifts are mentioned elsewhere which are not found in this catalogue (compare Romans 12:4–8, and verse 28 of this chapter). Secondly, note that although the apostle appears to divide these gifts into three classes, the principle of classification is not discernible. That is, we can discover no reason why one gift is in one class rather than in another; why, for example, prophecy, instead of being associated with other gifts of teaching, is connected with those of healing and working miracles. The different modes of classification which have been proposed, even when founded on a real difference, cannot be applied to the arrangement given by the apostle. Some would divide them into natural and supernatural. But they are all supernatural, although not to the same degree or in the same form. There are gifts of the Spirit which are ordinary and permanent, such as those of teaching and ruling, but they are not included in this listing, which embraces nothing which was not miraculous, or at least supernatural. Others, such as Neander, divide them into those exercised by word, and those exercised by deeds. To the former class belong those of wisdom, knowledge, prophecy, and speaking with tongues; to the latter belong the gifts of healing and miracles. Others, again, propose a psychological division, that is, one based on the different faculties involved in their exercise. Hence they are distinguished as those which concern the feelings, those which pertain to the intelligence, and those which relate to the will. But this is altogether arbitrary, as all these faculties are concerned in the exercise of every gift. It is better to take the classification as we find it, without attempting to determine the principle of arrangement, which may have been partly fortuitous, or determined by the mere association of ideas, rather than by any characteristic difference in the gifts themselves. The Scriptures are much more like a work of nature than a work of art; much more like a landscape than a building. Things spring up where we cannot see the reason why they are there, rather than elsewhere, while everything is in its right place.

'To one there is given through the Spirit the message of wisdom, to another the message of knowledge by means of the same Spirit, to another faith by the same Spirit, to another gifts of healing by that one Spirit'
In verse 7, Paul had said, 'To each one the manifestation of the Spirit is given.' What follows is the illustration and confirmation of what he said there. The point to be illustrated is the diversity of forms in

which the same Spirit manifests himself in different individuals.

The message, or 'word', of wisdom is the gift of speaking or communicating wisdom; and the 'message', or 'word', of knowledge is the gift of communicating knowledge. However, it is not easy to decide what the difference is between wisdom and knowledge as used here. Some say that wisdom is practical, and knowledge speculative. Others say just the reverse. Passages may be cited in favour of either view. Others say that wisdom refers to what is perceived by intuition, that is, what is apprehended (they say) by reason, and knowledge is what is perceived by the understanding. The effect of the one is spiritual discernment, and of the other is scientific knowledge, that is, the logical nature and relationships of the truths discerned. Others say that wisdom is the gospel, the whole system of revealed truth, and the message of wisdom is the gift of revealing that system as the object of faith. In favour of this view are the following obvious facts:

1. Paul frequently uses the word in this sense. In chapter 2 he says that we speak wisdom, the wisdom of God, the hidden wisdom which the great of this world never could discover, but which God has revealed by his Spirit.

2. That gift stands first as the most important, and as the characteristic gift of the apostle, as may be inferred from verse 28, where the arrangement of functions to a certain extent corresponds with the arrangement of the gifts presented here. Among the gifts, the first is the 'message of wisdom', and among the functions, the first is that of the apostles. It is perfectly natural that this correspondence should be observed at the beginning, even if it is not carried through. This gift in its full measure belonged to the apostles alone; however, it belonged partly also to the prophets of the New Testament. Hence apostles and prophets are often associated as possessing the same gift, although in different degrees: 'built on the foundation of the apostles and prophets' (Ephesians 2:20); 'has now been revealed by the Spirit to God's holy apostles and prophets' (Ephesians 3:5; see also 4:11). The characteristic difference between these groups was that the apostles were endowed with permanent and plenary inspiration, and the prophets with occasional and partial inspiration.

'The message of knowledge', as distinguished from 'the message of wisdom', is probably to be understood of the gift which belonged to teachers. Accordingly, they follow the apostles and prophets in the list in verse 28. 'The message of knowledge' was the gift of understanding correctly and exhibiting properly the truths revealed by the apostles and prophets. This agrees with 13:8, where the gift of knowledge is represented as belonging to the present state of existence.

'By means of the same Spirit.' Literally, *according to* the same Spirit,' that is, according to his will, or as he sees fit; see verse 11. The Spirit is not only the author, but the distributor of these gifts. And therefore sometimes they are said to be given 'by', and sometimes 'according to', the Spirit.

'To another faith by the same Spirit, to another gifts of healing by that one Spirit'
In the Greek there is a distinction which is not expressed in our translation. The main divisions in this list seem to be indicated by a word which is a stronger expression of difference than between the other terms, although both words are translated 'another'. Therefore, where the stronger word is used, a new group seems to be introduced. The first class includes the message of wisdom and the message of knowledge; the second includes all the rest except for the last two.

'To another faith': as faith is mentioned here as a special gift some Christians have, it cannot mean saving faith, which is common to all. It is generally supposed to mean the faith of miracles to which our Lord refers in Matthew 17:19–20, and which the apostle mentions in 13:2 ('a faith that can move mountains'). But to this is also objected that the gift of miracles is mentioned immediately afterwards as something different from the gift of faith. Others say it is that faith which manifests itself in all the forms listed under this class, that is, in miraculous powers, in healing, in prophecy, and in distinguishing between spirits. But then it is nothing special; it is a gift common to all under this heading, whereas it is as much distinguished from them as they are from each other. Besides, no degree of faith involves inspiration which is supposed in prophecy. In the absence of clear evidence for deciding what faith is meant here, it is safest, perhaps, to stick to the simple meaning of the word, and assume that it means a higher measure of the ordinary grace of faith. Such a faith enabled people to become confessors and martyrs, and is fully illustrated in Hebrews 11:33—40. This is something truly as wonderful as the gift of miracles.

'To another gifts of healing': that is, gifts by which the sick were healed (Acts 4:30). This evidently refers to the miraculous healing of diseases.

'To another miraculous powers, to another prophecy, to another distinguishing between spirits, to another speaking in different kinds of tongues, and to still another the interpretation of tongues'
'Miraculous powers' — literally, 'effects which are miraculous', or which consist in miracles. This is more comprehensive than the preceding gift. Some merely had the gift of healing the sick, while others had the general powers of working miracles. This was exemplified in the death of Ananias, in raising Dorcas, in making Elymas blind, and in many other cases.

The nature of the gift of prophecy is clearly shown in chapter 14. It consisted in occasional inspiration and revelations, not merely or generally relating to the future, as in the case of Agabus (Acts 11:28), but either in some new communications relating to faith or duty, or simply an immediate impulse and aid from the Holy Spirit, in presenting truth already known, so that conviction and repentance were the effects aimed at and produced; compare 14:25. The difference between the apostles and the prophets was the apostles were permanently inspired, so that their teaching was always infallible, whereas the prophets were infallible only occasionally. The ordinary teachers were uninspired, speaking from the resources of their own knowledge and experience.

'To another distinguishing between spirits.' It appears, especially from the letters of the apostle John, that pretenders to inspiration were numerous in the apostolic age. He therefore exhorts his readers to 'test the spirits to see whether they are from God, because many false prophets have gone out into the world' (1 John

4:1). It was therefore important to have people with the gift of determining whether a person was really inspired, or spoke only from the impulse of his own mind, or from the dictation of some evil spirit. In 14:29, reference is made to the exercise of this gift. Compare also 1 Thessalonians 5:20–21.

'To another speaking in different kinds of tongues,' that is, the ability to speak in languages previously unknown to the speakers. The nature of this gift is determined by the account given in Acts 2:4–11, where it says that the apostles 'began to speak in other tongues as the Spirit enabled them'. People of all the neighbouring countries asked with astonishment, 'Are not all these men who are speaking Galileans? Then how is it that each of us hears them in his own native language?' It is impossible to deny that the miracle recorded in Acts consisted in enabling the apostles to speak in languages which they had never learnt. Unless, therefore, it is assumed that the gift which Paul is speaking about here was entirely different, its nature is beyond dispute. The identity of the two, however, is proved from the sameness of the terms by which they are described. In Mark 16:17 it was promises that the disciples would speak 'in new tongues'. Acts 2:4 says they spoke 'in other tongues'. Acts 10:46 and 19:6 say that those on whom the Holy Spirit came spoke 'in tongues'. It can hardly be doubted that all these forms of expression are to be understood in the same sense; that to speak 'in tongues' in Acts 10:46 means the same thing as speaking 'in other tongues' in Acts 2:4, and that this again means the same as speaking 'in new tongues' as promised in Mark 16:17. If the meaning of the phrase is thus historically and philologically determined for Acts and Mark, it must also be determined for the letter to the Corinthians. If 'tongues' means 'languages' in the former, it must have the same meaning in the latter. We thus have two arguments in favour if the old interpretation of this passage. First, that the facts narrated in Acts necessitate the interpretation of the phrase 'to speak in other tongues' to mean to speak with foreign languages. Second, that the interchange of the expressions 'new tongues', 'other tongues', and 'tongues', referring to the same event, shows that 'to speak in tongues' must have the same meaning as the previous two expressions, which can only mean to speak in new languages.

A third argument is that the common interpretation satisfies all the facts of the case:

1. What was spoken with tongues was intelligible to those who understood foreign languages, as appears from Acts 2:11. Therefore the speaking was not an incoherent, unintelligible rhapsody.

2. What was uttered was articulate sounds, the vehicle of prayer, praise, and thanksgiving (1 Corinthians 14:14–17).

3. They were edifying, and therefore intelligible to the person who uttered them (1 Corinthians 14:4).

4. They could be interpreted, which supposes them to be intelligible.

5. Though intelligible in themselves, and to the speaker, they were unintelligible to others, that is, to those not acquainted with the language used; and consequently they were unsuitable for an ordinary Christian meeting. The folly which Paul rebuked was speaking Arabic to people who understood only Greek. The speaker might understand what he said, but others were not profited (1 Corinthians 14:2, 19).

6. The illustration used in 1 Corinthians 14:7, 11, from musical instruments, and from the case of foreigners, requires the common interpretation. Paul admits that the sounds uttered were not without meaning (14:10). His complaint is that someone who speaks in an unknown tongue is a foreigner to him (verse 11). This illustration supposes the sounds uttered to be intelligible in themselves, but not understood by those to whom they were addressed.

7. The common interpretation suits even those passages which present the only real difficulty in the case, namely those in which the apostle speaks of the mind as being unfruitful in the exercise of the gift of tongues, and those in which he contrasts praying with the spirit and praying with the mind (14:14–15). Although these passages, taken by themselves, might seem to indicate that the speaker himself did not understand what he was saying, and even that his intellect was in abeyance, they may naturally mean only that the speaker's understanding was unprofitable to others; and speaking with the mind may mean speaking intelligibly. It is not necessary, therefore, to infer from these passages that to speaking

in tongues was to speak in a state of ecstasy, in a manner unintelligible to any human being.

8. The common interpretation is also consistent with the fact that the gift of interpretation was distinct from that of speaking with tongues. If a person could speak a foreign language, why could he not interpret it? Simply, because it was not his gift. What he said in that foreign language was said under the guidance of the Spirit; had he attempted to interpret it without the gift of interpretation, he would be speaking of himself, and not 'as the Spirit enabled them'. In the one case he was the organ of the Holy Spirit, in the other he was not.

The fourth argument is that those who depart from the common interpretation of the gift of tongues differ indefinitely among themselves as to its true nature. Some assume that the word 'tongues' does not here mean languages, but 'idioms' or peculiar and unusual forms of expression. To speak with tongues, according to this view, is to speak in an exalted poetic strain, beyond the comprehension of common people. But it has been proved from the expressions 'new' and 'other' tongues, and from the facts recorded in Acts, that the word 'tongues' must mean languages here. Besides, to speak in exalted language is not to speak unintelligibly. The Greeks understood the loftiest strains of their orators and poets. This interpretation also gives the word a technical sense foreign to all scriptural usage, and one which is entirely inadmissible, at least in those cases where the singular is used. Someone might be said to speak in 'phrases', but not in 'a phrase'.

Others say that the word means the tongue as the physical organ of utterance; and to speak 'with the tongue' is to speak in a state of excitement in which the mind and the will do not control the tongue, which is moved by the Spirit to utter sounds which are as unintelligible to the speaker as to others. But this interpretation does not suit the expressions 'other tongues' and 'new tongues', and is irreconcilable with the account in Acts. Besides, it degrades the gift. It is out of analogy with all scriptural facts. The spirits of the prophets are subject to the prophets. The Old Testament seers were not beside themselves, and the apostles in the use of the gift of tongues were calm and rational, speaking the wonderful works of God in a way which the foreigners gathered in Jerusalem easily understood.

Others, again, admit that the word 'tongues' means languages, but deny that they were languages foreign to the speaker. To speak with tongues, they say, was to speak in an incoherent, unintelligible manner, in a state of ecstasy, when the mind is entirely abstracted from the external world, and unconscious of things about it, as in a dream or trance. This, however, is liable to the objections already advanced against the other theories. Besides, it is evident from the whole discussion that those who spoke in tongues were self-controlled. They could speak or not as they pleased. Paul censures them for speaking when there was no occasion for it, and in such a manner as to produce confusion and disorder. They were, therefore, not in a state of uncontrollable excitement, unconscious of what they were doing or saying.

The arguments against the common view of the nature of the gift of tongues (apart from the exegetical difficulties with which it is thought to be encumbered) are not such as to make much impression on minds accustomed to reverence the Scriptures.

1. It is said the miracle was unnecessary, as Greek was understood wherever the apostles preached. This, no doubt, is in a great degree true. Greek was the language of educated people throughout the Roman empire, but it had not superseded the national languages in common life, nor was the preaching of the apostle confined to the limits of the Roman empire. Besides, this supposes that the only point of the gift was to facilitate the propagation of the Gospel. This was doubtless one of the purposes which it was intended to answer; but it had other important uses. It served to prove the presence of the Spirit of God; and it symbolized the calling of the Gentiles and the common interest of all nations in the Gospel. See the remarks on Acts 2:4.

2. It is said God does not usually remove difficulties miraculously, when his people can surmount them by labour.

3. Others pronounce it impossible that a man should speak in a language which he had never learnt. But does it follow that God cannot give him the ability?

4. It appears that Paul and Barnabas did not understand the

speech of Lycaonia (Acts 14:11–14). The gift of tongues, however, was not the ability to speak all languages. Probably most of those who received the gift could speak only in one or two. Paul thanked God that he had the gift in richer measure than any of the Corinthians.

5. The gift does not appear to have been made subservient to the missionary work. It certainly was in the first instance, as recorded in Acts, and may have been afterwards.

6. Paul, in 1 Corinthians 14:14–19, does not contrast speaking in tongues and speaking in one's own language, but speaking with the mind and speaking with the spirit; therefore, to speak in tongues is to speak without understanding, or in a state of ecstasy. This is a possible interpretation of this one passage considered in itself, but it is in direct contradiction to all those passages which prove that speaking with tongues was not an involuntary, incoherent, ecstatic mode of speaking. The passage referred to, therefore, must be understood in consistency with the other passages referring to the same subject. Though there are difficulties attending any view of the gift in question, arising from our ignorance, those connected with the common interpretation are incomparably less that those which beset any of the modern conjectures.

'To still another the interpretation of tongues.' The nature of this gift depends on the view taken of the preceding. Commonly, at least, the man using a foreign language was able to understand it (see 14:2, 4, 16), and may have had the gift of interpretation in connection with the gift of tongues. It is possible, however, that in some cases he did not himself understand the language which he spoke, and then of course he would need an interpreter. But even when he did understand the language which he used, he needed a distinct gift to make him the organ of the Spirit in its interpretation. If speaking in tongues was speaking incoherently in ecstasy, it is hard to see how what was said could admit of interpretation. Unless coherent, it was irrational, and if it was irrational, it could not be translated.

'All these are the work of one and the same Spirit, and he gives them to each one, just as he determines'
Despite the diversity of these gifts, they all have a common origin. They are the work of the same Spirit. Therefore, what verse 6 says is done by God, the present verse says is done by the Spirit. This is in accordance with constant scriptural usage. The same effect is sometimes attributed to one, and sometimes to another of the persons of the Holy Trinity. This supposes that, being the same in substance (or essence) in which divine power inheres, they cooperate in the production of these effects. Whatever the Father does, he does through the Spirit. The Holy Spirit not only produces these gifts in people's minds, but he distributes them 'to each one', that is, not according to people's merits or wishes, but according to his own will.

'Just as he determines.' This passage clearly proves that the Holy Spirit is a person. Will is attributed to him here, and this is one of the distinctive attributes of a person. Both the divinity and the personality of the Holy Spirit are therefore involved in the nature of the work here ascribed to him.

'The body is a unit, though it is made up of many parts; and though all its parts are many, they form one body. So it is with Christ'
Here is an illustration of the truth taught in the preceding verses. Every organism, or organic whole, supposes diversity and unity. That is, different parts united so as to constitute one whole. The apostle had taught that in the unity of the church there is a diversity of gifts. This is illustrated by a reference to the human body. It is one, yet it consists of many parts. And this diversity is essential to unity; for unless the body consisted of many members, it would not a 'body', that is, an organic whole.

'So it is with Christ.' That is, the body of Christ, or the church. As the body consists of many parts and yet is one, so it is with the church: it is one and yet consists of many members, each having its own gift and function. See Romans 12:4–5; Ephesians 1:23; 4:4, 16.

*'For we were all baptised by one Spirit into one body — whether Jews or
Greeks, slave or free — and we were all given the one Spirit to drink'*
This is the proof of what immediately precedes. The church is
one, 'for we were all baptised by one Spirit into one body'. This is
commonly understood (even by the modern commentators) to
refer to the sacrament of baptism; and the apostle is made to say
that by the Holy Spirit received in baptism we were made one
body. But the Bible clearly distinguishes between baptism with
water and baptism with the Holy Spirit. 'I baptise you with water
. . . He will baptise you with the Holy Spirit' (Matthew 3:11). 'The
one who sent me to baptise with water told me, "The man on
whom you see the Spirit come down and remain is he who will baptise with the Holy Spirit"' (John 1:33). 'For John baptised with
water, but in a few days you will be baptised with the Holy Spirit'
(Acts 1:5). These passages not only distinguish between the baptism of water and the baptism of the Spirit, but they disconnect
them. The baptism to which Acts 1:5 refers took place on the day
of Pentecost, and had nothing to do with the baptism of water. It
is not denied that the one is sacramentally connected with the
other, or that the baptism of the Spirit often accompanies the baptism of water; but they are not inseparably connected. The one
may be without the other. And in the present passage there does
not seem to be even an allusion to water baptism, any more than in
Acts 1:5. Paul does not say that we are made one body by baptism,
but by the baptism of the Holy Spirit; that is, by spiritual regeneration.

Any communication of the Holy Spirit is called a baptism,
because the Spirit is said to be poured out, and those on whom he
is poured out, whether in his regenerating, sanctifying, or inspiring influences, are said to be baptized. In all the passages quoted
above, the expression is 'by the Spirit', as it is here. It is not therefore by baptism as an external rite, but by the communication of
the Holy Spirit that we are made members of the body of Christ.

'Into one body' means 'so as to constitute one body'. No matter
how great may have been the previous difference, whether they
were Jews or Greeks, bond or free, by this baptism of the Spirit all
who experience it are merged into one body; they are all intimately

and organically united as partaking of the same life. Compare Galatians 3:28. And this is the essential point of the analogy between the human body and the church. As the body is one because it is pervaded and animated by one soul or principle of life, so the church is one because it is pervaded by one Spirit. And as all parts of the body which partake of the common life belong to the body, so all those in whom the Spirit of God lives are members of the church which is the body of Christ. And by the same reasoning, those in whom the Spirit does not live are not members of Christ's body. They may be members of the visible or nominal church, but they are not members of the church in that sense in which it is the body of Christ. This passage, therefore, not only teaches us the nature of the church, but also the principle of its unity. It is one, not as united under one external visible head, or under one governing tribunal, nor in virtue of any external visible bond, but in virtue of the indwelling of the Holy Spirit in all its members. And this internal spiritual union manifests itself in the profession of the same faith, and in all acts of Christian fellowship.

'And we were all given the one Spirit to drink.' This is a difficult clause. In some manuscripts it is 'into one Spirit', in others 'one Spirit'. If the latter is to be preferred, the sense is, 'We have all drunk one Spirit'. That is, we have all been made partakers of one Spirit. Compare John 7:37, and other passages, in which the Spirit is compared to water of which people are said to drink. The meaning of the passage according to this reading is simple and pertinent. 'By the baptism of the Holy Spirit we have all been united in one body and made partakers of one Spirit.' If the other text is preferred, the most natural interpretation would seem to be, 'We have all been made to drink so as to become one Spirit.' The words 'unto one Spirit' would then correspond to 'unto one body'. Luther, Calvin, and Beza suppose the allusion to be to the Lord's Supper. 'By baptism we become one body, and by drinking (of the cup, that is, by the Lord's Supper) we become one body.' But this allusion is not only foreign to the context but is not indicated by the words. How can the simple phrase 'made to drink', in such a context, mean to share in the Lord's Supper? Besides, as the modern commentators all remark, the tense of the verb forbids this interpretation. It must express the same time as the preceding verb. 'We were all baptised, and we were all made to drink.' It is something done in the past, not something continued in the present that the word expresses. If anything is to be supplied it is not the word 'cup', but 'the Spirit', that is, the water of life. 'We have been made to drink (that is, of the Spirit) so as to become one spirit.'

Another interpretation supposes that the phrase literally translated 'to drink into' is equivalent to 'drink of'. The sense is then, again, 'We have all drunk of one Spirit.' The doctrine taught is clear, namely, that by receiving the Spirit we are all made members of the body of Christ, and that it is in virtue of the indwelling of the Spirit that the church is one.

1 Corinthians (1857; Wheaton (IL): Crossway Books, 1995).

Commentary on 1 Corinthians 12:28–31

In Ephesians 4:11 Paul says, 'It was he [God] who gave some to be apostles, some to be prophets,' etc. Here, he began to use the same form – 'in the church God has appointed . . .' – but varies the construction, and says, 'first of all apostles'. This verse amplifies the previous one. In verse 27 he said the church is like the human body. Here he shows that the analogy consists in the common life of the church, or the indwelling Spirit of God, manifesting itself in a diversity of gifts and functions, just as the common life of the body manifests itself in different organs and members. In the church some were apostles, that is, immediate messengers of Christ, made infallible as teachers and rulers by the gift of plenary inspiration.

'Second prophets.' That is, people who spoke for God as the occasional organs of his Spirit.

'Third teachers.' That is, uninspired men who had received the gift of teaching.

'Then workers of miracles.' Here and in what follows abstract terms are used for concrete – literally, 'miracles', meaning people endowed with the power of working miracles.

'Also those having gifts of healing.' That is, people endowed with the power of healing diseases.

'Those able to help others.' That is, people qualified and appointed to help the other officers of the church, probably in the care of the poor and the sick. These, according to the common understanding from Chrysostom to the present day, were deacons and deaconesses.

'Those with gifts of administration.' 'Governments', that is, people who had the gift and authority to rule. As this gift and office are distinguished from those of teachers, it cannot be understood to mean the presbyter or overseers who were required to be 'able to teach' (1 Tim. 3:2). It seems to refer clearly to a class of officers distinct from teacher, that is, rulers, or as they are called in the Reformed churches, 'ruling elders'.

'Those speaking in different kinds of tongues.' That is, people having the gift of speaking in foreign languages. This is probably put last because it was so unduly valued and so ostentatiously displayed by the Corinthians.

Note that this list was not intended to be exhaustive. Gifts are mentioned in verses 8–10, and elsewhere, which have nothing to correspond to them here.

Secondly, every office necessarily supposes the corresponding gift. No one could be an apostle without the gift of infallibility; nor a prophet without the gift of inspiration; nor a healer of diseases without the gift of healing. We may appoint people to offices for which they have not the necessary gifts, but God never does, any more than he ordains the foot to see or the hand to hear. Therefore, if anyone claims to be an apostle, or prophet, or worker of miracles, without the corresponding gift, he is a false pretender. In the early church, as now, there were many false apostles, that is, people who claimed the honor and authority of the office without its gifts.

Thirdly, the fact that any office existed in the apostolic church is no evidence that it was intended to be permanent. In that age many spiritual manifestations and endowments were needed for the organisation and propagation of the church, which are no longer required. We no longer have prophets, nor workers of miracles, nor gifts of tongues. The only evidence that an office was intended to be permanent is the continuance of the gift of which it was the organ, and the command to appoint to the office those who are found to possess the gift. The only evidence that God intended the eye to be a permanent organ of the body is that he has perpetuated the faculty of vision. Had the gift of sight been discontinued, it would be no good our calling the mouth and nose 'eyes', and demanding that they should be recognised as such. This is precisely what Roman Catholics and others do when they call their bishops 'apostles', and require people to honour and obey them as though they were.

Fourthly, the only evidence of a call to an office is possessing the requisite gifts. If someone received the gift of prophecy, he was thereby called to be a prophet; or if he received the gift of healing, he was thereby called to exercise that gift. So if anyone has received ministerial gifts, he has received a call to the ministry. The Bible has taught us what those gifts are. They include soundness in the faith, competent knowledge, ability to teach, the love of Christ and zeal for his glory, an intelligent conviction of an obligation to preach the gospel, and in short the qualifications which are necessary in one who is to be an example and guide of the flock of Jesus Christ. The office of the church in the matter is, first, to examine whether the candidate for the ministry really possesses ministerial gifts; and then, if satisfied on that point, authoritatively to declare its judgment in the appointed way. The same is true of a call to missionary work or to any other form of labour in the church of Christ. The fundamental idea is that the church is the body of Christ, filled by his Spirit, and that the Spirit distributes variously, as he wills, to each person the gifts which he intends him to exercise for the edification of the whole.

'Are all apostles? Are all prophets? Are all teachers? Do all work miracles? Do all have gifts of healing? Do all speak in tongues? Do all interpret?'
As in the body all is not eye, or all ear, so in the church all have not the same gifts and functions. And as it would be preposterous in all the parts of the body to aspire to the same function, so it is no less preposterous in the members of the church that all should covet the same gifts. It is the apostle's purpose to suppress, on the

one hand, all discontent and envy, and on the other all pride and arrogance. God distributes his gifts as he pleases; all are necessary, and the recipients of them are mutually dependent.

'But eagerly desire the greater gifts. And now I will show you the most excellent way'
All cannot have every gift, but eagerly desire the better ones. To 'eagerly desire' implies corresponding effort to obtain. The extraordinary gifts of the Spirit were bestowed according to his own good pleasure. But so also are his saving benefits. Yet both may, and should, be sought in the use of the appointed means.

'The greater gifts.' From 14:5 we see that these were the ones which were the more useful. The Corinthians had a very different standard of excellence, and sought most eagerly the gifts which were the most attractive, although the least useful.

'And now I will show you the most excellent way.' Whether it is excellent compared to something else, or most excellent, depends on the context. Here no comparison is implied. The idea is not that he intends to show them a way that is better than seeking gifts, but a way *par excellence* to obtain those gifts. Calvin and others do indeed adopt the other view, but it supposes the preceding imperative ('eagerly desire') to be merely concessive, and is contrary to 14:1, where the command to seek the more useful gifts is repeated. The sense is, 'Seek the better gifts, and moreover I show you an excellent way to do it.'

1 Corinthians (1857; Wheaton (IL): Crossway Books, 1995).

Commentary on 1 Corinthians 14:1–25

The superiority of the gift of prophecy to that of tongues is based on the following considerations:

1. A person who speaks in tongues speaks to God, whereas a person who prophesies speaks to other people (verses 2–3).

2. A person who speaks in tongues edifies only himself, whereas a person who prophesies edifies the church (verses 4–5). This is proved in the following ways:

a. By an appeal to their own judgment and experience. If Paul came to them speaking in a way which they could not understand, what good could it do them? But if, as a prophet, he brought them a revelation from God, or as a teacher, set before them a doctrine, they would be edified (verse 6).

b. From the analogy of musical instruments. It is only when the sounds are understood that they produce the desired effect. If a person does not know that a given note of the trumpet is a signal for battle, he will not prepare himself for the conflict (verses 7–9).

c. From their experience of dealing with strangers. If someone comes to me speaking a language which I do not understand, no matter how polished or significant that language may be, he is a foreigner to me, and I to him (verses 10–11).

In their zeal for spiritual gifts, therefore, they should have regard to the edification of the church (verse 12). Hence, anyone who had the gift of tongues should pray for the gift of interpretation, as, without it, however devotional, his prayers could not profit other people (verses 13–14). It was not enough that the prayers and praises should be spiritual; they must be intelligible; otherwise those who were unlearned could not join in them (verses 15–17). For himself, the apostle says, although more richly endowed with the gift of tongues than any of his readers, he would rather speak five words so as to be understood than ten thousand words in an unknown tongue (verses 18–19). It was mere childishness in the Corinthians to be so delighted with a gift which they could not use in any practical way (verse 20). They should learn wisdom from the experience of the Hebrews. It was as a judgment that God sent among them teachers whom they could not understand. So long as they were obedient, or there was hope of bringing them to repentance, he sent them prophets speaking their own language (verses 21–22). Their experience would not be dissimilar. If they came together, each speaking in an unknown tongue, the effect would be only evil. But if, when they assembled, all the speakers spoke so as to be understood, and under the influence of the Spirit, then people would be convinced and converted, and God glorified (verses 23–25).

In the comment on 12:10, reasons have already been presented for sticking to the common view that the gift of tongues was the gift miraculously conferred of speaking in foreign languages. Everyone must feel, however, the truth of Chrysostom's remark in his commentary on this chapter: 'This whole passage is very obscure; but the obscurity arises from our ignorance of the facts described, which, though familiar to those to whom the apostle wrote, have ceased to occur.' This gift is specially connected with prophesying ('they spoke in tongues and prophesied', Acts 19:6). This is because all speaking under divine, supernatural influence was included under the head of prophesying; and all who spoke in tongues spoke 'as the Spirit enabled them', so they all prophesied in the wide sense of the term. But it is not so easy to understand why this gift should have been so common, nor why it should so often accompany conversion (see Acts 10:46; 19:6). There are many things also in this chapter which it is not easy to understand on any theory of the nature of the gift. Under these circumstances it is necessary to hold fast what is clear, and to make what is certain our guide in explaining what is obscure. It is clear –

1. That the word 'tongues' in this context, as already proved, means languages.

2. That the speaker with tongues was in a state of calm self-control. He could speak, or be silent (14:28).

3. That what he said was intelligible to himself, and could be interpreted to others.

4. That the unintelligibleness of what was said arose not from the sounds uttered being inarticulate, but from the ignorance of the hearer. The interpretation of particular passages must, therefore, be controlled by these facts.

'Follow the way of love and eagerly desire spiritual gifts, especially the gift of prophecy.'
In the preceding chapters Paul had taught the following:

1. That all the extraordinary gifts of the Spirit were proper objects of desire.

2. That they were of different relative importance.

3. That love was of greater value than any gift.

In accordance with these principles, the apostle exhorts his readers to 'follow the way of love', that is, to press forward towards it, as people do towards the goal in a race (Philippians 3:12, 14). Pursue it earnestly as the greatest good. But at the same time, 'desire spiritual gifts'. Because love is more important than miraculous gifts, it does not follow that the latter were not to be sought. The same word is used here as in 12:31.

'Especially the gift of prophecy.' The two gifts specially in the apostle's mind were the gift of speaking in tongues and that of prophecy, that is, the gift of speaking as the organ of the Spirit in a way that would instruct and edify the hearer. Of these two gifts, he says, the latter is to be preferred. The reason for this preference is given in what follows.

'For anyone who speaks in a tongue does not speak to men but to God. Indeed, no one understands him; he utters mysteries with his spirit'
This teaches:
1. That he who speaks in tongues speaks not to men, but to God.
2. That this means that men do not understand *him*.
3. That the reason he is not understood is in the medium of communication, not in the things communicated.

'Does not speak to men but to God.' Or, speaks not *for* men but *for* God. His communion is with God, and not with man.

'No one understands him.' Literally, 'no man *hears*', that is, hears any articulate sounds. He hears the sound, but does not distinguish the words. This, however, does not imply that the sounds uttered were in themselves unintelligible, so that no living person (unless inspired) could understand them. When the apostle spoke in tongues on the day of Pentecost, what they said was understood. The meaning is not that no living person, but that no one *present*, could understand. It is not the use of the gift of tongues that he censures, but the use of that gift when no one was present who understood the language used.

'He utters mysteries with his spirit.' 'Spirit' does not mean the man's spirit as opposed to his understanding. The Scriptures do not distinguish between these faculties. The 'spirit' is not the higher spiritual powers of our nature, but the Holy Spirit; compare 2:14. The following considerations favour this interpretation:

1. The prevailing use of the word 'spirit' in reference to the Holy Spirit in all Paul's letters, and especially in this whole context.

2. The expression 'to speak in (or by) the Spirit' is an established scriptural phrase, meaning to speak under the guidance of the Holy Spirit.

3. When 'spirit' is to be distinguished from the understanding, it designates the affections – a sense which would not at all suit this passage.

4. The meaning arrived at by this interpretation is natural, and suits the context. 'Although he who speaks in tongues is not understood, he still is guided by the Spirit, and speaks mysteries.'

'Mysteries' means divine truths, things which God has revealed. In Acts 2:11, they are called 'the wonders of God'. To make the word mean 'things not understood by the hearer' is contrary to the usage of the word. A secret disclosed is no longer a secret; and a mystery revealed ceases to be a mystery, for a mystery is something hidden. Besides, Paul would then say, 'No one understands him, yet he speaks what is not understood.' The meaning is obviously that although what he says is not understood, it contains divine truth. The difficulty was in the language used, not in the absence of meaning, or in the fact that inarticulate sounds were used. This verse, therefore, contains nothing inconsistent with the commonly received view of the nature of the gift in question. 'He who speaks in tongues speaks to God and not to men, for no one (in the case supposed) understands him, although what he says is replete with the highest meaning.' The implication is that these 'tongues' were foreign to the hearers; and that is why it says 'no one understands him'.

'But everyone who prophesies speaks to men for their strengthening, encouragement and comfort'

The prophet spoke in the native language of his hearers; the speaker in tongues spoke in a foreign language. This made the difference between the two cases. The one was understood and the other was not. The prophet spoke with a view to 'strengthening'. This is a general term including the sense of the next two. He strengthened the church either by encouragement or by comfort, either by arousing believers to do or suffer, or by pouring into their hearts the consolations of the Spirit.

'He who speaks in a tongue edifies himself, but he who prophesies edifies the church'
This follows from what had been said. The speaker in tongues did not edify the whole church, because he was not understood; he did edify himself, because he understood himself. This verse, therefore, proves that the understanding was not in abeyance, and that the speaker was not in an ecstatic trance.

'I would like every one of you to speak in tongues, but I would rather have you prophesy. He who prophesies is greater than one who speaks in tongues, unless he interprets, so that the church may be edified'
'I would like every one of you to speak in tongues.' It was not to be inferred from what he had said, that the apostle undervalued this gift. He admitted its importance as one of the manifestations of the Spirit, and in verse 18 he gives thanks that he himself possessed it in rich measure. From this it is evident that it was something of a higher nature than modern theories would represent it.

'He who prophesies . . .' He is more useful than the speaker in tongues, unless the latter interprets. Speaking under the supernatural influence of the Spirit was common to both gifts; the only difference was in the language used. If the speaker interpreted, then he prophesied.

'So that the church may be edified.' This proves that the contents of these discourses, delivered in an unknown tongue, were edifying; and therefore did not consist in mysteries in the bad sense of that term, that is, in enigmas and dark sayings. This passage also proves that the gift of interpretation, although distinct from that of tongues, might be, and doubtless often was, possessed by the same person, and consequently that he understood what he said. The absence of the gift of interpretation does not prove that the speaker himself in such cases was ignorant of what he uttered. It only proves that he was not inspired to communicate in another language what he had delivered. Had he done so, it would have been on his own authority, and not as an organ of the

Spirit. It is conceivable that a man might speak connectedly in a foreign language under the inspiration of the Spirit, so as to be perfectly understood by those acquainted with the language, though he himself did not understand a word of what he uttered. But this hypothesis, though it would suit some passages in this chapter, is inconsistent with others, and therefore cannot be adopted.

'Now, brothers, if I come to you and speak in tongues, what good will I be to you, unless I bring you some revelation or knowledge or prophecy or word of instruction?'
'Now.' Since things are so, that is, since speaking with tongues without interpreting is unedifying, what good will I do you, asks the apostle, if I should come to you speaking in a language which you do not understand? He then varies the question: 'What good will I do you unless I speak to you as a prophet, by (or rather, *with*) a revelation, or as a teacher with a doctrine?' There are not four, but only two modes of address in this verse. Revelation and prophecy belong to one; and knowledge and doctrine to the other. He who received revelations was a prophet, and he who had 'a word of instruction' was a teacher.

'Even in the case of lifeless things that make sounds, such as the flute or harp, how will anyone know what tune is being played unless there is a distinction in the notes?'
In the Greek, this verse begins with the word 'yet', which is explained in various ways. The most natural interpretation is to assume that the word here, as in Galatians 3:15, is out of its logical place, and that the sentence should read thus: 'Things without life-giving sound, *yet*, unless they give a distinction of sound, how shall it be known . . .' The obvious intention of the illustration is to show the uselessness of making sounds which are not understood. But what is the point of the analogy? According to some, it is that as musical instrument emit a mere jargon of sounds, unless the regular intervals are observed, so the speaker in tongues utter a mere jargon. The sounds which they utter are not articulate words, but a confused noise. From this it is inferred that speaking in tongues

THE CLASSICS ON REVIVAL

was not the gift of speaking foreign languages. This would make Paul wish (verse 5) that all the Corinthians would utter unmeaning sounds, and give thanks that he produced more such jargon than any of them! It is clear from what follows, as well as from the drift of the whole discourse, that the simple point of the analogy is that, as we cannot know what is piped or harped, or benefited by it, unless we can discriminate the sounds emitted, so we cannot benefit by listening to one who speaks a language which we do not understand. The point the apostle is making is not about the nature of the gift but the folly of its use.

'Again, if the trumpet does not sound a clear call, who will get ready for battle?'
This confirms the last clause of the previous verse. The sound emitted does not produce its proper effect if it is unintelligible or uncertain. This teaches us the point of the whole illustration. The trumpet may sound the battle call, but if that call is not understood, who will take any notice? So the speak in tongues may announce the most important truths, he may unfold mysteries, or pour out praises as from a harp of gold, but what good can it do those who do not understand him?

'So it is with you. Unless you speak intelligible words with your tongue, how will anyone know what you are saying? You will just be speaking into the air'
This is the application of the preceding illustration, and affords another proof of what the apostle intended to illustrate. It was not the nature of the sounds uttered, but their unintelligibleness to the hearer, which was to be considered.

'With your tongue.' That is, by means of the tongue as the organ of speech.

'Intelligible words.' Or rather, an intelligible discourse. This does not imply, as the advocates of modern theories contend, that those who spoke in tongues uttered inarticulate sounds. The opposite of the Greek word is not inarticulate, but unintelligible, that is, what is not in fact understood.

'You will just be speaking into the air.' That is, in vain. Your words are lost in the air, no ear receives them. In 9:26, the man who struck in vain is said to beat the air.

'Undoubtedly there are all sorts of languages in the world, yet none of them is without meaning'
'Undoubtedly.' The Greek is properly translated 'it may be'; the phrase is often used to make a statement indefinite, where precision is impossible or unimportant. It was not matter, so far as the apostle's object was concerned, whether there were more or less.

'There are all sorts of languages.' Or, 'There are ever so many languages.' Calvin understands this to refer to the voices or natural cries of animals. All animated nature is vocal; no living creature is mute or utters unintelligible sounds. The context, however, shows that the reference is to human speech.

'Yet none of them is without meaning.' Literally, 'a language which is no language', that is, without significance, which is the essence of a language. The illustration contained in this verse goes to prove that speaking in tongues was to speak in foreign languages. The very point is that all languages are significant, so the languages used by those who spoke in tongues were significant. The difficulty was not in the language used, but in the ignorance of the hearer. This is still clearer from what follows.

'If then I do not grasp the meaning of what someone is saying, I am a foreigner to the speaker, and he is a foreigner to me'
'If then.' That is, because the sounds uttered are significant, because the person is not making a mere senseless noise, but is speaking a real language, therefore, if I do not know the meaning of the language, I shall be like a foreigner to him and he to me. Otherwise it would not be so. If someone utters incoherent, inarticulate sounds, which no one alive could understand, that would not make him a foreigner. It might prove him to be deranged, but not a stranger.

'So it is with you. Since you are eager to have spiritual gifts, try to excel in gifts that build up the church'
'So it is with you.' As the person who speaks a language which I do

not understand if a foreigner to me, and I to him, so it is with you. You too are foreigners to those who do not understand the language which you use. As all such unintelligible speaking is worthless, the apostle exhorts them to seek to edify the church.

'Since you are eager to have spiritual gifts.' Literally, 'As you are zealous of spirits.' The most probable explanation of this expression is to be sought from 12:7, where it says that to each one the manifestation of the Spirit is given. One and the same Spirit manifests himself in different ways in different people; and these different manifestations are called spirits. Somewhat analogous are the expressions 'spirits of prophets' (verse 32), 'distinguishing between spirits' (12:10), 'test the spirits' (1 John 4:1), and 'the seven spirits' (Revelation 1:4). In all these cases 'spirits' means manifestations of the Spirit, or forms under which the Spirit manifests himself. It is not an unusual figure of speech when the effect receives the name of its cause.

'Try to excel [or 'abound'] in gifts that build up the church.' This is the common explanation of this clause. But taking the words in their order the passage reads, 'Seek (these gifts) with a view to the building up of the church, in order that you may excel.' The former explanation is the more natural. The end of object to be sought is not 'that they might excel'; that is not the ultimate object, but the building up of the church. 'Seek that you may abound to the edification of the church,' that is, so that you may possess in rich abundance those gifts which are useful.

'For this reason anyone who speaks in a tongue should pray that he may interpret what he says'
This is an inference not only from the preceding verse but from the whole preceding argument, which was intended to show how useless it is to speak in a language which no one present understands. The verse can be interpreted in two ways. It may mean that anyone who speaks in tongues should pray for the gift of interpretation; or, that he should pray with the purpose of interpreting what he said. The principal reason for this second interpretation is the assumption that the gift of tongues was exercised only in prayer and praise; in other words, that it consisted in an ecstatic

but unintelligible and unintelligent outpouring of the heart to God. It is therefore inferred that 'to speak in a tongue' (verse 13) and 'to pray in a tongue' (verse 14) mean exactly the same thing, the former being no more comprehensive than the latter. But this whole assumption is not only gratuitous but contrary to Scripture. The gift of tongues was, according to Acts 2:5–11, exercised in 'declaring the wonders of God'. It is also apparent from what is said in this chapter (verses 22–5 and 27) that the gift in question was not confined to acts of devotion. The first interpretation is therefore to be preferred: 'Let him pray that he may interpret.'

'For if I pray in a tongue, my spirit prays, but my mind is unfruitful'
This is the reason why the speaker in tongues should pray for the gift of interpretation. Unless he interprets, his prayer can do no good; or, as the same idea is expressed in verses 16–17, those who are unlearned cannot join in it. Praying in a tongue is specified, by way of example, as one way of speaking in tongues. Though the general meaning of this verse is thus clear, it is the most difficult verse in the whole chapter. What does Paul mean by saying his spirit prays? There are three answers given:

1. That 'spirit' here means the higher intellectual powers of the soul, as distinguished from the understanding. This verse and those which come immediately afterwards are the principal basis of the theory that the speaker in tongues was in a state of ecstatic excitement in which his understanding was not exercised, so that he did not know what he was saying or doing. It has already been shown how inconsistent this theory is with the facts of the case. This view of the passage, therefore, cannot be accepted. Besides, it has already been noted that the Scriptures know nothing of this distinction between the 'reason' and the 'understanding'.

2. Others say that 'spirit' here means the affections: 'My feelings find utterance in prayer, but my understanding is unfruitful.' This would make good sense, but this meaning of the word 'spirit' occurs only rarely. In most of the passages quoted by lexicographers as examples of this use of the term, it really means the Holy Spirit. And in this whole discussion 'spirit' is not once used for the feelings.

3. 'My spirit' may mean the Holy Spirit in me; that is, my
spiritual gift; or, my spirit as the organ of the Spirit of God. Each
person has his own spirit (compare verse 12), that is, has his own
spiritual gift. And Paul means to say that when someone prays in
an unknown tongue, his spiritual gift is indeed exercised; in other
words, the Holy Spirit is active in him, but others do not benefit.
The person who speaks in tongues is not to be regarded as in a
frenzy, or, as the mockers said, as full of new wine. He is really the
organ of the Holy Spirit. But as the influence of the Spirit under
which he acts is not irresistible, he should not exercise his gift
where it can do no good to others. He may pray in silence (verse
28). This interpretation seems much more in accordance with the
use of the word and with the whole drift of this chapter.

'My mind is unfruitful.' This may mean, 'My understanding
does not benefit, gains no fruit; that is, I do not understand what
I am saying.' Though the words in themselves may have this meaning, this interpretation contradicts all those passages which teach
that the person speaking in tongues did understand himself. The
words, therefore, must be understood to mean, 'my understanding produces no fruit', that is, it does not benefit others. This is in
accordance with all that precedes, and with the uniform use of the
word (Eph. 5:11; Titus 3:14; 2 Pet.1:8; Matt. 13:22). From the
beginning, Paul had been urging his readers to have regard to the
edification of the church, and here he says that if he prayed in an
unknown tongue, though he acted under the guidance of the
Spirit, his prayer could not benefit others. We have already noted
that this interpretation is confirmed by verses 16–17, where the
same idea is expressed by saying that those who do not understand
could not say 'Amen' to such a prayer. By his mind being unfruitful, therefore, he means that others did not understand what he
said.

The great objection to the preceding interpretation is that '*My*
spirit' and '*my* mind' must be explained in the same way. If the latter means '*my own* mind', the former must mean '*my own* spirit'.
The Holy Spirit, it is said, never is, and cannot be, called '*my* spirit',
for the very reason that it is distinct from the human spirit. The
interpretation given above, however, does not suppose that 'my

spirit' means the Holy Spirit as a person, but the Holy Spirit as a manifestation; it is the way in which the Spirit manifests himself in me. In other words, it is my spiritual gift. The objection, if it has any force, bears as much against the agreed meaning of the phrase 'the spirits of prophets' as it does against the explanation just given of the expression, 'my spirit'. The spirits of prophets means the Holy Spirit as manifested in the prophets, or the spiritual influence of which they were the subjects. And that is just the meaning of 'my spirit' in this passage.

'So what shall I do? I will pray with my spirit, but I will also pray with my mind; I will sing with my spirit, but I will also sing with my mind'
'So what shall I do?' That is, what is the practical conclusion from what has been said? That conclusion is expressed by Paul's avowal of his own purpose. The interpretation of this verse of course depends on how we understand the previous verse. Accordingly, some say, the meaning is that I will pray not only with the reason, but with the understanding also – that is, not only exercising the higher powers of my nature, but also with such a command of the understanding as to be able to comprehend and to interpret what I say. (This view of the subject supposes that people who spoke in tongues were in a state rather like that of sleep-walkers, whose spiritual nature is active, but their ordinary intellectual consciousness suspended, so that when they recover, they do not remember anything they said or did when in their sleep-walking state.)

Others say the passage means, 'I will pray with the heart and with the understanding; my mind and feelings will unite in the exercise.' This makes very good sense, but is entirely foreign to the context. The idea is correct in itself, but it is not what Paul says here.

According to the third interpretation, the sense is, 'I will not only pray in the exercise of my spiritual gift, but so as to be understood by others.' That is, not only spiritually but intelligibly. If 'with my mind' may mean 'with a view to interpret', as Meyer and others say it does, then it may certainly mean 'with a view to being understood'. That is, this is what is implied and intended in what the apostle says. When someone spoke 'with the Spirit', the Spirit

was the moving principle, making him speak and telling him what
to say. When he spoke 'with the mind', the mind was that controlling principle. These two could be combined. The person could
speak like this under the guidance of the Spirit in such a way as to
be intelligible to others.

'I will sing.' The Greek word meant 'to touch'; then 'to touch the
cords' of a stringed instrument, that is, to play it; then to sing or
chant in harmony with such an instrument; and then to sing or
chant. This last is its New Testament meaning. It appears from
this as well as from other passages that singing was part of Christian worship from the beginning.

*'If you are praising God with your spirit, how can one who finds himself
among those who do not understand say 'Amen' to your thanksgiving, since
he does not know what you are saying? You may be giving thanks well
enough, but the other man is not edified'*
'Praising God.' The word includes praise and thanksgiving. The
word translated *'thanksgiving'* in the last clause of the verse expresses
the same idea.

'With your spirit.' That is, under the influence of the Spirit, or
exercising your spiritual gift, as in the previous verse.

'Those who do not understand.' The Greek word means someone who is out of office, as opposed to officers; and in general,
anyone who does not have the distinguishing characteristic of the
class to which it is opposed. Here it means the ungifted, in contrast
to those who had the gift of tongues; or rather, it applies to anyone
who was ignorant of the language used by the speaker. Compare
verses 23–4; Acts 4:13; 2 Corinthians 11:6. The context shows that
Paul is not referring to laymen as opposed to church officer; for
the officers were just as likely as anyone else to be ignorant of the
language used.

'Say "Amen" to your thanksgiving.' That is, assent or respond to
it. 'Amen' is a Hebrew adjective meaning 'true' or 'faithful', often
used adverbially at the end of a sentence to express agreement
with what is said, in the sense of 'let it be so'. In the Jewish
synagogue it was the custom for the people to respond to the
prayers by audibly saying 'Amen', by which they indicated their

assent and participation in the petitions which had been offered. The Jews attached great importance to saying 'Amen', and numerous passages are quoted to show the superstitious extreme to which this was carried. 'He who says Amen is greater than he that blesses.' 'Whoever says Amen, to him the gates of Paradise are opened.' 'Whoever says Amen shortly, his days will be shortened; whoever answers Amen distinctly and at length, his days will be lengthened.' According to Justin Martyr, the custom passed over to the Christian church. This also seems to be indicated in this passage; the expression is, 'say *the* Amen', that is, utter the familiar formula of assent. Anyone who does not understand cannot assent, 'since he does not know what you are saying'. People cannot assent to what they do not understand, because when we assent to something it implies that we affirm it. Therefore it is impossible to join in prayers uttered in an unknown tongue. It is true that people say words can touch the feelings even if they do not convey any distinct notions to the mind; but we cannot say 'Amen' to such words, any more than we can to a flute. Such blind, emotional worship, if it can be called such, is far removed from the intelligent service which the apostle demands.

'You may be giving thanks well enough.' That is, in a way acceptable to God and profitable to yourself. This proves that the speaker must have understood what he said. For if the unintelligible is useless, it must be sot to the speaker as well as to the hearer. If it was necessary for them to understand in order to be edified, it was no less necessary that he should understand what he said in order to benefit. This verse is therefore decisive against all theories of the gift of tongues which assume that those who used them did not understand their own words. The Scriptures recognise no unintelligent worship of God, or any spiritual edification (in the case of adults) disconnected from the truth – whether that edification be sought by sounds or signs, whether by prayers or sacraments.

'I thank God that I speak in tongues more than all of you. But in the church I would rather speak five intelligible words to instruct others than ten thousand words in a tongue'

We cannot believe that Paul should thank God for the gift of tongues if that gift consisted in the ability to speak in languages which he himself did not understand, and which could therefore benefit neither himself nor others. It is equally clear from this verse that speaking in tongues was not speaking in a state of mental unconsciousness. The common doctrine of the nature of this gift is the only one consistent with this passage. Paul says that although he could speak in foreign languages more than the Corinthians, he would rather speak 'five intelligible words' than ten thousand words in an unknown language.

'In the church.' That is, in the assembly.

'To instruct others.' To instruct orally (see Galatians 6:6). This shows what is meant by speaking 'with the mind'. It is speaking in such a way as to convey instruction.

'Brothers, stop thinking like children. In regard to evil be infants, but in your thinking be adults'
Children have two characteristics: a disposition to be pleased with trifles, or to value things falsely; and comparative innocence. With regard to evil, there is a great difference between a little child and a full-grown man. The apostle wanted the Corinthians to lay aside the first characteristic. He wanted them to cultivate the second. They had shown themselves childish in valuing the gift of tongues above more useful gifts, and in using it when it could serve no good purpose. A little child, however, is something so lovely, and is so often held up in Scripture for imitation, that he could not say, without qualification, 'Stop being children.' He therefore says, 'Stop *thinking* like children.' But 'in regard to evil' (a comprehensive word for evil dispositions), they are to 'be infants'. Similarly, our Lord said, 'Unless you change and become like little children, you will never enter the kingdom of heaven' (Matthew 18:3).

'In the Law it is written: "Through men of strange tongues and through the lips of foreigners I will speak to this people, but even then they will not listen to me," says the Lord.'
'In the Law.' The word 'law' means something which binds, especially what binds the conscience as a rule of faith and practice.

That rule may be revealed in our hearts, in the whole Scriptures, in the Pentateuch, or in the moral law; and hence the word as used in Scripture may refer to any one of these forms in which the will of God is made known; or it may include them all. The context must decide its meaning in each particular case. Here, as in John 10:34, Romans 3:20, and elsewhere, it refers not to the Pentateuch but to the Old Testament. The passage quoted is Isaiah 28:11–12, which the NIV translates as 'with foreign lips and strange tongues God will speak to his people, to whom he said, "This is the resting place, let the weary rest"; and, "This is the place of repose" – but they would not listen.' The apostle gives a free translation of verse 11, and the concluding words of verse 12. He does not quote the passage as having any prophetic reference to the events in Corinth; much less does he give an allegorical interpretation of it in order to make it a condemnation of speaking in tongues. It is a simple reference to a signal event in the Jewish history from which the Corinthians might learn a useful lesson. The Jews had refused to hear the prophets speaking their own language, and God threatened to bring upon them a people whose language they could not understand. This was a judgment, a mark of displeasure intended as a punishment and not for their conversion. From this the Corinthians might learn that it was no mark of the divine favor to have teachers whose language they could not understand. They were turning a blessing into a curse. The gift of tongues was intended, among other things, to facilitate the propagation of the Gospel, by enabling Christians to address people of various nations in their own languages. Used for this purpose, it was a blessing; but to use it for the sake of display, in addressing those who could not understand the language used, was to make it a curse. The Spirit of God often confers gifts on people, and then holds them responsible for the way in which they exercise them.

'Tongues, then, are a sign, not for believers but for unbelievers; prophecy, however, is for believers, not for unbelievers'
'Then.' This word expresses the connection between this verse and what precedes it: 'wherefore', or, 'so that'. The inference may be drawn either from the immediately preceding clause, namely,

'"Even then they will not listen to me," says the Lord'; or from the historical fact referred to in the whole verse. If the former, then the apostle's intention is to show that as teaching the Hebrews by people of other languages did not make them obedient, so speaking in other tongues would not profit the Corinthians. If the latter, then the intention is to show that as sending foreigners among the Hebrews was a mark of God's displeasure, so speaking in foreign languages in the Christian meetings would be a curse and not a blessing. The latter view is demanded by the whole context.

The inference from the preceding verse is that tongues are a sign not to the believing but to the unbelieving, and prophesying just the reverse. This difficult verse is explained in various ways.

1. The word 'sign' is taken in the sense of 'mark' or 'proof', as when it says, 'the things that mark an apostle' in 2 Corinthians 12:12. Compare Luke 2:12 and 2 Thessalonians 3:17. The passage would then mean, 'Tongues are a proof that those among whom they are used are not believers, but unbelievers; and prophesying is a proof that they are believers, and not unbelievers.' But when the word is used in this sense, the thing of which it is a sign is put in the genitive. It is a sign *of*, not *to* or *for*.

2. It may mean a 'prodigy' or 'wonder'. This is a very common sense of the word, as in the familiar phrase 'signs and wonders'. The meaning is then commonly made to be, 'Tongues are a wonder designed not for the benefit of believers, but for unbelievers; and on the other hand, prophecy is a wonder designed not for the benefit of unbelievers, but for the benefit of believers.' But this is neither true nor in accordance with verse 24. It is not true that the gift of tongues was designed exclusively for the conversion of unbelievers. Why should not that gift be exercised for people's edification as well as their conversion? Conversion would not enable them to understand the native language of the apostles. Much less is it true that prophecy was designed exclusively for the edification of believers. The prophets and apostles were sent out for the conversion of the world. And in verse 24 the conversion of unbelievers is specified as the very effect to be anticipated from the use of this gift. A still more decisive objection to this interpretation is that it does not give the true conclusion from the preceding

verse. The nature of the premises must decide the nature of the inference. God sent foreigners to teach the Hebrews, but they still remained disobedient; but it is not fair to infer from this that foreign tongues were designed for the conversion of unbelievers. The very opposite conclusion would naturally follow from that fact.

3. 'Sign' here may mean a warning, or sign of punishment. 'Tongues are a warning, designed not for believers, but for unbelievers,' who are understood to be not just those without faith but positive infidels, or obstinate rejecters of the truth. To this, however, it may be objected that the word 'unbeliever' is used in verse 24 for those without faith, and that to assume a change of meaning in the same context is most unnatural. A still more serious objection is that this interpretation cannot be carried out. It cannot be said that prophecy is a warning designed for believers. The two parts of the sentence are so related that whatever is said of the gift of tongues must be true also of prophecy.If one is a punishment designed for unbelievers, the other must be a punishment designed for believers.

4. The most satisfactory explanation is to take 'sign' in the general sense of any indication of the divine presence. 'Tongues are a manifestation of God, applying to believers but to unbelievers; and prophecy is a similar manifestation, applying not to unbelievers but to believers.' By 'tongues', however, we are not to understand the gift of tongues, but, as verse 21 requires, foreign languages, that is, languages unknown to the hearers. The meaning, therefore, is that when a people are disobedient, God sends them teachers whom they cannot understand; when they are obedient, he sends them prophets speaking their own language. This is the natural conclusion from the premises contained in verse 21. When the Hebrews were disobedient, God sent foreigners among them; when they were obedient, he sent them prophets. Hence it follows that unintelligible teachers are for the unbelieving; those who can be understood are for the believing. This view is also consistent with what follows, which is intended to show that speaking in a language which those who hear cannot understand is the cause of evil; whereas speaking intelligibly is the source of good. It must be remembered that it is not the gift of tongues that the apostle is

talking about, but speaking to people in a language which they do not understand. Therefore this interpretation does not imply any disparagement of the gift in question. When used aright – that is, when used to address those to whom the language was intelligible – it was prophecy.

The obscurity of this passage arises in a great measure from the ambiguity of the expression 'to speak in tongues'. It means to speak in foreign or unknown languages. But a language may be said to be unknown either by the speaker or by the hearer. It is said to be unknown to the speaker if it has not previously been acquired; and it is said to be unknown to the hearers if they do not understand it. The apostle uses the expression sometimes in one sense and sometimes in the other. When it says that the apostles, on the day of Pentecost, spoke in tongues, it means that they used languages which they had never learned; but when Paul says he would rather speak five intelligible words than ten thousand words in a tongue, he means in a language unknown to the hearers. Speaking in tongues in the one sense was a grace and a blessing; in the other sense, it was a folly and a curse. In these verses the apostle deals with speaking in tongues in the latter sense.

'So if the whole church comes together and everyone speaks in tongues, and some who do not understand or some unbelievers come in, will they not say that you are out of your mind?'
'So.' The inference from the preceding argument is that speaking in languages not understood by the people is undesirable and useless. To show how right this conclusion is, the apostle supposes the case which follows.

'If the whole church comes together.' That is, if all the Christians of the place, or the whole congregation, is assembled. This is one of the conditions of the hypothesis. Another is that 'everyone speaks in tongues'. This does not necessarily imply either that all present had the gift of tongues, or that all who possessed the gift spoke at one and the same time, although from verses 27 and 30 it may be inferred that this was sometimes done. All that the words here require is that all who spoke used foreign languages. 'To speak in tongues' must mean to speak in languages unknown to the hearers.

The third condition of the case supposed is that 'some who do not understand or some believers' should come into the meeting. Who are the people 'who do not understand'?

1. Some say they were Christians ignorant of the gift of tongues, because they are distinguished from 'unbelievers', or those not Christians.

2. Others say that they are those who were ignorant of Christianity, and the 'unbelievers' are those who knew and rejected it, that is, infidels. This is giving the word a meaning which it does not have in itself, and which the context does not give it.

3. The simplest explanation is that those 'who do not understand' were those ignorant of the language spoken, and the 'unbelievers' were those who were not Christians, whether Jews or Gentiles. Such people were doubtless often led, from curiosity or other motives, to attend the Christian meetings. The two groups are not so distinguished that the same person might not belong to both. The same people were either people 'who do not understand' or 'unbelievers' according to which aspect was considered. Considered in relation to the languages spoken, they were people 'who do not understand'; considered in relation to Christianity, they were 'unbelievers'. The apostle asks what impression such people, in the case supposed, would receive. Would they not say 'you are out of your mind'? See John 12:20; Acts 12:15; 26:24.

'But if an unbeliever or someone who does not understand comes in while everybody is prophesying, he will be convinced by all that he is a sinner and will be judged by all, and the secrets of his heart will be laid bare. So he will fall down and worship God, exclaiming, "God is really among you!"'
This is another part of the inference from what was said in verses 21–22. Speaking in languages unknown to the hearers is suitable for producing the happiest effects.

'While everybody is prophesying.' That is, if all the speakers speak under the guidance of the Spirit in a language which the hearers can understand.

'If an unbeliever or someone who does not understand comes in.' From these words it is clear that the latter were not Christians as distinct from Jews or Gentiles, here called 'unbelievers', for the same effect is said to be produced on both. Therefore those who do not understand were as much the subjects of conversion as the unbelieving. The meaning is, if anyone, either ignorant or without faith, should come in, he would be 'convinced by all'. That is, what he heard from all would carry conviction to his mind. He would be convinced of the truth of what he heard; convicted of guilt in regard to sin and righteousness and judgment (John 16:8); convinced that Jesus is the Christ, the Son of the living God (Acts 9:20, 22); and that it is a trustworthy saying that deserves full acceptance, that Jesus Christ came into the world to save sinners (1 Timothy 1:15).

'Will be judged by all.' That is, examined, searched into; for the Word of God is judges the thoughts and attitudes of the heart (Hebrews 4:12). The result of this searching examination is that 'the secrets of his heart will be laid bare'; that is, they will be revealed to himself. His real character and moral state, which he was ignorant of before, will be made known to him. The effect of this is humility, contrition, self-condemnation, and turning to God. This is expressed by saying, 'So' (that is, in this condition of a convinced sinner who has been brought to the knowledge of himself) 'he will fall down and worship God.' The first step in religion is entire self-abasement – a conviction of sin (that is, of guilt and pollution) that leads to self-condemnation and self-abhorrence, and to a complete renunciation of all dependence on our own righteousness and strength. When the soul is humbled in this way, God reveals himself sooner or later, in mercy, as reconciled in Jesus Christ; and then we worship him. This expresses reverence, love, and confidence. It is the return of the soul to the favor and fellowship of God. One who has had such an experience cannot keep it to himself. The apostle therefore describes the convert as 'exclaiming, "God is really among you!"' 'It is with your heart that you believe and are justified, and it is with your mouth that you confess and are saved' (Rom. 10:10). It is not enough to believe the truth; it must be publicly professed, because confession is the natural fruit of faith. When there is a proper apprehension of the value of the truth, and a sincere appropriation of the promises of

God to ourselves, there will be the desire to acknowledge his goodness and to proclaim the truth to others. The thing acknowledged
is that 'God is really among you,' that is, that Christianity is divine;
that Christians are not deluded by his Spirit. The convert therefore joins himself to them to share their fate, to take part in whatever reproach or persecution falls to their lot. This confession is
made with confidence. It is not a mere conjecture, but a firm conviction, based on experience, that is, on the demonstration of the
Spirit (2:4).

1 Corinthians (1857; Wheaton (IL): Crossway Books, 1995).

Camp meetings at Cane Ridge, Kentucky
(1801)

*Camp meetings took place between 6th and 12th August 1801, in Cane
Ridge, Kentucky, which included drunkenness and sexual promiscuity. But
one Presbyterian minister counted three thousand people on the ground,
calling out for God's mercy with tears in what was then termed a 'falling
exercise'.*

A non-Christian, James B. Finley's eyewitness account of Cane Ridge

The noise was like the roar of Niagara. The vast sea of human
beings seemed to be agitated as if by a storm. Some of the people
were singing, others praying, some crying for mercy in the most
piteous accents, while others were shouting vociferously. While
witnessing these scenes, a peculiarly strange sensation, such as I
had never felt before, came over me. My heart beat tumultuously,
my knees trembled, my lip quivered, and I felt as though I must
fall to the ground. A strange supernatural power seemed to pervade the entire mass of mind there collected. Soon after I left and
went into the woods, and there I strove to rally and man up my
courage.

After some time I returned to the scene of excitement, the waves of which, if possible, had raised still higher. The same awfulness of feeling came over me. I stepped up on to a log, where I could have a better view of the surging sea of humanity. The scene that then presented itself to my mind was indescribable. At one time I saw at least five hundred, swept down in a moment as if a battery of a thousand guns had been opened upon them, and then immediately followed shrieks and shouts that rent the very heavens.

Quoted in Charles A. Johnson, *The Frontier Camp Meeting* (Dallas: Southern Methodist University Press, 1955), p. 55.

A first-hand account of a camp meeting of 4,000 people in June 1801

The meeting continued five days, and four nights; and after the people generally scattered from the ground, numbers convened in different places, and continued the exercise much longer. And even where they were not collected together, these wonderful operations continued among every class of people, and in every situation; in their houses and fields, and in their daily employments, falling down and crying out, under conviction, or singing and shouting with unspeakable joy, were so common, that the whole country round about, seemed to be leavened with the spirit of the work.

Richard M'Nemar, *The Kentucky Revival, or, A Short History of the Late Extraordinary Outpouring of the Spirit of God* (New York, 1846), pp. 24–5.

Peter Cartwright

A frontiersman and leading evangelist in the 'Second Great Awakening' of 1801, who travelled by horse around the circuits of the Methodist Episcopal Church in Kentucky.

God's mighty hand seen at the camp meetings, including 'jerks'

A new exercise broke out among us, called the 'jerks', which was overwhelming in its effects upon the bodies and minds of the people. No matter whether they were saints or sinners, they would be taken under a warm song or sermon, and seized with a convulsive jerking all over, which they could not by any possibility avoid, and the more they resisted the more they jerked. If they would not strive against it and pray in good earnest, the jerking would usually abate. I have seen more than five hundred people jerking at one time in my large congregations.

I always looked upon the jerks as a judgement sent from God, first, to bring sinners to repentance; and, secondly, to show professors that God could work with or without means.

The Autobiography of Peter Cartwright (Nashville (TE): Abingdon, 1956), pp. 45–6.

Henry Prince

Leader of an English perfectionist movement that grew out of a group of students at St David's Theological College, Lampeter. Prince founded the Agapemone, and lived in a country house in Somerset, at Spaxton, where communal marriages were reputed to take place.

Sinlessness

[Soon after his first marriage Henry Prince told Hepworth Dixon:] As he told me himself, . . . died to the flesh, and was born a second time to the Spirit. He put off the old man, he discarded self, he ceased to commit sin, and even to be capable of sin.

W. Hepworth Dixon, *Spiritual Wives* (London, 1868), vol. 1, p. 271.

J. C. Ryle
(1816–1900)

Bishop of Liverpool from 1880 to 1900, Ryle was called by the Baptist C. H. Spurgeon, 'the best man in the Church of England.' Author of Expository Thoughts on the Gospels.

The work of the Holy Spirit and the work of Christ

We need the work of the Holy Spirit as well as the work of Christ; we need renewal of the heart as well as atoning blood.

Holiness: Its Nature, Hindrances, Difficulties, and Roots (1879), p. 23.

True holiness is much more than tears and sighs . . . A holy violence, a conflict, a warfare, a fight, a soldier's life, a wrestling are spoken of as characteristic of the true Christian.

Holiness: Its Nature, Hindrances, Difficulties, and Roots (1879), pp. x, xvi.

C. H. Spurgeon
(1834–92)

English Baptist preacher, author of The Treasury of David.

Preaching is totally dependent on the divine Spirit sent from above

Once, while preaching in Scotland, the Spirit of God was pleased to desert me; I could not speak as usually I have done. I was obliged to tell the people that the chariot wheels were taken off, and that the chariot dragged along very heavily. I have felt the benefit of that experience ever since. It humbled me bitterly; and if I could, I would have hidden myself in any obscure corner of the earth. I felt as if I should speak no more in the name of the Lord; and then the thought came, 'Oh, thou art an ungrateful creature! Hath not God spoken by thee hundreds of times? And this once, when he would not do so, wilt thou upbraid him for it? Nay, rather thank him that he hath so long stood by thee; and if once he hath forsaken thee, admire his goodness, that thus he would keep thee humble.'

Some may imagine that want of study brought me into that condition, but I can honestly affirm that it was not so. I think that I am bound to give myself unto reading, and not to tempt the Spirit by unthought-of effusions. I always deem it a duty to seek my sermons from my Master, and implore him to impress them on my mind; but on that occasion, I think I had prepared even more carefully than I ordinarily do, so that unpreparedness was not the reason for the lack of force I then mourned.

The simple fact is this, 'The wind bloweth where it listeth'; and, sometimes, the winds themselves are still. Therefore, if I rest on the Spirit, I cannot expect that I should always feel his power alike. What could I do without his celestial influence? To that, I owe everything. Other servants of the Lord have had experiences similar to mine. In the Life of Whitefield we read that, sometimes, under one of his sermons, two thousand people would profess to be saved, and many of them were really so; at other times, he preached just as powerfully, and no conversions were recorded. Why was that? Simply, because, in the one case the Holy Spirit went with the word; and in the other case, he did not. All the heavenly result of preaching is due to the divine Spirit sent from above.

The Autobiography of C. H. Spurgeon, ed. R. Backhouse (London: Hodder & Stoughton, 1993), pp. 146–7.

Test the spirits

Observe how sovereign the operations of God are. He may in one district work a revival, and people may be stricken down, and made to cry aloud, but in another place there may be crowds, and yet all may be still and quiet, as though no deep excitement existed at all. God can bless as he wills and he will bless as he wills. Let us not dictate to God. Many a blessing has been lost by Christians not believing it to be a blessing, because it did not come in the particular shape which they had conceived to be proper and right.

C. H. Spurgeon: The Early Years, 1834–1859 (Edinburgh: Banner of Truth, 1962), p. 328.

Spurgeon's assessment of the great revival of 1858 in the USA

In the United States of America there has been a great awakening.

Two hundred and fifty thousand people – that is a quarter of a million – profess to have been regenerated, and have united themselves with different sections of God's church. And that which makes me believe the work to be genuine is just this – that the enemies of Christ's holy gospel are exceedingly wroth at it. When the devil roars at anything, you may rest assured there is some good in it. The devil is not like some dogs we know of; he never barks unless there is something to bark at. When Satan howls, we may rest assured he is afraid his kingdom is in danger.

Now this great work in America has been manifestly caused by the outpouring of the Spirit, for no one minister has been a leader in it. All the ministers of the gospel have co-operated in it, but none of them have stood in the van. God himself has been the leader of his own hosts.

It began with a desire for prayer

It began with a desire for prayer. God's people began to pray; the prayer-meetings were better attended than before; it was then proposed to hold meetings at times that had never been set apart for prayer; these also were well attended. And there has been real prayer. Sinners beyond count, have risen up in the prayer-meetings, and have requested the people of God to pray for them; thus making public to the world that they had a desire after Christ; they have been prayed for, and the church has seen that God truly hears and answers prayer.

The need for ministers to be anointed by the Holy Spirit

. . . If you would have the Holy Spirit exert himself in our midst, you must first of all look to him and not to instrumentality. When Jesus Christ preached, there were very few converted under him, and the reason was, because the Holy Spirit was not abundantly poured forth. He had the Holy Spirit without measure himself, but on others the Holy Spirit was not as yet poured out. Jesus Christ said, 'Greater works than these shall ye do because I go to my Father, in order to send the Holy Spirit'; and recollect that those few who were converted under Christ's ministry, were not converted by him, but by the Holy Spirit that rested on him at that time. Jesus of Nazareth was anointed by the Holy Spirit. Now then, if Jesus Christ, the great founder of our religion, needed to be anointed by the Holy Spirit, how much more our ministers?

Never preach without the Holy Spirit

. . . Until our churches honour the Holy Spirit, we shall never see it abundantly manifested in our midst. Let the preacher always confess before he preaches that he relies on the Holy Spirit. Let him burn his manuscript and depend on the Holy Spirit. If the Spirit does not come to help him, let him be still and let the people go home and pray that the Spirit will help him next Sunday.

The Treasury of the New Testament (London: Marshall, Morgan & Scott, 1933), Sermon on Acts 10:44.

Calvinism and revival

In the history of the church, with but few exceptions, you could not find a revival at all that was not produced by the orthodox faith. If you turn to the continent of America, how gross the falsehood that Calvinistic doctrine is unfavourable to revivals! Look at that wondrous shaking under Jonathan Edwards.

The Autobiography of C. H. Spurgeon, vol. 2: The Full Harvest (Edinburgh: Banner of Truth, 1973), p. 46.

His power is by no means diminished

From the descent of the Holy Spirit at the beginning we may learn something concerning his work at the present time. Remember at the outset that whatever the Holy Spirit was at the first that he is now, for as God he remaineth for ever the same: whatsoever he then did he is able to do still, for his power is by no means diminished. As the prophet Micah says, 'O thou that art named the house of Jacob, is the spirit of the Lord straitened?' We should greatly grieve the Holy Spirit if we supposed that his might was less today than in the beginning. Although we may not expect, and need not desire, the miracles which came with the gift of the Holy Spirit, so far as they were physical, yet we may both desire and expect that which was intended and symbolised by them, and we may reckon to see the like spiritual wonders performed among us at this day.

The Treasury of the New Testament (London: Marshall Morgan & Scott, 1933), Sermon on Acts 2:2–4.

Flooded by the Holy Spirit

Ask God to make you all that the Spirit of God can make you, not only a satisfied believer who has drunk for himself, but a useful believer, who overflows the neighbourhood with blessing. I see here a number of friends from the country who have come to spend their holiday in London. What a blessing it would be if they went back to their respective churches overflowing; for there are numbers of churches that need flooding; they are dry as a barn-floor, and little dew ever falls on them. Oh that they might be flooded!

Oh, for a flood of grace

What a wonderful thing a flood is! Go down to the river, look over the bridge, and see the barges and other craft lying in the mud. All the king's horses and all the king's men cannot tug them out to sea. There they lie, dead and motionless as the mud itself. What shall we do with them? What machinery can move them? Have we a great engineer among us who will devise a scheme for lifting these vessels and bearing them down to the river's mouth? No, it cannot be done. Wait till the tide comes in! What a change! Each vessel walks the water like a thing of life. What a difference between the low tide and the high tide. You cannot stir the boats when the water is gone; but when the tide is at the full see how readily them move; a little child may push them with his hand. Oh, for a flood of grace! The Lord send to all our churches a great springtide! Then the indolent will be active enough, and those who were half dead will be full of energy. I know that in this particular dock several vessels are lying that I should like to float, but I cannot stir them. They neither work for God nor come out to the prayer-meetings, nor give of their substance to spread the gospel. If the flood would come you would see what they are capable of: they would be active, fervent, generous, abounding in every good word and deed. So may it be! So may it be! May springs begin to flow in all our churches, and may all of you who hear me this day get your share of the streams. Oh that the Lord may now fill you and then send you home bearing a flood of grace with you. It sounds oddly to speak of a man's carrying home a flood within him, and yet I hope it will be so, and that out of you shall flow rivers of living water. So may God grant for Jesus' sake. Amen.

The Treasury of the New Testament (London: Marshall, Morgan & Scott, 1933), Sermon on John 7:38–9.

Two kinds of perfection

There are two kinds of perfection which a Christian needs – one is the perfection of justification in the person of Jesus; and the other is, the perfection of sanctification worked in by the Holy Spirit. At present corruption still rests even in the breast of regeneration. At present the heart is partially impure. At present there are still lusts and evil imaginations. But, oh, my soul rejoices to know that the day is coming when God will finish the work which he has begun; and he will present my soul, not only perfect in Christ, but, perfect in the Spirit, without spot or blemish, or any such thing.

And is it true that this poor depraved heart is to become as holy as that of God? And is it true that this poor spirit, which often cries, 'O wretched man that I am, who shall deliver me from the body of this sin and death!' shall get rid of sin and death – I shall have no evil things to vex my ears, and no unholy thoughts to disturb my peace? Oh, happy hour! Oh, to be washed white, clean, pure, perfect! Not an angel more pure than I shall be – yes, not God himself more holy! And I shall be able to say, in a double sense, 'Great God, I am clean – through Jesus' blood I am clean, through the Spirit's work I am clean too!' Must we not extol the power of the Holy Spirit in thus making us fit to stand before our Father in heaven?

The Treasury of the New Testament (London: Marshall, Morgan & Scott, 1933), Sermon on 'The power of the Holy Spirit' Romans 15:13.

If ye then, being evil, know how to give good gifts unto your children: how much more shall your heavenly Father give the Holy Spirit to them that ask Him?' (Luke 11:11–13)

a. God will give the Holy Spirit to those who ask for him

The Holy Spirit is sometimes represented as the wind, the life-giving breath. He blows on the valleys filled up with the slaughtered and they are brought to life. You and I, though we are made to live often feel that life is flagging, and almost dying. The Spirit of God can bring us to life, revive in us the spark of divine life, and strengthen in our hearts God's life. Pray for this quickening breath, and God will give it to you. As surely as you sincerely pray you will have and feel the revival of the life within.

The Spirit of God is sometimes compared to water. It is he who applies the blood of Jesus and sanctifies us. He cleanses us, fertilises us. Well, he will come to us in that capacity. Do we feel that our sin has much power over us? O Spirit of God, destroy sin within us and work purity in us. You have already given us the new birth by water and the Spirit, go on and complete your work until our whole nature is formed in the image of the Great Firstborn. You will have it if you seek it; God will give you this Spirit if you seek for this.

The Holy Spirit is revealed to us under the image of light; he illuminates the mind, he makes our natural darkness flee. Wait upon him, O child of God, that you may be led into all truth. He can make what now perplexes you to become plain; he can enlighten you about truths which are beyond you at the moment. What on him! As God's child, long to be taught by God. I do not know how to communicate to you the sense I feel just now about the deep condescension of God in promising to give us the Holy

Spirit. He has given us his Son, and now he promises his Spirit. Here are two gifts, unimaginable in preciousness. Will God dwell with humankind on the earth? Will God dwell in people? Can it be that the infinite Spirit, God over everyone, blessed for ever, will dwell in my poor heart, and make my body to be his temple? It is certainly so; for as certain as it is that God will give good things to those who ask for good things, he will certainly give the Holy Spirit to those who ask for the Holy Spirit. Sit not in the dark then when God's light will shine on you if you seek it.

The Holy Spirit is described as fire, and in this capacity he kindles enthusiasm of spirit, and burning zeal in the hearts of God's people. The tongue of fire speaks with a matchless might; the heart of flame conquers the sons of men. O that we had this fire! It is to be had. The Spirit of God will come in answer to our cries. He will come and fire the church, and each individual member of it.

Often the Spirit of God is likened to oil. Through God's Spirit we have the divine anointing. The prayer that the pastor may be anointed with fresh oil is a very welcome one, but it is equally needed that you yourselves have your lamps supplied, that your light may not go out. This desire will be fulfilled. He will give the Holy Spirit in this way to those who ask him for it. As the gentle dropping dew that cheers and refreshes the grass, so the Spirit will come and console our spirits, as they are tired by the heat of this world's busy day. The Holy Spirit will come and fall on us like dew if we seek him. As the blessed dove, bearing peace on his wings, so God's Spirit will come to us. In fact, there is no work of God's Spirit done in us unless we seek it. All of the attributes of God's Spirit can come to us if we ask for them. He will give the Holy Spirit to those who ask him.

b. It will truly be the Holy Spirit

From the context in which this verse comes I deduce that 'it will be truly be the Holy Spirit.' Go back again to that first thought. The child asks for bread and does not receive a stone; you ask for the Holy Spirit, and you will receive the Holy Spirit. Some people have been misled by an evil spirit. I believe that a great deal of the recent ranting about the date of the second coming of Christ came from an evil spirit. I doubt if there was any humble laying down of minds before God's throne to seek the Holy Spirit. There was probably too much self-sufficiency and a great desire for something that would make the person important. This had led many preachers into vain imaginings and fanatical ranting. You will not receive an evil spirit in place of the good Spirit, if you humbly and patiently wait on the Most High. Neither will you be misled by fancy. People will tell you that you are deluded when you experience deep joys, but if you have sincerely and intensely sought the Spirit, then God will give you the Spirit. You do not need to be afraid that when you bow before Jehovah's throne in Jesus' name, and ask for the Holy Spirit, that you will be sent away with anything other than that Holy Spirit who comes from the Father and the Son.

c. This Holy Spirit is given in answer to prayer

But it appears clearly enough from the text that 'this Holy Spirit is given in answer to prayer.' Did we not hear some time ago from certain wise brethren that we were never to pray for the Spirit? I think I heard it often said, 'We have the Holy Spirit, and therefore we are not to pray for it.' This is similar to that other statement from some of these brethren, that we have pardon for sin, so we are not to pray for pardon for sin, just as if we were never to pray for what we have! If we have life we are to pray that we have it more abundantly. If we have pardon in one respect we are to ask for a fuller appreciation of it; and if we have the Holy Spirit so that we are quickened, and saved, we do not ask him in that respect, but we ask for his power in other directions, and for his grace in other forms. I do not go before God now and say, 'Lord, I am a dead sinner, quicken me by your Spirit,' for I trust I am already alive by his Spirit; but as I am quickened I now cry, 'Lord, let not the life you have given me ebb away until it becomes very feeble, but give me your Spirit that the life within me may become strong and mighty, and may subdue all the power of death within my members, that I may be strong and vigorous as a result of your

Spirit.' O you who have the Spirit, you are the very people to pray that you may experience more of his matchless work and gracious influences, and through his indwelling may seek to know him better and better. Be encouraged by this: God will give the Holy Spirit to those who ask him. Ever since certain brethren gave up asking for the Holy Spirit they have not had it, and they have wandered into many errors. If they will not ask they will not have, but may we wait humbly and patiently on the Lord that he may daily give us his Spirit.

d. Know how to give

I desire earnestly to call your attention to one thing which our Saviour says: 'If ye being evil "know how to give" good gifts unto your children,' how ought the sentence to be completed? 'how much more shall your heavenly Father "know how to give" the Holy Spirit to them that ask him?' Is that not the right way to complete the sentence? Of course it is, but Jesus does not say that. He very kindly puts it, in the first place, that we 'know how to give good gifts,' for sometimes we know how to give them, but we cannot do it. It is a bitter thing, and yet it has sometimes happened that the child has said, 'Father, give me bread' and with a breaking heart the father has had to reply, 'My child, there is none.' It must be one of the hardest human trials, and yet it is the trial that tens of thousands of people in this city have to endure, as they say, 'No, there is not even a crust of bread for my child.' You see the father knows how, but he cannot do it. But the text does not say that God knows how to give the Holy Spirit, it says a great deal more than that, it declares that he does give, because with him to know how is the same thing as to do it. He gives the Holy Spirit to those who ask him. He does not only know how, but he does it. Never does he have to say to his child, 'My child, I cannot.' The poor sinner says, 'Lord, help me to repent,' and the Lord never says, 'I have not enough of the Holy Spirit as that.' Boundlessly will he give if faith only dares to open her mouth wide. You are not straitened in him; you are straitened in yourselves.

I am not telling you anything new, but a very simple truth, and yet for all that a truth which we do not put into practice. We may have the Spirit of God resting on us. As Stephen was a person filled with the Holy Spirit, even so may we be. We seek all the spiritual uplifting which the Holy Spirit gave to people of old, and he can give it to us still. Though he will not reveal new truths – for we do not ask this from him, as we already have the complete gospel revealed – he will bring home the old truths to our souls and make them potent in our consciences, in our lives, and this is what we want. If you are only just Christians, and are not glorifying God, nor living near him, nor mighty in prayer, nor well taught in Scripture, more useful in your lives; I beseech you to remember, if you do not have the Spirit it is because you do not seek him importunately, and do not seek him with a deep sense of your need of him. If you, being evil, give your children bread, how much more will God give you the Spirit; and as you, being evil, do not mock your child by putting him off without bread, and giving him something else, neither will your heavenly Father. He will give you the real Spirit; his own gentle, truthful, infallible, Holy Spirit he will give to those who ask him.

The Treasury of the New Testament (London: Marshall, Morgan & Scott, 1933).

John Noyes
(1811–86)

John Noyes was founder of a community at Oneida Greek, USA, and its most famous prophet. This branch of American perfectionism came to public attention through the 1834 revivalist meetings in the village of Manlius.

Perfectionism and religious love

Religious love is very near to sexual love, and they always get mixed in the intimacies and social excitements of revivals. The next thing a man wants, after he has found the salvation of his soul, is to find his Eve and his Paradise. Revivals lead to religious love; religious love excites the passions; the converts, finding themselves in theocratic liberty, begin to look about for their mates and their Paradise. Here begins divergence. If women have the lead, the feminine idea that ordinary wedded love is carnal and unholy rises and becomes a ruling principle. Mating on the spiritual plan, with all the heights and depths of sentimental love, becomes the order of the day. On the other hand, if the leaders are men, the theocratic impulse takes the opposite direction, and polygamy in some form is the result.

W. Hepworth Dixon, *Spiritual Wives* (London, 1868), vol.2, p. 177 (extract from a letter from Noyes to Dixon).

'Spiritual' union

The marriage supper of the Lamb is a feast at which every dish is free to every guest. Exclusiveness, jealousy, quarrelling, have no place there . . . I call a certain woman my wife; she is yours, she is Christ's, and in him she is the bride of all saints.

W. Hepworth Dixon, *Spiritual Wives* (London, 1868), vol. 2, p. 56.

Andrew Murray
(1828–1917)

Preacher in South Africa and prolific writer of Christian books.

The greatest need of the church, and the thing which, above all others, believers ought to seek for with one mind and with their whole heart, is to be filled with the Spirit of God . . . Every day ought to be a Pentecostal season in the church of Christ.

The Believer's Full Blessing of Pentecost (Basingstoke: Lakeland, 1984), pp. 9–10.

Filled with the Spirit

The Spirit did it all, on the day of Pentecost and afterwards. It was the Spirit who gave the boldness, the Spirit who gave the wisdom, the Spirit who gave the message, and the Spirit who gave the converting power.

And now, to those who feel the need of power, I would say: Is not your whole heart ready to say, 'That is what I want. I see it. Jesus did not send me to the warfare on my own charges; he did not bid me go and preach and teach in my own strength; Jesus meant me to have the fullness of the Holy Spirit. Whether I have a little Sunday School class or a Bible class, or some larger work, the one thing I need is the power of the Holy Spirit, to be filled with the Spirit.'

Are you ready to receive this from our Jesus? He loves to give it. God delights in nothing so much as to honour his Son, and it is honour to Jesus when souls are filled with the Holy Spirit, because then he proves what he can do for them.

Step One: I must be filled
Say it to God in the depth of your heart. God commands it; I cannot live my life as I should live without it.

Step Two: I may be filled
Then, say as the second step: *I may be filled.* It is possible: the promise is for me. Settle that, and let all doubt vanish. These apostles, once so full of pride and of self-life, were filled with the Holy Spirit because they clave unto Jesus. And, with all your sinfulness, if you will but cling to him, you *may be filled.*

Step Three: I would be filled
Them, thirdly, say: *I would be filled.* To get the 'pearl of great price' (Matt. 13:46) you must sell all, you must give up everything. You are willing, are you not? Everything, Lord, if I may only have that. Lord, I would have it from you today.

Step Four: I shall be filled
And then comes the last step: *I shall be filled.* God longs to give it; I shall have it. Never mind whether it comes immediately, as a flood, or in deep silence; or whether it does not come today, because God is preparing you for it tomorrow. But say, *I shall be filled.* If I entrust myself to Jesus he cannot disappoint me. It is his very nature, it is his work in heaven, it is his delight to give souls

the Holy Spirit in full measure. Claim it at once; *I shall.* My God, it is so solemn, it is almost awful; it is too blessed and too true — Lord, will you not do it? My trembling heart says, *I shall be filled* with the Holy Spirit. Say to God, '*Father, I shall,* for the name of my Saviour is Jesus, who saves from all sin, and who fills with the Holy Spirit. Glory to his name!'

Absolute Surrender; included in *Reviving the Soul: The Best of Andrew Murray's Devotional Writings,* ed. Robert Backhouse (London: Marshall Pickering, 1995), pp. 127–8.

Retaining the full Blessing of Pentecost

'*Praying in the Holy Ghost, keep yourselves in the love of God . . . Now to him that is able to keep you from falling . . . to the only wise God our Saviour, be glory . . . now and for ever. Amen*' *(Jude 20–1, 24–5).*
Can anyone who has had the full Pentecostal Blessing lose it? Without a doubt he can. God does not give this blessing with such force that people must keep it whether they are willing or unwilling. The blessing is given to the believer like a talent which should be used and looked after and which can bring happiness only by being used. Just as the Lord Jesus, after being baptised with the Holy Spirit, had to be made perfect by obedience and subjection to the guidance of the Spirit, so the Christian who receives the Pentecostal Blessing has to take care that he looks after what has been given to him.

Scripture shows us that we can only keep the blessing we have received by entrusting it to our Lord for sake keeping. Paul wrote to Timothy, 'He is able to keep that which I have committed unto him . . . That good thing which was committed unto thee keep by the Holy Ghost which dwelleth in us' (2 Tim. 1:12, 14). Jude advises his readers, 'Keep yourselves in the love of God . . . [who] is able to keep you from falling.' What we must do is to be humbly dependent upon the Lord who keeps us and through whom alone we are able to retain the blessing. As with the manna in the Old Testament, so too with this blessing: it must be renewed from heaven every day. Just as our bodies must inhale fresh air from outside us every moment, so our spirits must inhale the Holy Spirit. Let us see how this everlasting, uninterrupted keeping of the blessing is achieved.

The only purpose of the Pentecostal Blessing is to manifest Jesus in us as Saviour, in order that he may manifest his saving power in and through us to the world. The Spirit did not come instead of Jesus, but only and wholly in order to make the disciples more intimately and perfectly in relationship with the Lord than they had been when he was on earth. The power from on high did not come as a power which they could consider as their own: that power was bound inseparably to the Lord Jesus and the Spirit. Every action of the power was an immediate action of Jesus in them. All the aspects of the relationship which the disciples had had with Jesus when he was on the earth – following him, receiving his teaching, doing his will, sympathising with his suffering – were to continue even more powerfully, since through the Spirit the life of Jesus was now inside them. And it is the same with us. The Spirit in us will always glorify Jesus, always show that he alone must be Lord, that everything that is beautiful comes only from him. We must be faithful in seeking his words and his will in Scripture, in sacrificing effort and time we could spend with other people in order to spend time with him, if we are to keep the blessing. Jesus wants us to occupy ourselves wholly with him. Anyone who loves communion with Jesus above everything else will find that Jesus will maintain the Pentecostal Blessing in him.

The Promise of the Spirit; included in *Reviving the Soul: The Best of Andrew Murray's Devotional Writings*, ed. Robert Backhouse (London: Marshall Pickering, 1995), pp. 129–30.

Increasing the full Blessing of Pentecost

'He that believeth on me shall never thirst' (*John 6:35*).
'He that believeth on me . . . out of his belly shall flow rivers of living water' (*John 7:38*).
Can the full blessing of Pentecost be still further increased? Can anything that is full become still fuller? Yes: undoubtedly. It can

become so full that it always overflows. This is especially the characteristic and law of the blessing of Pentecost.

The words of our blessed Lord Jesus which have been quoted, point us to a double blessing. First, Jesus says that he who believes in him shall never thirst: he shall always have life in himself – that is to say, the satisfaction of all his needs. Then he speaks of something that is grander and more glorious: he that believeth in him, out of his heart shall flow rivers of living water to quench the thirst of others. It is the distinction betwixt full overflowing. A vessel may be full and yet have nothing over for others. When it continues full, and yet has something over for others, there must be in it an over-brimming, ever-flowing supply. This is what our Lord promises to his believing disciples. At the outset, faith in him gives them the blessing that they shall never thirst. But as they advance and become stronger in faith, it makes them a fountain of water out of which streams flow to others. The Spirit who at first only fills us will overflow out of us to souls around us.

It is with the rivers of living water as with many a fountain on earth. When we begin to open them, the stream is weak. The more the water is used, and the more deeply the source is opened up, the more strongly does the water flow. I should like to inquire how far this principle holds good in the realm of the spiritual life and to discover what is necessary to secure that the fullness of the Spirit may constantly flow more abundantly from us. There are several simple directions which may help us in reaching this knowledge.

1. Hold fast to that which you have

See to it that you do not misunderstand the blessing which God has given you. Be sure that you do not form any wrong conceptions of what the full blessing is. Do not imagine that the animation, and joy, and power of Pentecost must be felt and seen immediately. No: the church at present is in a dead-and-alive condition, and the restoration often comes slowly. At first, indeed, one receives the full blessing only as a seed: the full life is wrapped up in a little invisible capsule. The quickened soul has longed for it; he has surrendered himself unreservedly t; he has believed in silence that God has accepted his consecration and fulfilled his promise. In that faith he goes on his way, silent and happy, saying to himself: 'The blessing of the fullness of the Spirit is for me.' But that actual experiences of the blessing did not come as he had anticipated; or they did come, but lasted only for a short time. The result was that he began to fear that his surrender was not a reality; that he had been rejoicing in what was only a transient emotion; and that the real blessing was something greater and more powerful than he had yet received. The result is that very speedily the blessing becomes less instead of larger, and he moves further back rather than forward through discouragement on account of his disappointment.

The cause of this condition is simply lack of faith. We are bent on judging God and his work in us by sight and feeling. We forget that the whole process is the work of faith. Even in its highest revelations in Christians that have made the greatest progress, faith rests not on what is to be seen of the work of God or on the experiences of it, but on the work of God as spiritual, invisible, deeply hidden, and inconceivable. To you, therefore, my friend, who desires in this time of discouragement to return to the true life according to the promise, my counsel is not to be greatly surprised if it comes to you slowly or if it appears to be involved in darkness. If you know that you have given yourself to God with a perfect heart, and if you know that God, really and with his whole heart, waits to fulfil his promise in you with divine power, then rest in silence before his face and hold fast your integrity. Although the cold of winter appears to bury everything in death, say with the prophet Habakkuk: 'Although the fig tree shall not blossom, neither shall fruit be in the vines . . . yet I will rejoice in the Lord, I will joy in the God of my salvation' (Hab. 3:17–18). Do this, and you shall know God, and God will know you. If you are sure that you have set yourself before God as an empty, separated, purified vessel, to become full of his Spirit, then continue still to regard yourself so and keep silence before him. If you have believed that God has received you to fill you as a purified vessel – purified through Jesus Christ and by your entire surrender to him – then abide in this attitude day by day, and you may reckon upon it that the blessing will grow and being to flow. 'He that believeth on him shall not be confounded' (1 Pet. 2:6).

2. *Regard yourself as living only to make others happy*

God is love. His whole being is nothing but a surrender of himself in love to be the life of the creature, to make the creature participate in his holiness and blessedness. He blesses and serves all that lives. HIs glory as God is that he puts all that he has at the disposal of his creatures.

Jesus Christ is the Son of God's love, the bearer, the bringer, the dispenser of the love. What God is as invisible in heaven, he was a visible on earth. He came, he lived, he suffered and died only to glorify the Father – that is, to let it be seen how glorious the Father in his love is, and to show that in the Godhead there is no other purpose than to bless men and make them happy; to make it manifest that the highest honour and blessedness of any being is to give and to sacrifice.

The Holy Spirit came as the Spirit of the Father and the Son to make us partakers of this divine nature, to shed abroad the love of God in our hearts, to secure the indwelling of the Son and his love in our hearts to such an extent that Christ may verily be formed within us, and that our whole 'inner man')Ephesians 3:16) shall bear the impress of his disposition and his likeness.

Hence, when any soul seeks and receives the fullness of the Spirit, and desires to have it increased, is it not perfectly evident that he can enjoy this blessing only according as he is prepared to give himself to a life in the service of love? The Spirit came to expel the life of self and self-seeking. The fullness of the Spirit presupposes a willingness to consecrate ourselves to the blessing of others and as the servants of all, and that in a constantly increasing and unreserved measure. The Spirit is the outflowing of the life of God. If we will but yield ourselves to him, he will become rivers of living water, flowing from the depths of our heart.

Christian reader, if you will have the blessing increased, begin to live as a man who is left here on earth only in order that the love of God may work by you. Love all around you with the love of God which is in you through the Spirit. Love the children of God cordially, even the weakest and most perverse. Exercise and exhibit your love in every possible way. Love the unsaved. Present yourself to the Spirit to love him. Then will love constrain you to speak, to work, to give, and to pray. If there is no open door for working, or if you have not the strength for it, the door of prayer is always open, and power can be obtained at the mercy-seat. Embrace the whole world in your love, for Christ, who is in your heart, belongs also to the heathen. The Spirit is the power of Christ for redeeming them. Like God and Jesus and the Spirit, live wholly to bless others. Then the blessing shall stream forth and become overflowing.

The Full Blessing of Pentecost; included in *Reviving the Soul: The Best of Andrew Murray's Devotional Writings,* ed. Robert Backhouse (London: Marshall Pickering, 1995), pp. 139–43.

Filled with the Spirit

'Be not drunken with wine, but be filled with the Spirit, speaking one to another in psalms and hymns and spiritual songs' (Eph. 5:18–19)
To understand the command: 'Be filled with the Spirit.' we need only turn to the Day of Pentecost, where the disciples were all 'filled with the Holy Spirit'. We know what that meant to them. For three years they had lived day and night in closest fellowship with their Lord. His presence had been everything to them. When he spoke of his departure their hearts were sad. He promised that the Spirit would come, not to take his place, but to reveal himself as their Lord, ever present with them as much as when he was upon earth, only far more intimately and more gloriously. He would henceforth not be near them and beside them, without the power of enabling them to do what he had taught them, but would live and work in them, even as the Father had lived and worked in him as man. To be filled with the Spirit would mean to them that Christ on the throne would be to them an ever-present living reality, filling their hearts and life with all his heavenly love and joy. Their fellowship with him on earth would prove to have been but the shadow of that intense and unceasing union with him, which the Spirit would reveal in power.

The command: 'Be filled with the Spirit,' is a pledge that all that the disciples received and enjoyed at Pentecost is indeed for us too.

The Church has sunk down from the level of Pentecost to a life in which the spirit of the world and of human wisdom is, alas, far too prevalent. Few believe in the possibility of the unbroken presence of Christ dwelling in the heart, conquering sin by his holy presence, inspiring to devotion and perfect selfsacrifice by the fire of his love, guiding each hour into all his will and work by the leading of his blessed Spirit. The heavenly vision of Christ at the right hand of God, ministering, in the power of his infinite redemption, not only salvation to the penitent, but full salvation to all whom he has sanctified by his one offering, is scarcely known. And, as the result of this, there are but few found to witness to 'the exceeding greatness of his power toward us who believe'.

The condition, too, on which this blessing is to be received cannot be better studied than in the disciples. They had turned their back upon the world, and forsaken all to follow Christ. They had learnt to know and love him, and do his will. As our Saviour said himself: 'If ye love me, ye will keep my commandments, and I will pray the Father, and he will give you another Comforter.' They had continued with him in his temptations; he carried them with him through death and the grave; the joy and the power of the resurrection life filled their hearts with confidence and hope. Their whole being was yielded up and, one might say, lost in the ascended Lord upon the throne – they were indeed ready, fully prepared, to receive the wondrous gift that was to come upon them.

The Church of our day, how sadly it is lacking in that separation from the world, in that intense attachment and obedience to Christ, in that fellowship with his suffering and conformity to his death, in that devotion to Christ on the throne, and in that confident expectation of the never-ceasing flow of the water of life from under the throne, which gives the assurance that the fullness of the Spirit will not be withheld! No wonder that the mighty power of God is so little known and felt in our church life!

Let us turn once again to Pentecost, and think what the great gift was that was bestowed. Though they knew not at once to say in words what it meant, the Spirit woke in them the consciousness that he, in whom the Son and the Father had come to dwell in them, was himself indeed true God, the overflowing fountain, from whom rivers of life flowed through them, and from them on to the world. Coming fresh from the throne of our Lord in heaven, he rested on them as the Spirit of glory and of God, and filled their hearts with the very love and power of Christ in glory. As the mighty power of God dwelling within them, he convinced the world by their boldness, by their love, that God was indeed in their midst.

How different the conception of most Christians of what the Spirit is, and oh, how different their experience of the presence and the power of Christ that he imparts. How much the thought of the Spirit is little more than a mental conception, or a passing emotion, with its sense of power or of happiness. How little there is of the consciousness that fills the soul with deep reverence and quiet rest, with heavenly joy and strength, as the natural and permanent possession of the life of the believer . . .

'Be filled with the Spirit.' This filling has its very great difference in degree, from the first joy of a new but ignorant convert in a revival, through all the experiences by which he is taught what more is needed and is waiting for him, on to being filled with all the fullness of God as that comes through the dwelling of Christ in the heart.

In all filling we know how two things are needed. The one that the vessel be clean and empty and ready, even in its posture, to receive the water that is waiting for it. The other that the water be near and ready to give away itself in full measure to the waiting vessel. In the great transaction between God and man for the filling of the Spirit, man needs first of all to know how complete the surrender if that is needed, and how, even to the death to self and the world, the yielding up of the whole being is indispensable. And then how willing and ready, and oh, so able, the Holy God is to take possession of our being, and to fill it with himself.

When our Lord Jesus said: 'He that believeth on me, out of him shall flow rivers of living water,' he made the on condition of being filled with the Spirit to overflowing, nothing more and nothing less than simple faith in himself. Faith is not an imagination, not an argument or an intellectual conviction; it claims the whole heart, it yields up the whole being; it entrusts itself unreservedly to the power that seeks to take possession of it. *It is in the life of faith, cultivated in secret fellowship and adoring worship, in unceasing dependence and whole-hearted surrender, that the blessing will be found.*

Aids to Devotion; included in *Reviving the Soul: The Best of Andrew Murray's Devotional Writings,* ed. Robert Backhouse (London: Marshall Pickering, 1995), pp. 168–71.

Sealed with the Spirit

'In whom having also believed, ye were sealed with the Holy Spirit of promise' (Eph. 1:13).

When a king appoints an ambassador or a governor, his commission is sealed with the king's seal, bearing the king's likeness. The Holy Spirit is the seal of our redemption, not in the sense of giving us the assurance of our sonship as something apart from himself: *he himself* by his life in us is the seal of our sonship. His work is to reveal and glorify Christ in us, the image of the Father, and by fixing our heart and our faith on him, to transform us into his likeness. What a wonderful thought. None less than the Spirit of the Father and the Son, the bond of union between them, comes to us as the bond of our union with them, giving us the witness of the divine life within us, and enabling us to live out that life here in the body. *In the Christian life everything depends on knowing the Holy Spirit and his blessed work aright.*

First of all, we need to know that he comes to take the mastery of our whole being – spirit, soul and body – and through it all to reveal the life and the power of God as it works in our renewed nature. Just as Christ could not be glorified and receive the Spirit from the Father for us until he had died upon the cross, and parted with that life in which he had borne our sin and the weakness of our nature, so the coming of the Holy Spirit into our hearts in power implies that we yield ourselves to the fellowship of the cross, and consent *to die entirely to that life of nature in which self and sin have their power,* that through the Spirit, the new, the heavenly, life may take complete possession of us.

This entire mastery implies on our side complete surrender and obedience. Peter speaks of the 'Holy Ghost, whom God hath given to them that obey him'. Even as Christ came to do God's will alone, and humbled himself to the perfect obedience of the cross, that he might receive the Spirit from the Father and we through him, so the full experience of the Spirit's power rests entirely on our readiness in everything to deny self, in everything to yield to his teaching and leading. The great reason that believers are so feeble, and so ignorant of the blessings of the Spirit, is this, that at conversion and in their Christian life the question was never faced and settled that by the grace of God they would in everything, in every place, and at every moment, yield themselves to the control of the Spirit. Oh that God's children might accept of God's terms, *the undivided mastery of the Spirit,* the unhesitating surrender of the whole being to his control.

In this connection we need specially to understand that the degree or measure in which the working of the Spirit is experienced may vary greatly. A believer may rejoice in one of the gifts of the Spirit, say peace or joy, zeal or boldness, and yet may be extremely deficient in the other graces which his presence bestows. Our true position towards the blessed Spirit must be that of perfect teachableness, waiting to be led by him in all the will of God, with the consciousness of how much there still is within the heart that needs to be renewed and sanctified, if he is to have the place and the honour that belong to him.

There are specially two great enemies under which man was brought by his fall. These are the world and self. Of the world Christ says, 'The Spirit of truth, whom the world cannot receive because it knoweth him not'. *Worldliness is the great hindrance that keeps believers from living the spiritual life.* Of self Christ said, 'Let a man deny himself', 'Let a man hate his own life'. *Self, in all its forms – self-will, self-pleasing, self-confidence – renders a life in the power of the Spirit impossible.* And from these two great enemies, the power of the world and the power of self, nothing can deliver us but the cross of Christ. Paul boasts in the cross by which he has been crucified to the world. And he tells us: 'They that are Christ's have crucified the flesh,' in which self has its seat and power. To live the spiritual life, nothing less is needed than the entire giving up of the old life to the death, to make room for the blessed Spirit to renew and transform out whole being into the will of God.

Without the Spirit we can do nothing acceptable to God in things great or little. 'No man can say that Jesus is Lord but by the Holy Ghost.' No man can truly say 'Abba, Father,' but by the Spirit of God's Son sent into our hearts. In our fellowship with God, and as much in our fellowship with men, in our religious worship and our daily avocations, in the highest pursuit that life can offer and as much in the daily care of our bodies, everything must bear the seal of the Holy Spirit.

Of the Son we read, 'Him hath God the Father sealed.' It is 'in Christ' that we are sealed. As he, when the Spirit had descended upon him at his baptism, was led by the Spirit to the wilderness, thence by the Spirit to the synagogue at Nazareth, and thence through his whole life to the cross, 'where by the Eternal Spirit he offered himself a sacrifice unto God',. so we too are to live our daily life as those who are sealed by the Spirit. As true as it is of Christ, 'Him hath God the Father sealed,' is it true of every believer – the New Testament standard of the Christian life and its devotion is to be that it is all to bear the stamp of the Holy Spirit.

Let us learn the precious lesson that the Holy Spirit cannot inspire our devotions, except as he inspires our daily life. The Spirit of Christ claims and needs the rule of the whole man if he is to perform his blessed work in us. The indwelling of the Holy Spirit in us means nothing less than that in our religious life – and that means our whole life, nothing excluded – nothing is to be thought of, or trusted to, or sought after, but the immediate and continual dependence on his blessed working. The devotion of our public life will be the test of the uprightness of our secret devotion, and at the same time the means of strengthening our confidence in God who works in us through his blessed Spirit. Every thought of faith in the power of the Spirit must find its expression in prayer to God, who will most surely give us his Spirit when we ask him and work in us through the Spirit what we need.

A seal, attached to a document, gives validity to every sentence and every word it contains. Even so the Holy Spirit of promise, with which we are sealed, ratifies every promise that there is in Christ. And this is now one of the great differences between the Bible and the human standard of the Christian life, that while in the former the seal of the Spirit is accepted in his control of every movement and every moment of our life, in the latter we are content with but a very partial surrender to his guidance.

Aids to Devotion; included in *Reviving the Soul: The Best of Andrew Murray's Devotional Writings*, ed. Robert Backhouse (London: Marshall Pickering, 1995), pp. 165–8.

The daily renewal

To be filled with heaven, the life must be emptied of earth. We have this truth in Romans 12:2, 'Be ye transformed in the renewing of your mind.' An old house may be renewed, and yet keep very much of its old appearance, or the renewal may be so entire that men exclaim: What a transformation! The renewing by the mind of the Holy Spirit means an entire transformation, an entirely different way of thinking, judging, deciding. The fleshly mind gives place to a 'spiritual' understanding (Col. 1:9; 1 John 5:20). This transformation is not obtained but at the cost of giving up all that is of nature. 'Be not fashioned according to this world, but be ye transformed.' By nature we are of this world. When renewed by grace we are still in the world, subject to the subtle all-pervading influence from which we cannot withdraw ourselves.

And what is more, the world is still in us, as the leaven of the Holy Spirit, filling us with the life of heaven. Let us allow the truth to take deep hold of us. The divine transformation of the daily renewing of our mind into the image of him who is from above, can proceed in us no faster and no further than our seeking to be freed from every vestige of conformity to this world. The negative, 'Be not fashioned according to this world' needs to be emphasised as strongly as the positive 'Be ye transformed'. The spirit of this world and the Spirit of God contend for the possession of our being. Only as the former is known and renounced and cast out can the heavenly Spirit enter in, and do his blessed work of renewing and transforming. The whole world and whatever is of the worldly spirit must be given up. The whole life and whatever is of self must be lost. This daily renewal of the inward man costs much, that is, as long as we are hesitating, or trying to do it in our own strength. When once we really learn that the Holy Spirit does all, and in the faith of the strength of the Lord Jesus have given up all, the renewing becomes the simple, natural, healthy growth of the heavenly life in us.

Prayer's Inner Chamber; included in *Reviving the Soul: The Best of Andrew Murray's Devotional Writings,* ed. Robert Backhouse (London: Marshall Pickering, 1995), pp. 126–7.

Spiritual Gifts

'Now concerning spiritual gifts, brethren, I would not have you ignorant' (1 Cor. 12:1).

For a right understanding of the place these gifts held in the church, and of the teaching of Paul with regard to them, we must first think of their relation to the whole work of the blessed Spirit as that has been set before us in this epistle. We shall then have the right standpoint for answering more than one important question that may arise.

Paul's first mention of the Holy Spirit is where he speaks of him as a Spirit of power. He had preached to them the gospel in demonstrations of the Spirit and of power. Their conversion had been the proof of the mighty power of God bringing them to the obedience of faith.

The next thought is that he is not only the power but the wisdom of God. As the Spirit of revelation, he unveils the hidden mystery of the cross and shows forth the deep things of God. And that not only in the Apostle himself, but in all believers who yielded themselves fully to become spiritual men with the power of spiritual discernment.

In chapter 3 he is spoken of as the Spirit of holiness; 'the Spirit of God dwelleth in you . . . the temple of God is holy, which temple ye are.' Or, as is put in chapter 6, 'Ye are sanctified, ye are justified in the name of our Lord Jesus, and by the Spirit of God.' The whole life, both of justification and sanctification, depends upon him and his indwelling.

And then we have him as the Spirit of life. 'He that is joined unto the Lord is one spirit'; 'Your body is the temple of the Holy Ghost which is in you.' The indwelling of the Spirits is the indwelling of Christ in us, making us one Spirit with him. In these four words Paul teaches us how the spiritual life has as its essential and indispensable condition the faith and the full surrender to the mastery of the Holy Spirit.

In chapter 12 Paul's teaching concerning spiritual gifts leads us a step further on. There is a diversity of gifts, and yet the body is one. 'By one Spirit are we all baptised into one body . . . and have been all made to drink into one Spirit.' 'Ye are the body of Christ, and members in particular.' In summing up the diversity of gifts, Paul gives a list of some nine workings of the selfsame Spirit. And later on in the chapter he gives another list of eight ministrations with the view of pressing deeply upon them the thought of how the body of Christ needs every member for the full development of its health and the work it has to do in the world.

The great curse of sin is selfishness. Even in the church of Christ it still prevails. Men think of themselves and their own salvation, and rejoice in the gifts they possess. Many enter the church without understanding that as members of a body they are to care for each other, to use all their gifts for the help of those who have less. Their first object is to be the building up of the body of Christ in love. The great mark and happiness of their life is to be a love like that of Christ, who gave himself away for others. Gifts, however truly they may come from God, and however indispensable for the welfare of the church, are nothing without love. It is in the exercise of love that they are to find their true worth and beauty.

In chapter 13 Paul sounds the praises of love. A man may speak with tongues and have the gift of prophecy, and understand all mystery, and have all faith, so that he could remove mountains, and bestow all his goods on the poor, and give his body to be burnt, yet if he have not love, it availeth nothing, he is nothing. Knowledge and gifts tend to puff up; it is only love that seeketh not its own, that never faileth and is the greatest of all. Amid all the contentions and self-exaltation of these carnal Corinthians Paul lifts their thoughts to that one Spirit into which they had been baptised, and that one holy Body of which they are now members, and that divine love in which alone the likeness of God consists. 'Be ye therefore followers of God, as dear children; And walk in love, as Christ also hath loved us.' The spiritual growth of a church depends not only on the preaching, but on the life of fellowship and love, into the healthy exercise of which believers are led.

In chapter 14 Paul descends to particulars, dealing specially with the question of the gift of tongues and of prophecy. The Corinthians had evidently allowed themselves to be drawn away by what appeared miraculous and special. The gift of prophecy, as Paul defines it, 'speaketh edification, and exhortation, and comfort,' was not held in equal honour. Paul says that he would rather speak five words 'with my understanding, that I might teach others also, than ten thousands words in an unknown tongue'. The edification of the church is to be the highest law; those who can speak in tongues are to remember that the speaking in tongues, unless there be an interpreter, does not bring comfort or instruction to others. And in passing he gives us a picture of what a church meeting could be, and doubtless often was, where the spirit of love was allowed to rule. 'If all prophesy, and there come in one that believeth not, or one unlearned, he is convinced of all, he is judged of all: And thus are the secrets of his heart made manifest; and so falling down on his face he will worship God, and report that God is in you of a truth' – a pledge of what can be true of the church in our time, too, where the Spirit of the Lord is allowed free course.

The passage ends with a reminder that as God is not a God of confusion, but of peace, so those who first prophesy are also to learn to be subject one to another. Then he closes with words that have often been terribly abused, and yet have their divine worth in their own place – in all the churches of the saints 'Let all things be done decently and in order.' The chapters on spiritual gifts, on the supremacy of love, on the sacrifice of everything and everyone to the edification of the body, have been of untold value in the church of God, and in the full harmony of the truths they contain, are still essential to the building up of the Body of Christ.

Aids to Devotion; included in *Reviving the Soul: The Best of Andrew Murray's Devotional Writings*, ed. Robert Backhouse (London: Marshall Pickering, 1995), pp. 162–5.

E. D. Starbuck

A luminous element

I had been clearly converted twenty-three years before, or rather reclaimed. My experience in regeneration was then clear and spiritual, and I had not backslidden. But I experienced entire sanctification on 15th day of March 1893, about eleven o'clock in the morning. The particular accompaniments of the experience were entirely unexpected. I was quietly sitting at home singing selections out of Pentecostal Hymns. Suddenly there seemed to be a something sweeping into me and inflating my entire being – such a sensation as I had never experienced before. When this experience came, I seemed to be conducted around a large, capacious, well-lighted room. As I walked with my invisible conductor and looked around, a clear thought was coined in my mind, 'They are not here, they are gone.' As soon as the thought was definitely formed in my mind, though no word was spoken, the Holy Spirit impressed me that I was surveying my own soul. Then, for the first time in all my life, did I know that I was cleansed from all sin, and filled with the fullness of God.

The Psychology of Religion (1899), p. 310.

Stephen H. Bradley

An unlettered American.

One Sabbath, I went to hear the Methodist preacher at the Academy. So awakened were all the powers of my mind that I trembled involuntarily on the bench where I was sitting, though I felt nothing at heart. I will now relate my experience which took place on the same night. Had anyone told me before this that I could have experienced the power of the Holy Spirit in the manner which I did, I could not have believed it, and should have thought the person deluded that told me so. I went directly home after the meeting, and when I got home I wondered what made me feel so stupid. I retired to rest soon after I got home, and felt indifferent to the things of religion until I began to be exercised by the Holy Spirit, which began in about five minutes after, in the following manner.

At first, I began to feel my heart beat very quick all on a sudden, which made me at first think that perhaps something is going to ail me, though I was not alarmed, for I felt on pain. My heart increased in its beating, which soon convinced me that it was the Holy Spirit from the effect it had on me. I began to feel exceedingly happy and humble, and such a sense of unworthiness as I never felt before. I could not very well help speaking out, which I did, and said, Lord, I do not deserve this happiness, or words to that effect, while there was a stream (resembling air in feeling) came into my mouth and heart in a more sensible manner than that of drinking anything, which continued, for five minutes, which seemed to be the cause of my heart palpitating.

It took complete possession of my soul, and I am certain that I desired the Lord, while in the midst of it, not to give me any more happiness, for it seemed as if I could not contain what I had got. My heart seemed as if would burst, but I did not stop until I felt as if I was unutterably full of the love and grace of God.

A sketch of the life of Stephen H. Bradley, from the age of five to twenty-four years, including his remarkable experience of the power of the Holy Spirit on the second evening of November, 1829 (Madison (CO), 1830).

The Second Evangelical Awakening

In the year 1858 an extraordinary religious Revival swept every state in the United States of America, adding a million converts to the churches, accomplishing untold good, yet being utterly free from the fanaticism which had marred earlier American awakenings.

In the year 1859 a similar movement began in the United Kingdom, affecting every county in Ulster, Scotland, Wales and England, adding a million accessions to the evangelical churches, accomplishing a tremendous amount of social uplift, and giving an effective impulse to home and foreign missionary activity. [Out of this movement grew such organisations as the Children's Special Service Mission (now the Scripture Union), the Salvation Army, and the China Inland Mission (now the Overseas Missionary Fellowship).]

Among the converts and products of the revival were such outstanding men as Tom Barnardo, founder of Barnardo's Homes; James Chalmers, the pioneer missionary to New Guinea; Hugh Price Hughes, the Methodist stalwart; and Evan Hopkins, the founder of the Keswick Convention.

The religious Revival of 1859–65 equalled in magnitude the famed eighteenth-century Evangelical Revival.

J. Edwin Orr, *The Second Evangelical Awakening in Britain* (London: Marshall, Morgan and Scott, 1949), pp. 5–6.

The awakening in Ireland

Letter from the Very Rev. D. H. S. Cranage, D.D., former Dean of Norwich.

The Old Rectory
Winkfield, Windsor
1st May 1948

Dear Dr Orr,

It is a particular satisfaction to me that, fifty-six years after his death, the memory of my father should be commemorated in the important research you are engaged in . . .

The year 1859 was certainly the greatest epoch in the life of Dr Cranage. An extraordinary movement took place in Ireland at this time. It was a religious Awakening which pervaded all classes, and which baffles description. Dr Cranage had his first experience of it in a small building near Belfast. It was an evening meeting and a very ordinary preacher was presiding over a crowded audience. Before long, one and another began to cry for mercy, and many were so overcome that they were carried out in a fainting condition. There was the greatest physical as well as mental prostration, but the only cure was the clear preaching of the Gospel of Christ. When once the doctrine of atonement was laid hold of, and Christ seen as the sinner's substitute, all fear vanished and the people went away rejoicing.

Dr Cranage, in common with many others, first viewed the movement with suspicion, but was soon convinced of his divine origin, and joined heart and soul in the work. He had been a decided Christian for years, but he looked back to 1859 as the time when he first received assurance of salvation, through the merits of Jesus Christ. Writing about this time, he said: 'Through great mercy and love, I have been able to the last hour to say with humble, tearful, hopeful confidence,

> Thou, O Christ, art all I want,
> More than all in Thee I find.'

On his return to England after the summer holidays, he was asked to give an account of the Revival in a country school-room. It had never entered his head that he would become a public preacher, and he was hardly persuaded to accept the invitation. One meeting led to another, and he soon found the Irish work spreading to Wellington. A small town was rented in New Street, and the Town Hall often engaged. The Doctor was led on step by step till the New Hall was built in 1862. The day the foundation stone was laid witnessed a most remarkable scene. The religious awakening was so great that many were on their knees in the streets crying for mercy; there was quite a street prayer-meeting.

One little thing I may add. My father told me that, when his Mission Hall was opened in 1862, the crowd was so great that you could walk along the heads of the people.

Yours very sincerely,

D. H. S. Cranage

J. Edwin Orr, *The Second Evangelical Awakening in Britain* (London: Marshall, Morgan and Scott, 1949), pp. 284–5.

'Singular physical features' and the revival in Northern Ireland, August 1859

Too little as well as too much has been made of the singular physical features of this great revival. By some they are regarded as abnormal and excessive. I do not think so. They have accompanied all revivals.

I care not what sceptics may say, or little-faith Christians, who have no confidence in the extraordinary influences of the Spirit. I believe, as firmly as I believe in my own existence, that the Holy Spirit would never have permitted his work to be entangled with such perplexing and seemingly incredible phenomena, had he not had a most important end to serve them.

Authentic Records of Revival, ed. William Reid (London: Nisbet, 1860), pp. 47, 49.

Revival at Ahoghill

The outbreak of Revival: Extraordinary religious excitement at Ahoghill
To the Editor of the *Ballymeena Observer*
26th March 1859

Sir,
I beg permission, through the columns of your enlightened journal, to narrate, for the information of the public, a few extraordinary facts connected with a very singular and mysterious movement, of a religious character, now in progress throughout the neighbourhood of Ahoghill. The astounding occurrences may be for good, or for evil – I do not pretend to offer an opinion upon that point; but the present state of matters is generally attributed to the influence of well-intended lectures, sermons, and addresses recently delivered throughout various portions of this country, descriptive of the religious revivals in America.

The movement in this immediate neighbourhood has assumed the startling character of unexpected and instantaneous 'conversions', accompanied by the physical and spiritual operations of some overwhelming power upon the minds and bodies of the parties so converted. I may remark that manifold symptoms of this character, so far as the mental operations are concerned in the matter, became perceptible, some two or three years ago, in the neighbourhood of Kells and Connor, where they were followed by practical reformation, and much apparent good. A spirit of genuine religion appeared to have fallen upon many of the people; and the work was regarded as the power of godliness upon the human heart. Men of irregular habits became suddenly and permanently changed; institutions for prayer were established throughout the parish, and very numerously attended; drunkards became peaceable, sober, and religious members of society; houses once the habitations of wickedness, became sanctuaries of praise, and roofs that formerly echoed with songs of obscenity, now cover altars of family worship, and resound with the anthems of the royal psalmist. So far as Connor is concerned, therefore, all appears to be a steady, sober, and promising progression towards good.

By degrees the influence of these proceedings throughout Connor extended into the adjoining parish of Ahoghill; in some townlands of which the very astonishing developments, which I now purpose to relate, commenced about six week ago. The work of 'conversion', as it is called, here assumed the form of a supernatural intervention and miraculous agency. Men were suddenly 'struck' with an overwhelming and terrifying conviction of their sin and danger; and directly thrown into a state of intense bodily excitement, and mental frenzy – in short they became, as it were, 'possessed'. In this state the whole frame is shaken by some species of uncontrollable convulsion; very muscle quivers; one feels impelled by some irresistible influence to pray – and does pray, loudly, unceasingly, and with desperate earnestness, for pardon of sin and acceptance by the mercy of God through Jesus Christ.

In this extraordinary agitation of mind and body, the penitent continues to struggle for an indefinite period – generally less than two days; and finally becomes impressed with a gladdening sense of peace, and grace, quite as suddenly as he had previously been impressed with fear. From that moment he is apparently a changed and converted man; he has been as he affirms, born anew; and he proclaims his 'conversion' as having been accomplished by the direct intervention and visible agency of the Holy Spirit. The parties so 'converted' at present number about thirty-five.

It is a remarkable fact that a majority of these 'converts' are people in comfortable circumstances, people of intelligence, and generally of good moral character. Some of them had laboured in sabbath schools, where, they had acquitted themselves as 'workmen who need not be ashamed', but they have since declared before large assemblies, that, with all their former seeming good qualities, they were then only as 'dry bones in the valley of vision', but are now clothed with flesh and sinew, and have experienced the 'wonderful power of reanimating God'.

I have now fairly and candidly described the one side of the picture; but truth compels me to exhibit the reverse with like fidelity. It is greatly to be feared that there is something seriously wrong – that a species of self delusion or superstitious fanaticism is prevalent in this neighbourhood. The local clergy appear to be aware of this; and possibly with a view to present the realities of genuine religion in a proper light, a public meeting, under the direction and management of Presbyterian ministers, was held in the first Presbyterian Church of Ahoghill in the evening of the 14th instant – professedly upon the subject of 'Revivals'.

The congregation in attendance was immense – hundreds were unable to obtain admittance, and the new converts – the 'confirmed' from all parts of the neighbourhood were present on the occasion. Soon after the commencement of the services an impulse to address the audience fell suddenly, and apparently with all the power of prophetic inspiration, upon one of the 'converted' brethren. Every attempt to silence or restrain him was found utterly impossible. He declared that a revelation had been committed to him, and that he spoke by the command of a power superior to any ministerial authority. Defying every effort at control he proceeded to vociferate religious phrases with a rapidity and fluency which excited the most intense astonishment, and created a pan of very serious alarm among the audience. A rush was made towards the front of the galleries, and under an apprehension that they mighty possibly bread down, the presiding clergyman gave a peremptory order that the house should be vacated. A scene of terrible confusion immediately ensued.

Then the premises were ultimately cleared, the streets of

Ahogill presented another scene which baffles all powers of description, and such as the oldest inhabitant had never witnessed. The leading 'convert' – who is a comfortable farmer and a member or the congregation – assisted by several other speakers of the confirmed class, addressed the people, then numbering about 3,000 and comprising people of every creed from the Episcopalian to the Roman Catholic. The chief speaker vehemently proclaimed pardon to all sinners, inviting them to come forward and receive the spirit of adoption, which he declared himself commissioned to impart – occasionally holding up his hands, and bidding the people to receive the Holy Spirit. The immense assemblage appeared to be thoroughly paralysed. Amid a chilling rain, and on streets covered with mud, fresh 'converts', moved by the fervency and apostolic language of the speaker, fell upon their knees in the attitude of prayer; a spark of electricity appeared to have animated and impressed a large number of the audience; and it is confidently affirmed that some who went there to mock, were heard to pray. Such, and such like, are the local effects of this extraordinary movement, and the result is that the devotees continue firmly rooted and grounded in the belief that they are under the immediate inspiration and guidance of Divine Spirit. Their meetings are multiplied in number; and the 'new births', are daily upon the increase.

'Spectator'

J. Edwin Orr, *The Second Evangelical Awakening in Britain* (London: Marshall, Morgan and Scott, 1949).

The Ulster Revival, 1860

The old prayer meetings began to be thronged, and many new ones established. No difficulty now to find people to take part in them. The winter was past; the time of the singing of birds had come. Humble, grateful, loving, joyous converts multiplied. the awakening to a sight of sin, the conviction of its sinfulness, the illumination of the soul in the knowledge of a glorious Saviour, and conversion to him – all this operation, carried on by the lifegiving Spirit, was in the Connor district, for more than eighteen

months, a calm, quiet, gradual, in some cases a lengthened process, not commencing in, or accompanied by, a 'smiting down' of
the body, or any extraordinary physical prostration more than
what might be expected to result form great anxiety and deep
sorrow.

The awakening thus commenced and spread over a district in
which there was a good degree of preparation for its advent. It
may be observed generally that the characteristic forms of the
physical phenomena took place in every possible variety of circumstances – at home, abroad, in the church, in the market-place; in
the crowded meeting, and the seclusion of retirement. one is
stricken as he plies the shuttle or the loom; another as his eye falls
on some familiar passage, or his ear is arrested by some oft-
repeated invitation of the Word; a third while he is engaged in secret meditation or prayer. 'I have known the case of a man,' says the
Rev. John Macnaughtan of Belfast, referring to another class of
instances, after his visit to Ballymeena, 'going home from the
market after he had sold his produce, passing along the road-side,
and counting his money to see whether it was all right, when he
sunk down as if sun-struck, and his money was scattered on the
road.'

The first stage
Of the several stages in the experience of those who have been
the subjects of physical prostration, the first is characterised by
an awful apprehension of impending evil, a fearful looking for
a judgment and fiery indignation, accompanied by a crushing
pressure on the region of the heart, inducing the loud despair-
ing cry, or the groan of agony. In this state the sufferer is overwhelmed as by the billows of divine wrath, so that human help
is for the time of no avail, and all that man can do is to await
the issue, committing it to him who causeth light to arise in the
darkness. Then is the period also of fierce wrestling, real or
imagined, with the Evil One, whose personality is apprehended
with terrible distinctness, insomuch that the soul is as an arena in
which a death struggle is being carried on between the powers of
light and darkness.

The second stage
In the second stage, which is generally very sudden in its development, there is a transition from the deep depression before experienced to a calmer state of feeling, and some object earnestly desired and longed for, stand out before the view – the intensity of the mind's gaze being such that no human presence, although many may be intently waiting by, is reallised. It is a sort of waking dream, in which the steadfast countenance and upturned eye denote the character of the inner exercise. The labouring chest no longer heaves under its oppressive burden; there is a subsidence of the sob, the groan, the wail of lamentation, and the cold damps are passing off the brow. The arms that tossed about so wildly, are now stretched forth as if to embrace the prized and cherished object, and utterances like these drop from the lips in melting cadence, – 'O blessed Jesus, come! Thou art my hope, my life, my all; wash me in thy most precious blood; take away this filthy garment, and cover me with thine own pure righteousness;' or more affecting still, as in the case of that little girl, but eight years old, who exclaimed imploringly, in her native patois, 'O Christ, come to me! and when you come, O dinna lea' me, but aye stay wi' me.' It is in this stage that images flit before the mind with all the vividness of reality, and as if possessed of shape and substance; insomuch that the person, subsequently referring to his experience, will speak as if he had seen the dread realities of heaven and hell, although assured on calm reflection that the objects before his vision have only been his own toughts embodied in that form.

The third stage
And now a third experience ensues. It is that of sensible relief, a lightsome and liberated feeling, of which the chief ingredient is the assurance of forgiveness prompting to the outburst of rapturous praise. The fountains of the soul seem to be opened, and forth flows in unrestrained exuberance the gushing fulness of its joy. The bodily sensations correspond with the inner ecstasy, and even the plainest features glow as with an unearthly beauty. The heavy load, the incubus that weighed down all the spirit's energies, is lifted off, and there is a buoyancy and elasticity proportionate to

the depressing burden. The new-born happiness seeks audible expression. The language of the lips is all in unison with the serenity that reigns within. 'Christ and him crucified' being once apprehended, the grand, the dominant desire is to commend him to all around. How often, then, are heard such words as those in which a Sabbath-school girl, some thirteen years of age, was addressing her little companions by her bedside, as she lay in much exhaustion after a season of mental agony, while a gleam of spiritual joy played over her pale countenance, – 'O Annie! O Jane, dear, come to Jesus! He'll not put you away. Oh, give him your heart, give him all your heart, and he'll take away all your sins, and make you as happy as he has made me. Oh that all the sinners about here would come to him! He has room for them all. He would save them all.'

The fourth stage

To the above may be added a fourth stage in the prostration – namely, the languor and exhaustion which are the natural reaction from the intense excitement by which the frame has been agitated, and by reason of which not only delicate females, but strong and stalwart men have often been dor days unfitted for any manner of work.

Such bodily affections were almost universally associated with the awakening, when, for the first time, it appeared in any neighbourhood; although in many places the work proceeded most satisfactorily without their presence, and they generally subsided as it advanced. From their novelty and publicity they naturally attracted a large share of attention, serving, no doubt, an important purpose, but often stimulating an idle curiosity, and in the case of the uneducated and ill-informed, leading to a confounding of the spiritual process with the physiological characteristics by which it was accompanied.

W. Gibson, *The Year of Grace: A History of the Ulster Revival of 1859* (Edinburgh: Andrew Elliot, 1860), pp. 18, 24, 50–3; quoted in James R. Moore, *Religion in Victorian Britain: III Sources* (Manchester University Press, 1988), pp. 254–8.

The awakening in Scotland

The General Assembly of the Free Church of Scotland
Two years ago, our Assembly was deeply stirred by the intelligence of what God was doing in the United States of America. One year ago, the impression was deepened ... the pregnant cloud had swept onwards and was sending down upon Ireland a plenteous rain. This year, the same precious showers have been and are even now falling within the limits of our own beloved land.

We, as a church, accept the Revival as a great and blessed fact. Numerous and explicit testimonies from ministers and members alike bespeak the gracious influence on the people. Whole congregations have been seen bending before it like a mighty rushing wind.

James Buchanan, incoming Moderator, addressing the May 1860 General Assembly of the Free Church of Scotland, in *Proceedings and Debates in the General Assembly of the Free Church of Scotland* (Edinburgh, 1860), pp. 9ff.

Revival from Ireland

The wave of divine blessing came to us apparently from Ireland four or five years ago. It struck first the west coast of Scotland, then spread over a great part of the country. It was a very blessed season, perhaps the most extensive in its operation that we have ever known among us.

But it has, in a great measure, passed away. Still the fruits remain – living, active, consistent Christians who keep together, cherishing the memory of the time, blessing and praying for its return ... The number of students entering our divinity halls this season will be double or triple that of former years; this is a blessed fruit of the Revival.

The Revival, 19th January 1865.

There is a divine mystery about revivals

Alexander Whyte, himself revived in the Scottish Awakening of 1859, wrote his *Reminiscences of the Revival of '59*, some fifty years later. As an old man he wrote, 'A Revival quickens dead men, touches men's imaginations and sets loose their hearts. There is a divine mystery about Revivals. God's sovereignty is in them.

G. F. Barbour, *Life of Alexander Whyte* (London, 1932), pp. 88ff.

The awakening in Wales

There were loud cries from souls in agony
I saw there the most terrible spectacle of my experience; some on their knees, some on their faces completely overpowered. The succeeding week was a strange one, and the following Sabbath was unparalleled to me and terrible to the Dolgelly congregation. There were loud outcries from souls in agony, and thirty-five sought a place in God's house.

J. J. Morgan, *The '59 Revival in Wales* (Mold, 1909), p. 113.

The awakening in Southern England

I must not close without a memory, however meagre, of one wonderful epoch in the parish. It was the Revival. The year was 1859, that 'year of the right hand of the Most High' Ulster was profoundly and lastingly moved and blessed. Here and there in England it was the same; and Fordington, in 1860, was one of the scenes of divine awakening.

For surely it was divine. No artificial means of excitement were dreamt of; my Father's whole genius was against it. No powerful personality, no Moody or Aitken, came to us. A city missionary and a London Bible-woman were the only helpers from a distance. Hundreds of people were awakened, awed, and made conscious of eternal realities. A great social uplifting, wholesome and permanent, followed the revival.

Handley C. G. Moule, *Memorials of a Vicarage,* pp. 48ff.

The awakening in East Anglia and the Midlands

When I arose from my knees, and before the first verse of the hymn 'There is a fountain filled with blood' was finished, the power of God had come down in such a remarkable manner on the whole assembly, that when I looked over the hall sinners were prostrated in every part.

The Record, 20th April 1861.

Societies and the revival

They had heard of those blessed outpourings in America, in Sweden, in Ireland, in Scotland, in various parts of the metropolis, and other places. They had come together, know that God would bless them and be with them from day to day. Let all differences be forgotten: let them not remember that they were Churchmen or Dissenters, Baptists or Wesleyans, Presbyterians or Episcopalians.

Eugene Stock, *History of the Church Missionary Society* (London: CMS, 1899), vol. 2, pp. 32ff. (quoting Dr Arthur Tidman relating the spirit of Revival to the spirit of unity).

Revival in the West Indies

The next year, indeed, saw the outbreak of a remarkable spiritual Revival, general throughout the churches of the island [Jamaica]. It began in a Moravian church, and spread from the south coast to the central provinces, to Spanish Town and Savanna-la-Mar, from Montego Bay to Ann's Bay, and finally right through the country. Chapels became one more crowded. There was a widespread conviction of sin. As the movement spread, unhealthy excitement and religious hysteria showed themselves in places, but the testimony of almost all observers, of whatever denomination, was that the Revival was a real blessing from God and did permanent good.

Ernest Payne, *Freedom in Jamaica* (London, 1946), pp. 88ff.

Dwight L. Moody
(1837–99)

American evangelist; toured England and America with Ira Sankey.

Love, hope, liberty

The Spirit of God first imparts love; he next inspires hope, and then gives liberty; and that is about the last thing we have in many of our churches.

'Be filled with the Spirit' (Ephesians 5:18)

Ephesians 5:18 is not just an experience to be enjoyed but a command to be obeyed. If we do not open ourselves to a daily encounter with the Holy Spirit, then the inevitable conclusion is that we are disobedient Christians.

My baptism in the Holy Spirit

I began to cry as never before, for a greater blessing from God. The hunger increased; I really felt that I did not want to live any longer. [Although he was a Christian, a minister, and saw people being converted, he wanted more people to be converted.] I kept on crying all the time that God would fill me with his Spirit. Well, one day in the city of New York – oh! what a day, I cannot describe it, I seldom refer to it. It is almost too sacred an experience to name. Paul had an experience of which he never spoke for 14 years. I can only say, God revealed himself to me, and I had such an experience of his love that I had to ask him to stay his hand. I went preaching again. The sermons were not different; I did not present any new truths, and yet hundreds were converted. I would not now be placed back where I was before that blessed experience if you should give me all the world – it would be small dust in the balance.

W. R. Moody, *The Life of D. L. Moody* (New York: Fleming H. Revell, 1900), p. 149.

Martyn Lloyd-Jones, commenting on Moody's experience

It was so overwhelming, he felt as if he was going to be physically crushed. The love of God! That is what is meant by 'the love of God in your hearts'. That is the baptism of the Spirit. That is what turned D.L. Moody from a good, regular, ordinary minister, into the evangelist who was so signally used of God in this and in other countries.

Joy Unspeakable (Eastbourne: Kingsway, 1984), p. 80.

When the Spirit came

When the Spirit came to Moses, the plagues came upon Egypt, and he had power to destroy men's lives; when the Spirit came upon Elijah, fire came down from heaven; when the Spirit came upon Joshua, he moved around the city of Jericho, and the whole city fell into his hands. But when the Spirit came upon the Son of Man, he gave his life, he healed the broken-hearted.

Holy Spirit as evangelist

There is not a better evangelist in the world than the Holy Spirit.

R. A. Torrey

US evangelist.

The baptism with the Holy Spirit

The baptism with the Holy Spirit is an operation of the Holy Spirit distinct from and subsequent from his regenerating work . . . an impartation of power for service. This baptism was not merely for the apostles, not merely for those of the apostolic age, but for 'all that are afar off; even as many as the Lord our God shall call.' It is for every believer in every age of the church's history.

The Person and Work of the Holy Spirit (New York: Revell, 1910), p. 176.

In my early study of the baptism with the Holy Spirit I noticed that in many instances those who were so baptised 'spoke in tongues,' and the question often came into my mind, if one is baptised with the Holy Spirit will he not speak with tongues? But I saw no one so speaking and I often wondered, is there any one today who actually is baptised with the Holy Spirit?

Baptism in the Holy Ghost (London: Nisbet, 1895), p. 16.

Torrey's assessment of Pentecostals

Founded by a sodomite.

Quoted by Synan Vinson, *The Holiness-Pentecostal Movement in the United States* (Grand Rapids (MI): Eerdmans, 1971), p. 145.

Efim Gerasemovitch Klubniken
(or Little Prophet)

A series of prophecies from Armenia, from 1855

It is recorded that in Armenia, which is [was] mainly in Russia but partly in Turkey, an eleven-year-old boy in the village of Kara Kala received a series of prophecies in 1855. He foretold that the Turks would turn on the Armenians, and warned the Christians to escape by crossing the seas. Little lasting effect was produced by these prophecies. In 1900, the same prophet, now middle-aged, named Efim Gerasemovitch Klubniken (or Little prophet), again began to pass on to his people more warnings. In the same year a mass emigration of Pentecostals began, and continued for twelve years. In April 1914 the Turks killed between one and a half and two million people from the remaining Armenian population. The people who remained in Kara Kala were among those massacred. But thanks to the prophecy of Efim the Pentecostal families had fled for safety too many countries in the Middle East, including Lebanon, and also to countries as far flung as Argentina and the USA.

Eric S. Fife, *The Holy Spirit: The Bible and Common Sense.* pp. 130–1.

J. G. Arintero
(1860–1928)

Spanish spiritual director and Dominican theologian, who taught at Salamanca.

Prayer of spiritual intoxication

Perhaps not quite to the same extent as when the first disciples received the Holy Spirit, but at least enough to inspire certain kinds of 'enthusiasm', not so contained, but that it will seem madness in the eyes of some. [These forms may take] shouts and groans and songs of praise and leaping about for joy.

Stages in Prayer, Conclusions 1; ch. 8; *La Evolucion Mistica* (1908).

Samuel Chadwick
(1860–)

Wherever whole-hearted, absolute, unquestioning, positive, final abandonment of the life to God obtains, the life becomes filled with the Spirit.

G. Campbell Morgan, *The Spirit of God*, p. 227.

Before Pentecost . . . after Pentecost

Before Pentecost we pray in the Spirit, after Pentecost the Spirit prays through us.

The Way to Pentecost (London, 1951), p. 41.

Indwelling presence and power

All fullness of life, all resources of vitality, all certainty of assurance, all victory over sin and the flesh, all prevailing power in prayer, all certitude of glory – all and everything is in the

Indwelling Presence and Power of the Holy Spirit of God in Christ Jesus our Lord.

The Way to Pentecost (London, 1951), p. 36.

The Welsh revival
(1904–5)

A future revival leader receiving God's power

One Friday night last spring, when praying by my bedside before retiring, I was taken up to a great expanse – without time and space. It was communion with God. Before this I had a far-off God. I was frightened that night, but never since. So great was my shivering that I rocked the bed, and my brother, being awakened, took hold of me thinking I was ill. After that experience I was wakened every night a little after one o'clock. This was most strange, for through the years I slept like a rock, and no disturbance in my room would awaken me. From that hour I was taken up into the divine fellowship for about four hours. What it was I cannot tell you, except that it was divine. About five o'clock I was again allowed to sleep on till about nine. At this time I was again taken up into the same experience as in the earlier hours of the morning until about twelve or one o'clock . . . This went on for about three months.

Evan Roberts; quoted in Eifion Evans, *The Welsh Revival of 1904* (Evangelical Press of Wales, 1969), pp. 65–6.

After a prayer meeting in Loughor

After many had prayed, I felt some living energy or force entering my bosom, restraining my breath, my legs trembling terribly; this living energy increased and increased as one after another prayed. Feeling strongly and deeply warmed, I burst forth in prayer.

George Jeffreys, *Healing Rays* (London: Elim, 1935), p. 55.

If you and I could stand above Wales, looking at it, you would see fire breaking out here and there, and yonder, and somewhere else, without any collusion or prearrangement. It is a divine visitation in which God – let me say this reverently – in which God is saying to us, 'See what I can do without the things you are depending on'; 'See what I can do in answer to a praying people'; 'See what I can do through the simplest who are ready to fall in line and depend wholly and absolutely upon Me.'

G. Campbell Morgan, 'The Revival: Its Source and Power', in *Glory Filled the land: A Trilogy on the Welsh Revival,* ed. Richard Owen Roberts (Wheaton (IL): International Awakening Press, 1989), p. 174.

Gipsy Smith

Answering the question, 'how do you have a revival?' Gipsy Smith replied, 'Kneel down and with a piece of chalk draw a complete circle all around you – and pray to God to send revival on everything inside the circle. Stay there until he answers, and you will have revival.'

Bibliography

Note: Works for which no publication details are given are those of classical authors whose works are available in a variety of editions and translations.

Ambrose, *The Holy Spirit*.

Apopthegmata Patrum.

Arintero, J. G., *La Evolucion Mistica* (1908).

Arsenev, N. S., *Mysticism and the Eastern Church* (London: SCM Press, 1926).

Athanasius, *Life of St Antony*.

Augustine, *The City of God*.

— . *Confessions*.

— . *Sermons*.

Authentic Records of Revival, ed. William Reid (London: Nisbet, 1860).

Backhouse, Robert, *Invaded by Love: A Collection of Christian Conversions,* (London: Marshall Pickering, 1993).

Baird, Henry, *The Huguenots* (New York: Charles Scribner, 1885).

Baker, Augustine, *The Confessions of Venerable Father Augustine Baker* (London: Burns & Oates, 1922).

Barbour, G. F., *Life of Alexander Whyte* (London, 1932).

Barclay, Robert, *Inner Life of the Religious Societies* (London: Hodder & Stoughton, 1912).

Basil the Great, *On the Holy Spirit*.

Bax, Belfort, *The Rise and Fall of the Anabaptists*.

Baxter, Richard. *Reliquiae Baxterianae* (1696).

— , *Works*.

Bickley, *The Independents Against the Quakers*.

371

Boehme, Jacob, *Aurora*.

The Book of Homilies.

Brainerd, David, *Journal*.

Braithwaite, William Charles, *Beginnings of Quakerism* (1912).

Brown, John, *John Bunyan* (London: Isbister, 1885).

Calvin, John, *Commentary on Acts*.

— , *Commentary on John*.

— , *The Institutes of Christian Religion*.

Cartwright, Peter, *The Autobiography* (Nashville (TE): Abingdon, 1956).

Chadwick, Samuel, *The Way to Pentecost* (London, 1951).

Chevreau, Guy, *Catch the Fire: Toronto Blessing – An Experience of Renewal and Revival* (London: Marshall Pickering, 1994).

Clement of Rome, *Letter to the Corinthians*.

Cyprian, *To Demetrianus*.

Cyril of Jerusalem, *Catechetical Lectures*.

Dallimore, Arnold A., *George Whitefield* (Edinburgh: Banner of Truth, 1980).

The Didache.

Didymus, *Of the Trinity*.

Dixon, W. Hepworth, *Spiritual Wives* (London, 1868).

Dwight, S. E., *The Life of President Edwards* (New York, 1830).

Dunn, James D. G., *Jesus and the Spirit: A Study of the Religious and Charismatic Experience of Jesus and the First Christians as Reflected in the New Testament* (London: SCM Press, 1978).

Edwards, Jonathan, *The Distinguishing Marks of a Work of the Spirit of God*.

— , *A Treatise Concerning Religious Affections*.

— , *Works*, edited by Henry Hickman (Edinburgh: Banner of Truth, 1974).

— , and S. E. Dwight, *Life of Brainerd* (New Haven, 1822).

Epiphanius, *Heresies*.

— , *Heretics*.

Erasmus, *Paraphrases*.

Eusebius, *Church History*.

Evans, Eifion, *The Welsh Revival of 1904* (Port Talbot: Evangelical Movement of Wales, 1969).

— , *Daniel Rowlands and the Great Evangelical Awakening in Wales* (Edinburgh: Banner of Truth, 1985).

Fife, Eric S., *The Holy Spirit: The Bible and Common Sense.*

Finney, Charles Grandison, *Autobiography* (Bethany, 1977).

— , *Lectures on Revivals of Religion* (Manchester: Simpkin, Marshall, 1840).

— , *Memoirs* (1875).

— , *Reflections on Revival.*

Fox, George, *Journal* (London, 1852).

Franke, August Hermann, *Sermon on Matthew 17:1–9.*

Free Church of Scotland, *Proceedings and Debates in the General Assembly* (Edinburgh, 1860).

Gewehr, Wesley M., *The Great Awakening in Virginia, 1740–1790* (Durham (NC), 1930).

Gillies, J. *Memoirs of the Life of George Whitefield.*

Gledstone, J. P., *Life and travels of Whitefield* (London, 1871).

Glory Filled the land: A Trilogy on the Welsh Revival, ed. Richard Owen Roberts (Wheaton (IL): International Awakening Press, 1989).

Gordon, A. J. *The Ministry of Healing* (Harrisburg: Christian Publications, 1902).

The Great Awakening: Documents on the Revival of Religion, 1740–45, ed. Richard Bushman (New York: Atheneum, 1970).

Gregory I (the Great), *Dialogues.*

Gregory of Nyssa, *On the Lord's Prayer and the Beatitudes.*

Gregory of Tours, *Dialogues.*

Harper, Michael, *As at the Beginning* (London: Hodder & Stoughton).

Hasse, E. R., *The Moravians* (London, 1911).

Hermas, *Shepherd.*

Hilary of Poitiers, *Tract on the Psalms.*

Hildegard of Bingen, *Life.*

Hippolytus, *The Apostolic Tradition.*

— , *Refutation of All Heresies.*

Hodge, Charles, *A Commentary on Romans* (1864; reprinted Edinburgh: Banner of Truth, 1972).

— , *1 Corinthians* (1857; Wheaton (IL): Crossway Books, 1995).

— , *Commentary on the Epistle to the Ephesians* (Wheaton (IL): Crossway Books, 1994).

Hort, F. J. A., *The Ante-Nicene Fathers* (1895).

Huntingdon, Selina, Countess of, *Life and Times* (1839).

Ignatius of Antioch, *To the Philadelphians*.

Il'in, V. N., *Prepodobnyi Serafim Sarovskii* (Paris, 1930).

Irenaeus, *Against Heresies*.

Isaac the Syrian, *The Monastic Life*.

James, William, *The Varieties of Religious Experience* (London: Collins, 1960).

Jeffreys, George, *Healing Rays* (London: Elim, 1935).

Jerome, *Life of Saint Hilarion*.

John of St Thomas, *Cursus Theologicus*.

John of the Cross, *The Dark Night of the Soul,* edited by Halcyon Backhouse (London: Hodder & Stoughton, 1989).

Johnson, Charles Λ., *The Frontier Camp Meeting* (Dallas: Southern Methodist University Press, 1955).

Julian, *Comfortable Words for Christ's Lovers, being the visions vouchsafed to Lady Julian, recluse at Norwich in 1373,* ed. Rev Dundas Harford (London, 1912).

Justin Martyr, *Dialogue with Trypho*.

— , *The Second Apology*.

Knox, R. A. *Enthusiasm* (Oxford: Clarendon Press, 1950).

The Lives of S. Francis of Assisi, Brother Thomas of Celano, translated by A. G. Ferrers Howell (London: Methuen, 1908).

Lloyd-Jones, D. Martyn, *Joy Unspeakable: Power and Renewal in the Holy Spirit* (Eastbourne: Kingsway Publications, 1985).

— , *The Puritans: Their Origins and Successors* (Edinburgh: Banner of Truth, 1987).

— , *Revival: Can We Make it Happen?* (London: Marshall Pickering).

Lunn, *John Wesley*.

Luther, Martin. *Letters of Spiritual Counsel*.

— , *Preface to the Magnificat*.

M'Nemar, Richard, *The Kentucky Revival, or, A Short History of the Late Extraordinary Outpouring of the Spirit of God* (New York, 1846).

Melito, *Prophecy*.

Milner, Joseph. *The History of the Church*.

Moody, W. R., *The Life of D. L. Moody* (New York: Fleming H. Revell, 1900).

Moore, James R., *Religion in Victorian Britain: III Sources* (Manchester University Press, 1988).

Morgan, G. Campbell, *The Spirit of God*.

Morgan, J. J., *The '59 Revival in Wales* (Mold, 1909).

Morgana, Alphonse, *Early Christian Mystics* (Cambridge: Heffer, 1934).

Moule, Handley C. G., *Memorials of a Vicarage*.

Murray, Andrew, *Reviving the Soul: The Best of Andrew Murray's Devotional Writings*, ed. Robert Backhouse (London: Marshall Pickering, 1995).

— , *The Believer's Full Blessing of Pentecost* (Basingstoke: Lakeland, 1984).

Novatian, *Treatise Concerning the Trinity*.

Origen, *Contra Celsum*.

— , *On First Principles*.

Orr, J. Edwin, *The Second Evangelical Awakening in Britain* (London: Marshall, Morgan and Scott, 1949).

Owen, John, *Works*.

Packer, J. I., *Among God's Giants: Aspects of Puritan Christianity*, (Eastbourne: Kingsway, 1991).

Pascal, Blaise. *Pensées*.

Payne, Ernest, *Freedom in Jamaica* (London, 1946).

Rupert of Deutz, *The Glory and Honour of the Son of Man*.

Ryle, John Charles, *Holiness: Its Nature, Hindrances, Difficulties, and Roots* (1879).

A sketch of the life of Stephen H. Bradley, from the age of five to twenty-four years, including his remarkable experience of the power of the Holy Spirit on the second evening of November, 1829 (Madison (CO), 1830).

Smedley, Edward, *History of the Reformed Religion in France* (1832–4).

Southey, Robert, *Life of Wesley*.

Spener, Philipp Jakob, *Sermon on Matthew 12:2*.

The Spirit of Enthusiasm Exorcis'd, (London: Richard Sare), 1709.

Spurgeon, Charles Haddon, *The Autobiography* (Edinburgh: Banner of Truth, 1973).

— , *C. H. Spurgeon: The Early Years, 1834–1859* (Edinburgh: Banner of Truth, 1962).

— , *The Treasury of the New Testament* (London: Marshall, Morgan & Scott, 1933).

Starbuck, E. D., *The Psychology of Religion* (1899).

Stock, Eugene, *History of the Church Missionary Society* (London: CMS, 1899).

Symeon the New Theologian, *Catechesis.*

Teresa of Avila, *The Interior Castle,* edited by Halcyon Backhouse (London: Hodder & Stoughton, 1988).

Tertullian, *Against Marcion.*

— ,*Apology.*

— , *De monogamia (On Monogamy).*

— , *De Praescriptione Haereticorum (A Demurrer to the Heretics' Plea).*

— , *Letters.*

— , *On Modesty.*

— , *On the Resurrection of the Body.*

— , *On the Soul.*

— , *On the Veiling of Virgins.*

— , *To Scapula.*

Tillemont, *Perseuction under Marcus Aurelius.*

Torrey, Reuben A., *Baptism in the Holy Ghost* (London: Nisbet, 1895).

— , *The Person and Work of the Holy Spirit* (New York: Fleming H. Revell, 1910).

Tyson, J. R. *Charles Wesley on Sanctification* (Grand Rapids, 1986).

Vinson, Synan, *The Holiness-Pentecostal Movement in the United States* (Grand Rapids (MI): Eerdmans, 1971).

Upham, T. C., *The Life and Religious Experiences of Madame de la Mothe Guyon* (New York, 1877).

Warner, Rob, *Prepare for Revival* (London: Hodder and Stoughton, 1995).

Wesley, John, *Collected Works.*

— , *Journals.*

— , *Letters*.

— , *A Plain Man's Guide to Christian Holiness*, ed. H. C. Backhouse (London: Hodder and Stoughton, 1988).

White, John, *When the Spirit Comes with Power, Signs and Wonders Among God's People* (London: Hodder and Stoughton, 1992).

Whitefield, George, *Journals*.

— , *Sermons on Important Subjects* (London, 1828).

— , *Works* (London and Edinburgh, 1771).

William of St Thierry, *Canticle 132*.

Wood, A. Skevington, *The Inextinguishable Blaze* (London: Paternoster Press, 1960).

Woolman, John, *Journal*.

Index